My **Championship** Year

# My **Championship** Year

## Jenson Button

Edited by Sarah Edworthy

# CONTENTS

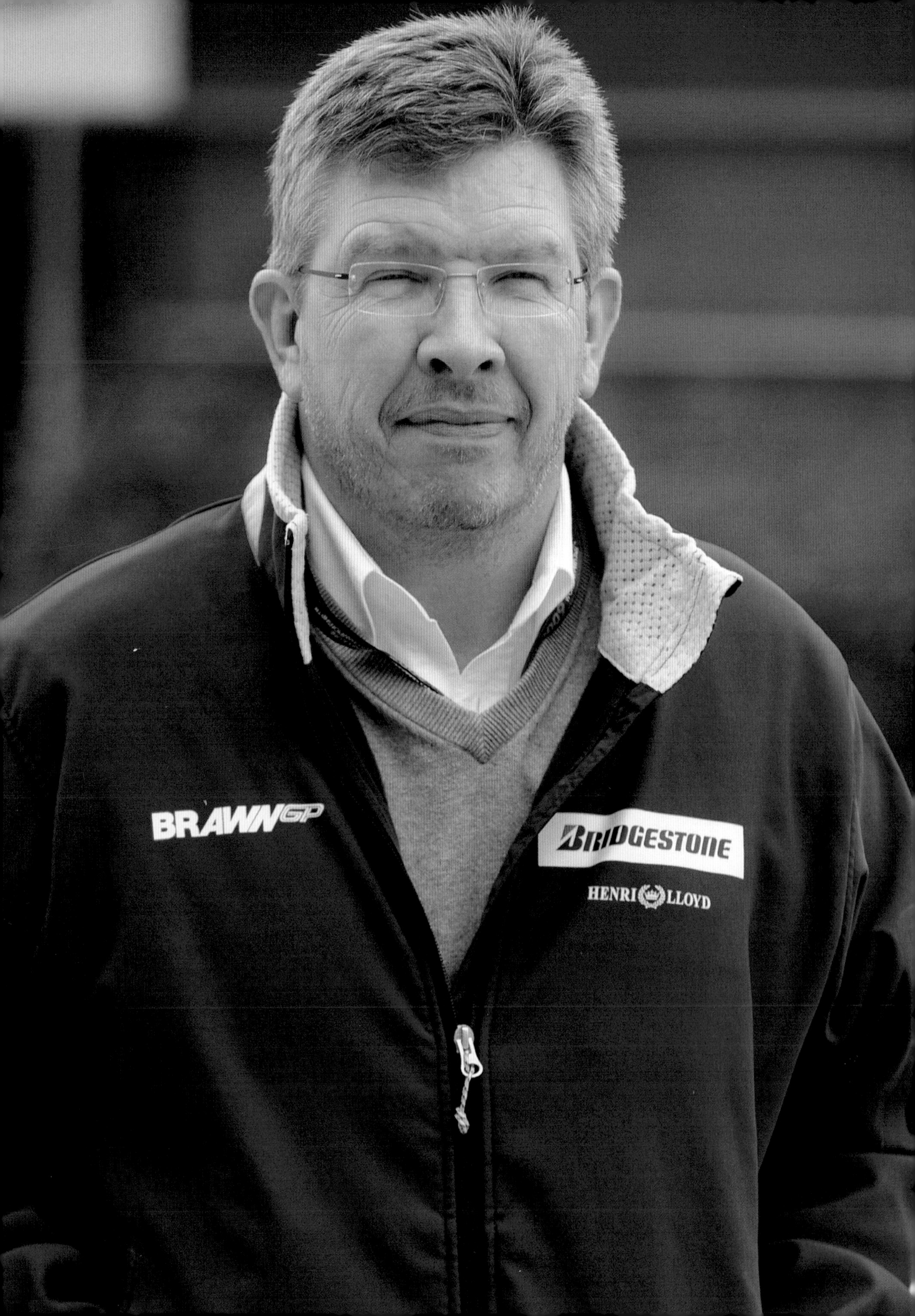
BRAWNGP
BRIDGESTONE
HENRI LLOYD

# Foreword

Jenson came into Formula One at the start of the 2000 season under the spotlight and he made an impression in his early days, finishing in a very credible eighth position in the Drivers' Championship in his first season. You could see instantly that Jenson was a fast driver and it was a boost for Britain to have such a young and talented driver competing in Formula One. I was working at Ferrari at the time and I only really saw Jenson from a distance. I've had the opportunity to get to know him well whilst we have been working together over the last two seasons and the qualities that I have always appreciated in him are his honesty, integrity and openness.

There is a very high level of admiration for Jenson at Brawn GP. His loyalty to our team is valued very highly and his support during our difficult days at the end of 2008 was a real credit to him and a boost for the team. Jenson is a genuine team member here, which is so important when you are fighting for the Championships. When he makes a mistake, he's the first to hold his hand up, just as he always praises the team when credit is due. In my first year here in 2008, we had a tough season with a difficult car and people at the team would tell me: 'You haven't seen what Jenson can really do.' What I have experienced this year is Jenson operating at the top of his game and able to show his talent in a good car.

Jenson is an incredibly smooth driver. His driving looks so controlled, which is impressive when you know how difficult Formula One cars can be to handle. He's very easy on the car and his smooth style looks after the tyres, but he is aggressive and assertive in his racing and very capable of holding his own on the track. For me, the highlights of Jenson's season would be the impressive six victories in the first seven races. Each win was an achievement. Whilst Australia and Monaco stand out for our one–two finishes, I thought Jenson drove exceptionally in Barcelona to take the win at the Spanish Grand Prix. Some of his wins might have looked straightforward but it was far from the case. Jenson was faced with not only a race-winning and vastly experienced team-mate in Rubens Barrichello, who had the same equipment as him, but also two very strong Red Bull cars driven by Sebastian Vettel and Mark Webber.

Until this season, Jenson hadn't fought for a Championship for a long time. He had a good year in 2004 but it was more about the race results than a potential title challenge. This year has been different. In any Championship season, you have strong periods and challenging times. One of the most impressive qualities which Jenson has shown has been his ability to deal with both scenarios and handle the attention which has come his way. He has maintained his controlled and measured approach when we were faced with races where our only objective was to consolidate and score a point or two. To achieve the results on the difficult days, when a couple of points is the full potential of the car, is what really counts in a Championship season and Jenson fully deserves the achievement of his first Drivers' Championship title.

Jenson is a straightforward guy. He's easy to work with and good company away from the track. He has his priorities sorted. Motor racing comes first but he enjoys life, much as I do, by keeping a balance and a strong circle of family and friends in this very intense world that we live and work in. 2009 has been an incredible year for Jenson and for Brawn GP. I hope you enjoy reading about the highs and lows, the victories and the challenges, the on-track action and the off-track stories of a wonderful season of Formula One racing.

Ross Brawn
Team Principal, Brawn GP

# Introduction

# The Phone Call

'I have some terrible news.' The voice was blunt.

Fairy tales usually begin with 'Once upon a time,' but this one, the story of my 2009 Formula One world championship season, started with an ominous voicemail message on my mobile phone: 'Jenson, please call me. We have to speak immediately.'

As with all life-changing moments, I can remember the circumstances in vivid detail. It was Thursday 4 December, 2008. I was at Gatwick returning from a training camp in Lanzarote. My mobile has the loudest message alert in the world, which is embarrassing when you accidentally forget to put it on silent. In that second when the seatbelt sign goes off, and everyone on the aeroplane switches on their telephones, mine went BING really loudly. As we filed off into Arrivals, I thought, 'Oh great, I've got a message.' It's always exciting to get off a flight and find you've got a message, isn't it?

Except that this one was from Richard Goddard, my manager. I could tell from the flat, serious tone of his voice that it wasn't a positive message. Something was wrong. I rang him and played it a bit stupid, light-heartedly saying, 'Hey Richard, what's up? What's the matter?'

He got straight to the point: 'I have some terrible news. Honda are pulling out of Formula One.'

At first I didn't believe him. I couldn't take it in. In shock, I dropped my mobile. I scrabbled around on the floor to pick up my phone while juggling hand luggage. I didn't say a word back to him. I had that tingly feeling you get all over when you're trying to absorb the implications of something horrendous. I stood there for what seemed like ages with my mouth open. Chrissy Buncombe, one of my oldest friends who'd come training with me, as he often does, looked at me and registered exactly what Richard had said just from the reaction on my face.

I finally managed to say to Richard, 'What does this mean?'

'Well, it means we don't have a drive in Formula One in 2009 – he always says 'we' – and there aren't really many options. Let's confer later in the day. There are two seats available, but not in places where you are going to further your career.'

It was shattering news, so unexpected. I was thinking, 'Oh my God, after two tough years in the sport with Honda in 2007 and 2008, when the prospects of the 2009 season have always been the light at end of the tunnel... this is unthinkable.' I had finished the 2008 season 18th in the world championship table with just three points. I had reached Q3, the third and final qualifying session at each grand prix, in which the fastest ten drivers shoot it out for pole position, just once. It had been a dispiriting campaign, but I'd been able to bide my time in a dog of a car because I knew 2009 would be the turning point. The introduction of new technical regulations was as close to a clean slate as the sport had experienced for decades – and would put all teams back on a level playing field. Having abandoned the development of the 2008 car a third of the way into the season, the team had directed resources to concentrate on the design of the 2009 car. With Ross Brawn leading the technical side, and immersing himself in the genesis of a daring new design, the team had a big head start. The new car was still under wraps, but from the wind-tunnel figures I knew we were building a fantastic machine. The boys at the factory in Brackley, near Silverstone, were doing a great job. Thanks to these funny looking wings, we had recovered a lot of the downforce that you lose under the new regulations. We were going to be very quick. Everything was looking very, very positive... and then came this news which picked me up and hurtled me down another slope on the emotional rollercoaster ride that I'd been on over the last few months.

As usual at Gatwick, I waited for my bags for a good hour, so I had plenty of time to think things over in Baggage Reclaim. As well as Chrissy, I was with Mikey Collier, my physio, and John Brame, my trainer, a triathlete who had just started to work with me on an intensive new programme designed so that I would start the new season fitter than ever before. We were exhausted after a challenging week of swimming, running and cycling, making the best possible use of Lanzarote's superb Olympic-standard facilities and gentle climate. When Mikey realised I had bad news to impart, he thought maybe I'd doubled the distance of the cycle race I'd challenged the team to join me on the next day around Silverstone ahead of a visit to the Honda factory at Brackley! Racing in 2009 had seemed such a formality; no one would have contemplated the nightmare scenario of a huge manufacturer like Honda pulling the plug on its Formula One operation. There were potentially awkward knock-on effects, too. Mikey and John work for me. I employ them. If I'm not working, nor do they, so it was an unsettling situation all round when I shared the news.

I rang my parents. My father, known as the old boy, and my mother Simone – who divorced more than twenty years ago – are always supportive. The old boy, a serious rallycross driver in the seventies and an F1 addict ever since the days of Stirling Moss, comes to all the races; my mum attends Barcelona, Monaco and Silverstone and calls in or texts before and after each race. I thought I'd better call them to let them know what was going on before they heard it on the news. At first, both were emotional, but very strong, too, which surprised me – especially my father. I didn't expect his reaction to be so positive and practical. He was at The Ship and Castle, his local in Monaco, when he took my call.

'Dad, brace yourself. There's a possibility I may not be in Formula One in 2009. Honda are pulling out.'

'100 per cent pulling out?' he asked.

'Yes, 100 per cent.'

He was clearly dumbfounded, but he could detect my anxiety and he quickly managed to put a very positive spin on it, saying there's always something you can retrieve from a bad situation. Obviously, he wasn't feeling that strong and positive, because he later said he went back to the bar, sank his drink and went straight home to ponder life without Formula One. But he wanted to sound bullish in front of me and that helped me as I stood there – still at the luggage carousel – thinking my F1 career might be over. I could race in other series, but if you go into Le Mans and Touring Cars, people tend to forget about you in Formula One. It is hard to come back from a year out. I didn't know what to do, and actually there was nothing I could do. Uncertainty clouded everything.

> Racing in 2009 had seemed such a formality; no one would have contemplated the nightmare scenario of a huge manufacturer like Honda pulling the plug on its Formula One operation.

I travelled back to Chrissy's house in London. Mikey was with us too. No one spoke in the car. Next morning I got up early and headed straight to the factory. It was a planned visit, but obviously now in very different circumstances. Originally I had challenged the team to race a lap of Silverstone on a bike. About 40 people were interested, but we called it off. No one was in the mood to be cycling around Silverstone in the pouring rain and 3°C.

I had intended to discuss the performance of the new car. Instead I went into the factory poised to chat with everyone, to raise spirits and help maintain morale. That makes me sound a bit like Prince Charles on a British industry tour, but factory visits are an integral part of a driver's role. I would like to go after every race to share my thoughts about the car and our performance, but the race schedule doesn't permit that. I probably go twenty times a year. The drivers' presence is a reminder of what the whole enterprise is about. A driver can push a team forward, inspire others by his own ambition. The guys always have lots of questions for me, and I bombard them with queries of my own. Our car is designed and built to compete against others; I'm entrusted with the fantastic job of racing it on the track. In between the drawing board and the race track, there's a long and close-knit chain of people giving their professional and emotional input. The Honda team comprised 700 hard-working, dedicated professionals, many with mortgages and young families. We're all involved in the process of trying to win – and in early December 2008 we all faced the loss of our jobs. I went to rally everyone, but deep down inside, I was not feeling optimistic at all. What chance was there of anyone buying the team less than three months before the first grand prix of 2009 at Melbourne, when the world was imploding financially? How could we possibly be racing in 2009?

I arrived at the factory. It is a hugely impressive glass and steel structure with state-of-the-art facilities for each department from design to engineering, workshop to component testing, carbon-fibre laboratory to the aerodynamicists' wind tunnel. I went round every department and I found it hard to gauge how to talk about the situation. The team had heard the news the same day as me, within an hour. I started by chatting to the guys in the engineering department. It's a big department of about 50 engineers. It's quite daunting trying to make a positive speech when you're feeling emotional yourself. I tried my best, but the voice went. I was a bit of a wreck. They looked at me and smiled. Then someone stepped forward and bailed me out, 'Well, Jenson, obviously it's an emotional time, but we're staying positive, and as soon as you leave this room we're going to get back to work. Nobody will be interested in buying this team or putting money into it unless we can prove to them that we're worth the investment.' They were working as normal, pushing 100 per cent despite the uncertainty about whether the car would ever race. Honda to their credit hadn't just switched off the lights and locked the factory doors. They had resolved on a window of time to help the management secure the future of the team in some form or other. The budgets were obviously much smaller during this period than when Honda were fully committed to the race programme, but the focus in the factory was inspiring. It helped me tremendously. The sight of their strenuous endeavour encouraged me to think, yes, we can find a sponsor. I'd gone to the factory to boost spirits, but the guys ended up bolstering my faith that a solution would be found.

The whole situation was a wake-up call. I had taken it for granted that we would be racing in 2009. In retrospect, I think Honda had too. I had signed a new three-year extension to my contract only weeks before Honda had announced it was pulling out. Early pre-season speculation and whispers were all about how good the car was going to be. I was pretty confident in my own ability and I assumed I'd be around with the team a lot longer. So Honda's withdrawal was a huge jolt, a life-changing moment. I couldn't just go and find another job. It was going to change my life completely if I wasn't racing in Formula One. I had achieved one grand prix victory in Hungary in 2006, but I was nowhere near finished. I had the same dream that I'd had ever since I was eight years old: to win the Formula One world championship. I had been working towards that dream for so many years that the prospect of no car, no team, no Formula One future put everything into a completely different and frankly horrifying perspective.

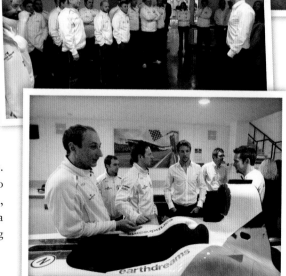

# The Uncertainty

Honda's sudden exit precipitated fears within Formula One that other manufacturers would pull out too. Right up to the nano-second of being informed of Honda's action, however, I had only heard positive vibes from them. The 2009 season was looking very promising and as everyone can now see the car that we'd built was incredibly competitive. I don't know if people at Honda went back to the big bosses and said the 2009 car was looking good but they couldn't be certain how it would measure up against the opposition or if the worldwide issue of selling road cars meant that they could not afford to be seen to be spending so much money in Formula One. It is very unusual for the Japanese to take any action that involves such public loss of face. Jessica Michibata, my half-Japanese, Tokyo-based girlfriend, said she was very surprised at what happened. We suspected that Honda must have had serious problems back at base, which was confirmed when company president Takeo Fukui gave a speech explaining the need to offer the team for sale. Fukui san – who is a massive motorsport fan of both motorbikes and cars – was very emotional as he declared that Honda had to protect its core business activities and secure its long-term future at a time of mounting uncertainty within the motor industry. Fine, I understood why they withdrew, but it was a bit late in the day to inform a racing team – although I'm sure that's because they had been trying to find a solution.

> There were already many talented people at Brackley, but Ross's arrival in 2007 lifted expectations.

The most difficult year had been 2007. Back then, the team had no leadership or direction. All decisions, big and little, went to committee. I couldn't see things ever getting done, never mind anything getting better. That's when Richard Goddard and I pushed hard to get Ross Brawn on board. He was then on a year's sabbatical from Ferrari. We worked hard to impress upon Honda the need to tempt him back into Formula One with a new challenge. At first, he was linked with Red Bull, but at the end of November 2007 he was named as the new team principal of Honda F1 Racing. What a coup!

As technical director, Ross had overseen a record seven world championship successes with Michael Schumacher both at Benetton (1994 and 1995) and at Ferrari (2000, 2001, 2002, 2003 and 2004). He is renowned for his organisational genius in the factory and for spontaneously adapting race strategy from the pit wall according to whatever dramatic circumstances a race produces. From his appointment onwards, I was confident that things would turn around. He radiates enormous influence. He doesn't need to say anything. He's a big bear of a man and his presence at the factory seemed to inspire everyone to push harder. The workforce have real belief in him and respect for what he achieved at Benetton and Ferrari. They can see what heights can be reached in Formula One. It seems a 'dream team' emerges wherever and whenever he is in charge. There were already many talented people at Brackley, but Ross's arrival in 2007 lifted expectations. Meanwhile the team was testing Lucas di Grassi and Bruno Senna, young stars from GP2, the Formula One feeder series. They still hadn't settled on my teammate for 2009, but a willingness to blood novices suggests a strong, forward-looking outfit that is prepared to take risks.

The car was still under embargo, but we knew it was strong. During the winter, I spoke to my race engineer Andrew 'Shov' Shovlin more than to Ross Brawn. Shov and I have worked together since 2003, back when the team was called BAR-Honda. 2009 would be his sixth season as my Senior Race Engineer. We're great mates and very close, which we need to be in order to understand each other in the heat of battle. Over the radio, it is Shov who tells me important facts, lap times of drivers in front and behind, and orders me to push. We tend to talk less than other driver-engineer partnerships because he knows I like it that way. But we get on so well. We're always taking the mickey out of each other, because you do with your mates, don't you?

I had also spent time at the factory with the aerodynamicists, running through the blizzards of data and sifting the reams of information and feedback from the wind tunnel. Formula One teams live or die by the data we get from our cars, whether from scale models in the wind tunnel or from telemetry while the car is testing or racing. I took great heart from the fact that we'd worked out why the 2008 car was such a failure, not only aerodynamically but also mechanically. All the little niggly problems that had plagued us over the past few years had been solved.

> Good cars don't happen by accident. They are the result of a supreme organisation of talent as well as a million and one gizmos, widgets and grommets working together harmoniously.

I think the Honda management expected Ross to turn everything upside down, but he found the systems in place were very, very good. The team lacked nothing in brainpower and resources. Areas like quality control, craftsmanship and component checking had many experienced people in place, seasoned veterans of multiple F1 campaigns as well as any number of bright young things. He didn't need to initiate any major changes, just a difference in approach – tweaks and fine-tuning rather than coarse adjustments. The preparation, design and systems were all first class and meticulously executed.

At the weekly concept meetings at the factory, which Ross chaired, designers and engineers would bring ideas to the table and sit around and discuss which way to go forward on development and design. Good cars don't happen by accident. They are the result of a supreme organisation of talent as well as a million and one gizmos, widgets and grommets working together harmoniously – a thing of beauty when it happens but notoriously hard to achieve. As soon as Ross was on board, there was a buzz about the future. It wasn't going to happen overnight – car design is a long process – so the 2008 season was our year of sacrifice, but, boy, could I see light at the end of the wind tunnel. And then, Honda's shock announcement.

While everyone at the factory tried to ignore the uncertainty surrounding the team's future and press on with that complex process of designing and testing and re-designing and re-testing that would eventually produce the 2009 car, I juggled three options. One was to seek a drive with another team. The problem was that the game of musical seats that determined who drove for which team in 2009 was all but over. While it would have been interesting to have driven for either of the two teams that had vacancies, neither of them would have furthered my career and helped me win the world championship. The second option was to hang on in at whatever became of Honda F1 and fasten my seatbelt for the white-knuckle ride that would be helping the team to find a sponsor in time to line up on the grid in Melbourne on 29 March. Failing that, the third 'option' was to take a year out.

The suspense was unsettling. Richard and I chewed over these possibilities endlessly. Always at the back of my mind was the car. It was so frustrating to think that we might not make it to the grid in this car, and that it might not turn a wheel in anger. I knew it was good. I'd seen the investment from Japan; I'd been in on the Brawn-led development right from the start. I'd felt the quality and knew that it went right through the entire Honda F1 organisation. I couldn't believe that no one would want to buy a team of hardworking, dynamic engineers. In the end, there was no decision to make. We stayed loyal to our team and, with a shake of the hand and firm look in the eye, determined to focus on getting that car to the grid in Melbourne.

The hat was brimming with names of potential buyers, headed by Sir Richard Branson, Dr Vijay Mallya, Achilleas Kallakis the Greek shipping magnate, Carlos Slim, the Mexican media tycoon (who a few years ago had been declared the richest man in the world); and Prodrive, the motorsport engineering group associated with World Rally Championship entries led by Dave Richards, himself the former team principal of the team when it was BAR-Honda. Richard, my manager, was on the case and would never let it go. He was pushing very hard to help interest a buyer in securing the team while keeping me informed as much as he could about which parties were shaping up, what the respective implications would be, and how much Honda would help us out with transitional financing.

On some days the news looked positive; on others, it looked anything but. We'd have three days of feeling positive and then four days of accepting that whatever scenario we were entertaining was not going to happen. You never knew which way it was going to swing. It didn't help that there was a lot of stuff going on in the upper echelons of the sport which we weren't party to. Honda's billion-dollar exit had prompted headlines like 'F1 in crisis!' And there were broader political issues. The Team That Was Once Honda had to line up on the grid in Melbourne in some shape or form, or Bernie Ecclestone would be penalised for not having twenty cars on the grid.

'Jenson, it's Frank. How are you feeling?'

One of the first people to call me after the initial news broke was Frank Williams, who had been responsible for giving me my Formula One break in 2000. 'Hope you are okay. I'm sure it will work itself out.' He was very positive. It was good to hear from Frank. When he gave me my Formula One debut I was nineteen, though twenty by the time of the first race in Melbourne. He was very paternal and he'd told me: 'Always work to be as fit as you can and spend time with the team, always pushing forward.' Frank's advice even fitted this strange set of circumstances. The team remained incredibly focused. Sometimes they didn't know as

much information as me, which is probably just as well. But Frank was right, you've got to push the team and stay as fit as possible. That is what I did. I spent another week in Lanzarote with Mikey and John, putting in the training hours – although I discovered how hard it is to train when you don't know what you're training for.

My family – mum, the old boy, my sisters Tanya, Samantha and Natasha – my mates and my girlfriend were all unerringly positive. Perhaps it's her Japanese upbringing, but Jessica is very philosophical and believes in star signs – which I don't so much. She was very confident things would turn around. She is a fashion model and a popular personality in Japan – her blog gets more than 100,000 hits a day! We met in a restaurant in Tokyo in February 2008 while I was fulfilling a PR engagement for Honda. She was with a female friend of mine. Later I spoke to my friend, got her number and called her a couple of times just for a friendly chat. We didn't meet again until the Japanese Grand Prix last year in November. I invited her. She came along, and... yeah! She's been with me through the really difficult winter months. She's very matter of fact, very positive. Overnight it felt like I'd known her for years. She understood me so quickly. And she absolutely loves racing. It's so important to me that my girlfriend cares about what I do.

I kept the old boy informed as much as I could. We never, ever, spoke in negative terms. In fact, we never dwelt on the subject at all. I was headlong into training. Triathlon is an all-consuming discipline which I had taken up when things were going badly at Honda. When it comes to training I have the lowest boredom threshold, but the mix of running, cycling and swimming is the perfect challenge. It was tough underachieving at race weekends but I found training and racing in triathlon got rid of the frustration, because there is a direct correlation between effort put in and reward taken out. If I achieved a goal, or a new personal best, it was down to me, not the bike, the trainers or the goggles! Triathlons give me a buzz, and I relish the hard training because I'm the one in control.

I didn't speak to any other driver during the winter. In our free time, we drivers are friendly, without being friends exactly – except perhaps for the poker gang led by Robert Kubica and Giancarlo Fisichella, which can involve Tonio Liuzzi, Fernando Alonso, Nico Rosberg, Adrian Sutil and Rubens. The driver I speak to most often is David 'DC' Coulthard. As fellow British drivers, we always got on well. We both made our Formula One debuts courtesy of Frank Williams. Our motorhomes were parked in the same FIA-alloted area at European grands prix and we are neighbours in Monaco. In his new role as BBC pundit alongside Eddie Jordan, he's been very encouraging. But I would rather hang out with my close friends Chrissy Buncombe – who runs Halycon Events, which organises corporate hospitality packages at grands prix – and Richie Williams, who races in Porsche Supercup, one of the motorsport categories that follows F1 around Europe. So they are always at a grand prix, and it's a good little family.

> Ever since the age of eight my life has been precisely attuned to the rhythms of the motorsport calendar, and now it was 'on hold'.

Formula One is nothing if not good at keeping up appearances, so despite the havoc that the credit crisis was causing to the motor industry, it was seemingly business as usual in the pre-season build-up. Other teams were launching their cars, Donington was given the green light as a venue for the British Grand Prix and the usual rumour-mill about the respective performances of each car was spinning with almost invisible speed. I preferred not to know about any of it. There was a tangible excitement about a new era, ushered in by new regulations which put all the teams back on a level. But I couldn't yet see a way to being part of it. I cut myself off. I didn't log on to Autosport or F1 Racing or anything on the internet. If I wasn't racing, I wasn't interested in racing at all. It was too painful. I avoided the motorsport magazines, which previously I had devoured hungrily. I shunned racing altogether. I was just training and keeping in touch with the factory. It was strange. Ever since the age of eight my life has been precisely attuned to the rhythms of the motorsport calendar, and now it was 'on hold'.

I rarely spoke to Nick Fry, the Chief Executive Officer of Honda F1 Racing, who was previously CEO of British American Racing before Honda bought out the team in late 2005, two seasons after my arrival from Renault in 2004. Nick knew where I was. He knew exactly where I wanted to be. It was not necessary to keep calling him, pushing him on points, so I just left him to it. I didn't speak much to Ross either. They knew I was focused on driving for the team. They knew I was prepared to play my part in helping the team secure its future, which was obviously to take a wage cut. By the end of the 2009 season, I will have earned some twenty per cent of what I would have earned under the terms of my previous contract with Honda. But I didn't – and don't – care. It helped the team, and it helped provide me with a car that I love to drive. Money means nothing when you have the chance to race in a front-running car with the world championship in your sights.

The potential buyout options now blur into one. I heard about Ross Brawn's offer of a management buyout from Richard. Other parties were still interested, however. Analysing the options, we agreed the management buyout offer was positive. It meant Ross would stay around and apply his inimitable focus to make it the best team in the world. But, with a small privateer team, you worry about money, and the sums that could be invested in development and upgrades for the car throughout the season. Maybe a tycoon-style buyer was a better option? It was hard weighing up which direction was best.

In the end, the management buyout with a little help from Honda won the day. Meanwhile, a deal with Mercedes-Benz had been swung to supply engines. Ross had actually rung Mercedes on the very day Honda pulled out, which shows how badly he wanted to see his first car race. The question soon arose as to what name to give the team. Ross considered 'Tyrrell', since the team's DNA goes back via BAR-Honda to the late Ken Tyrrell's team, which had enjoyed its heyday in the late 1960s and early 1970s with Jackie Stewart behind the wheel. But the feedback was that 'Tyrrell' was a name that no longer resonated with a modern F1 audience. A subsequent brainstorming of generic names produced Pure Racing, but that would mean we'd be the Pure-Mercedes team which Mercedes vetoed. At that point, Caroline, a secretary in the team's legal office handling the contracts, said: 'Why not Brawn?' I thought this was a very positive move. Brawn is a good strong name, not only in the literal sense but also because Ross is a legend in the sport – although people have turned it into Prawn Racing! With Ross owning the team and his name emblazoned across the car, he couldn't possibly screw up, could he?! As an engineer-turned-owner, he takes a lot of pressure, but he can handle it. He never looks ruffled. He's handled pressure for many years in Formula One. I think the buyout has made him even stronger. Now that Ross owns the team, he's become more of a facilitator than a designer. He has turned the team around. The name has puzzled a few observers, however. In Bahrain, I read an article in a local paper the day after the race. The columnist wrote that, of course, people will buy a Ferrari road car if Ferrari is racing in F1. But he couldn't figure out why someone would buy a shaver just because they sponsor an F1 team!

On the evening of Wednesday, 4 March Ross called me to request I come to the factory the next day. He said we were doing the shakedown test on Friday. 'We need to do it if we're going racing and we can afford to do it,' he said. On Thursday morning I arrived to find the entire workforce assembled in the car bays, the area where the cars get fondled. Ross stood up with Nick Fry and announced we would be racing in 2009, that our name would be Brawn GP and that we would have our shakedown at Silverstone the following day. Ross's speech prompted whoops of joy, but it was that last-minute. After weeks of uncertainty, worry, frustration and stress, it was a massive relief to read the official announcement released on 5 March:

*Honda Motor Company Limited and Ross Brawn are pleased to confirm that they have reached agreement to secure the future of the former Honda Racing F1 Team. With immediate effect, Honda will pass ownership to Ross Brawn, Team Principal of the new Brawn GP Formula One Team.*

*Brawn GP has agreed a partnership with Mercedes-Benz High Performance Engines, Brixworth, UK to supply the team with its 2.4-litre Mercedes-Benz FO108W Formula One engines.*

*The team can confirm that its race driver line-up for the 2009 season will combine the talents of two of Formula One's most experienced drivers in Jenson Button and Rubens Barrichello. The race-winning drivers continue their partnership at the team for a fourth consecutive year, forming the most experienced driver partnership on the grid with 423 grand prix starts between the pair.*

We also knew, however, that there would be cost cutting and job losses. It was an uneasy situation. Some people were very happy, others worried about their futures.

# The Car

Silverstone was absolutely freezing for the shakedown. Budgets being what they were, we had a little tent to base ourselves in. It was like Formula Ford days again with a limited number of people present for a private testing session. No press. No fans. Just team members. To hear the Mercedes engine fire up in the crisp spring air was a very special moment. It was very emotional to see the car hit the circuit for its maiden run. The BGP 001 was testimony to the collective pride of the team with its common spirit, courage, stamina, ambition and dream. Throughout that day, every single team member came up at some point to see the car go round.

The purpose of a shakedown is to run through a systems check on a new car and collect base data. It was amazing, at last, to drive the car, even though I couldn't get a feeling for how good it was when fully unleashed because we ran the shakedown on the club circuit at Silverstone – the school circuit – and not the grand prix track. We had no problems at all. It was a breeze. It was the first time out with the Mercedes-Benz engine and we very quickly ironed out the drivability issues with the engine. Working with Mercedes under the time constraints turned out exceptionally well. New partnerships can require familiarisation periods as engine manufacturer and chassis constructor learn to work together, but it was never a case of Brawn GP and Mercedes-Benz. It felt like we had been working together as Brawn-Mercedes for a decade.

**To hear the Mercedes engine fire up in the crisp spring air was a very special moment. It was very emotional to see the car hit the circuit for its maiden run.**

I have never got into a car for a shakedown feeling such a buzz. How often does a driver get to try out the first car of a team making its Formula One debut? Well, a lot of established Formula One drivers wouldn't want to, but Brawn GP wasn't really a new team except in name. Yet there was something new in the air – a freshness of approach and a feeling of pure excitement. The BGP 001 was painted in its new unfussy yellow and white livery. I like simple colour schemes, especially after the busy ones we'd had previously at Honda. The look and shape of the car appealed to me. The nose was very different to that of any other car. Everything was perfect. It all fitted together so well. You could see passion shining from the eyes of every member of the team as the car ran on the circuit for the first time.

Every previous car I've been involved with had been a slight rush to get ready. But when the mechanics put the engine cover and side pods on the BGP 001 – and we're talking fitting pieces together to within 0.1mm of each other – everything matched beautifully. There were no overlapping parts. Everything about the car had been thought out so carefully. There wasn't a single area that I could say was not perfect. This is almost incredible when you think the car had been designed for the Honda power unit, not the Mercedes. The gearbox was higher than it should be for the new engine. Everything had to be modified and thrown together at the last minute. It was thrown together very well I must say!

A seat fit can be a laborious process that takes a couple of days. You sit in a cockpit and wait as a foam mixture grows and hardens around you, taking a perfect mould of your shape in order to form a solid, supportive, comfortable seat. Often the first attempt is botched. You trim it, but still it doesn't quite work. You try again... and again. You need a few attempts to get it right, but this time it was all so easy, just a morning's work. They trimmed it up and it felt so comfortable. I sit much lower in the BGP 001 than in previous cars, which also makes me feel more comfortable. So it was all coming together nicely: my first drive at Silverstone, in the ideal position in the cockpit, in a great seat. None of those eve-of-season niggly little comfort issues was there. I was in a great place to concentrate on improving our performance.

# Barcelona

Monday, 9 March: the new Brawn GP-liveried trucks nosed their way into the Circuit de Catalunya, folded in the hills to the north-east of Barcelona. It was a milestone moment. Everyone we met was quick to congratulate us on being part of Formula One in 2009. Mechanics, engineers and the travelling workforce from rival teams came up to us, shook our hands and offered any help we needed, which was so uplifting. Formula One is a big family and we felt its embrace. The teams travel around the world fighting each other, but we are all in it together.

At first we felt very much like latecomers to the party. All our rivals had already been testing for months. Minutely attuned to what was going on in other factories, the engineers and mechanics at Brackley had clocked the testing times of the other teams and seen that they were very close. Only a few hundredths covered the entire field. This could mean two things: either that every other team had built an amazing car or that every other team had built a pretty average car.

Every driver will tell you the place they feel most comfortable on earth is in a racing car, helmet on, visor down, ready to prove they are the quickest. It is where you feel most relaxed, most yourself. It was a magical sensation climbing into the cockpit to pit the BGP 001 against the other cars. The plan for the first run was to drive five laps. 'Obviously everything's very different,' Shov said, 'especially the engine, the driveability, so just get a feel for it.' After two laps, I had the biggest smile on my face. The car was beautiful to drive. Wow! I thought, 'What have we done? We've built a car that is exceptional.'

I said to Shov: 'This is a great car. There are no areas that we need to improve. What a great base line!'

'Do you know how quick you are?'

'No...'

'You are six tenths quicker than anyone and they've been testing for four months,' he grinned.

Are you kidding? Then I realised that the other teams had built pretty average cars. It wasn't only the speed that blew my mind. I could also feel every bump, and I could do so much with the car because it did the same thing every time I hit the brakes. Five laps was all I needed to sense it was consistent and reliable, and just incredibly fast. Nothing went wrong. There were no reliability issues. Normally when you put a car together for the first time, the bodywork doesn't quite fit. It might be too close to the exhaust, which would burn the bodywork and the track rods, or the wishbones would overheat and have to be taped. There are always niggles

and snags. But the BGP 001 was faultless, which was almost incredible when you think the car was modified and re-built in a matter of weeks to incorporate the Mercedes engine. I've never driven a car like it. That was the moment I knew the 2009 season would be fun – although I was already wondering whether we, as a small team, had enough money to improve the car throughout the season and continue in the same vein.

I saw David Coulthard in the Barcelona paddock and couldn't resist walking over to rebuke him in jest. He's a mate, after all, and a few weeks earlier he had written an article in which he had speculated that were Brawn ever to make it to the grid in Melbourne, they should not be at the front but at the back – and that's if they can get the engine to fit in time for the first race. A knowing smile had come over my face when I read that, mindful of the exciting developments that were going on behind closed doors at Brackley. Long before the team was launched, we had snuck a Mercedes engine unit into the factory for the engineers to assess it vis-à-vis our chassis. There was no reason why DC should know this, and I couldn't blab it to him at the time, but after our pace had shocked everyone at Barcelona, I strolled over and said, 'You were wrong, weren't you?!' Thrilled to be wrong, DC said, 'I am shocked, first of all that you are here and secondly at the pace of the car. I'm so happy for you.'

Why is the BGP 001 so good? There are three main performance areas. 1) Aerodynamics. At Honda F1, we had decided early in 2008 to undertake an intensive aerodynamic programme and to exploit new technical regulations which in effect meant that every team had to develop their 2009 cars from scratch. It was a very intensive programme, and our early start gave us an advantage. 2) Engine. This had been a weakness last season but we expected the new rule changes to level the playing field over the winter. However, being able to use Mercedes-Benz gave us a top-level power unit. 3) Tyres. The Honda-turned-Brawn GP team always boasted a top-quality vehicle dynamics group, or chassis group, which works on suspension geometry, stiffness, et cetera, both to protect and to get the most out of tyre performance.

A strong, front-running car needs these three elements to be operating at a high level. If you bring them along to the race, and you haven't made a mistake along the way, you're in a great position. As well as the technical regulations, there were new sporting regs for the 2009 season, too, involving the use of tyres and engines, as well as a ban on testing. I'm a big fan of the change in tyres from groove tyres – which I've always had to drive on in my previous nine years in Formula One – to slicks, which are the tyres we should always use. A slick is a proper race tyre, a big, grippy tyre with no tread pattern so that more rubber is in contact with the track surface to maximise traction. With slicks back on the car, it felt like a proper racing machine. Rules dictating engine use changed. The two-races-per-engine rule was abandoned. We have limited engines – just eight 2.4-litre, V8 engines per driver for the whole 17-race season, and that includes practice, qualifying, the race. That allocation would have sounded crazy eight years ago, but the reliability of these engines now is fantastic. Mercedes-Benz began the season with certain engines marked for particular races and practice sessions.

The other major difference is the ban on testing during the season. The teams are also banned from testing post-season until the New Year, except for when they want to test a young driver. The outlawing of testing is a strange one. It makes my life quieter. My schedule is emptier. And it saves us money – but, pre-season, I can't imagine not being able to test our new aero parts in between races to see what effect they have on the performance chart.

Losing the test-team operation was a massive cut in costs. Supporting a race team and a test team was like running two Formula One teams: different cars, trucks, team, engines. Team personnel lost their jobs. Brawn GP sold the old Honda test trucks. It is a positive for F1. We need to be saving money, not spending £400m a year – and all this came about because Honda pulled out. The testing ban was a direct result of Honda's shock withdrawal from the sport.

# Other Cars...

I had closed my ears to the speculative chat that always precedes each season: about whether the new McLaren could provide Lewis Hamilton with back-to-back titles, or whether Renault had consolidated their end-of-2008 form, or whether the glory days would return to Williams. The only time I ever heard any whispers about pre-season testing was when I went to the factory and the team chatted to me about launches, testing times, design features. The first time I heard about the Red Bull being a beautiful car – as everyone called it – was at the factory when the boys showed me pictures. 'We think this is the one to beat,' they said. And they were right.

As soon as I drove our amazing car I thought, 'Wow, this is my opportunity to shine. This is my chance to win the world championship.' I rarely uttered those words to myself; in fact, I'd never uttered those words to myself. I was thinking things through race by race and I remained that way pretty much throughout the season. I get excited about every race that I go to, knowing that I'm competing to dominate that event. I'm always assessing whether there's a possibility we can win the next race, but not thinking too far beyond that. The path beyond about two races ahead is strewn with banana skins and oil slicks. You can't think too long term.

The third, and final, test was scheduled for 15–17 March at Jerez in Spain. Again, the car went like a dream. The winter testing season concluded with Autosport magazine declaring the fledging Brawn GP team the winners of the testing war. Andrew van de Burgt wrote in his editor's letter: 'A Brit is the bookies' favourite to win the opening race of the season, but it's not Lewis Hamilton that the smart money is going on, it's Jenson Button! The pace and reliability of the Brawn have been a revelation.'

I keep hearing of people who clocked our speed at Jerez and immediately called the bookies to bet on us to win the world championship at odds of 100-1. My sisters are still livid that I hadn't tipped them off!

We had got up to speed in the shortest possible time. In four months the world of Formula One had gone topsy-turvy. The McLaren was positively slow – Lewis Hamilton's title defence seemed to be in disarray before the season had even begun. Our team had responded best to the changes in technical regulations. There was an opportunity to be seized and I wasn't going to let it slip.

# To Australia

As soon as we realised Brawn GP was a runner, and that we would be competing in 2009, albeit on a fraction of Honda's budget, we frantically scoured the Internet for the cheapest deals on flights Down Under. Flying your gang – physio, manager, PA, family – to various races around the world is an incredibly expensive exercise. It comes in at about £80,000 for one assistant to attend every race. In the new downsized, cost-cutting era of Brawn GP, my manager Richard only attends a few races and my PA Jules operates from the United Kingdom. I travel economy, except long-haul, and book standard hotel rooms. We were prepared to haggle for cheap fares to Melbourne, but Emirates came up trumps and looked after us beautifully. It was fitting, because I had flown Emirates to my debut race in Formula One in 2000.

So Rubens and I would be on the grid in Melbourne, our fourth year as team-mates, with a car that was declared the one to beat – an almost unbelievable thought. I'd received a text from him five days after the Honda announcement in December saying, 'So what are we going to do?' My response was, 'Well, to start with you are my main competition to try and find a drive!' But it had turned out well in the end for both of us. Rubens only received the call close to the start of the season, but had kept fit over the winter and was raring to go. Thanks to our knowledge and experience – Rubens with his 266 grand prix starts and me with 149, both of us grand prix winners – ours was the perfect driver line-up for a new team. Our daily debrief sessions with the engineers at the track would be efficient and to-the-point. It's important to share information and move forward quickly from practice to find the best qualifying set-up and race trim. We both knew our team of engineers well – Rubens was to be reunited with his senior race engineer Jock Clear for a fourth season and I was going into my sixth season steered by Shov. Thanks to a perfect team effort we'd arrive on the start line in Melbourne in the best possible shape.

I was so excited I felt like a kid again. It was like preparing to fly off to my first race in Formula One nine years earlier, except I was in a better position – with a great team, a lot of experience and a genuine thrill about stepping into a Formula One car. I had never enjoyed that incredible feeling of anticipation about a race during 2008 because we'd never produced a car that was capable of troubling the front-runners. But that horrible, close-season limbo made me realise how much I love racing in Formula One.

Towards the end of 2008 Rubens had more often than not outqualified me. It wasn't a big deal, certainly not the sort of psychological battle that the paddock media like to whip up. There was a simple reason why he'd bettered me. Two thirds of the way through 2008 new aero parts arrived and we started tweaking the set-up. The parts gave the car more downforce, but the effect was to create oversteer (sliding rear end) which didn't suit my driving style. By that time, the team was already concentrating on the 2009 car, so it was too late to analyse and fix the problems, which meant a downbeat end to my season. I struggled to coax the best out of the car whereas Rubens, who likes a car with oversteer, had an easier time of it. The surest way to measure a driver is against his team-mate, who has the same equipment and the same resources to draw on. I'd always edged Rubens, but during this period he finished ahead of me more than he had ever done before. In 2009, I was determined to prevent that happening.

> The 2009 car suits me very well. From those two tests in Barcelona and Jerez I found a lot of confidence to push the car and easily find its limits.

I like the car to be stable at the rear. I'm not one to slide through a corner, like Sebastian Vettel. I try to be as smooth and precise and in-control as possible. That way you make fewer mistakes. I have driven like that ever since I was eight years old, when I started racing in karts. It's not a conscious driving style, it's just the natural way I drive. A stable rear end means you can brake hard, very late, and turn smoothly. The 2009 car suits me very well. From those two tests in Barcelona and Jerez I found a lot of confidence to push the car and easily find its limits. The problem with the 2008 car was that it was twitchy at the rear end. I'd hit the brakes, go into oversteer and start sliding, which meant I'd be wrongly positioned for the corner. I could not be precise. No way could I drive a car like that, whereas Rubens could. It's more his style. The joy of our new car is you can set it up how you want it over the weekend – and Rubens and I always set up slightly differently – and we both enjoy driving it because it reacts to changes. If you make a change, it affects performance positively or negatively. If you made changes on our previous cars, it felt like nothing happened.

I love the fact that we are a small private team rocking up to destroy the big boys, like Lord Hesketh's team, which was run from a stately home in the 1970s and delivered James Hunt his first grand prix victories, or the Williams team in its early years under Frank. The lack of a corporate approach has its advantages. As a driver in a small independent team with scarcely any sponsors, I have fewer obligatory PR functions to fill my schedule – that's always a positive for a racing driver! And it's such a close-knit, interdependent environment that we're like a little family. No one wants to let each other down. The original workforce has shrunk by 300. The job-shedding was traumatic, but it was the only way Ross could keep the team alive. As Honda F1, the team had grown too big for a Formula One team. I still have 400 people back at the factory watching me race, 400 people for whom I want to do a special job as much as for myself.

> I love the fact that we are a small private team rocking up to destroy the big boys.

The legality of our rear diffuser was brewing up a storm pre season. The diffuser is the part of the floor at the rear of the car that curves upwards and generates downforce. I reasoned, 'Everyone can see we are quick and everyone's worried they're not. Our rivals might focus on 'grey' areas of interpretation of the new rules, but I had to focus on the racing and forget about paddock politics. We'd sacrificed our 2008 season to concentrate on 2009. McLaren, Ferrari and Renault had not been working on their car so long, and there were mutterings about the unfairness of this. But that is how it is in Formula One. The established teams thought they might never catch up with the teams who had this kind of diffuser (Toyota and Williams had controversial diffuser components as well) so decided to protest instead! But the big teams quickly catch up. They always do.

I just focused on doing my job where it counted – on the circuit. I ignored the diffuser issue unless specifically asked. But I did dwell on reliability... We knew our Mercedes engine was dependable, but our gearbox was brand new. The mechanical side of the car was new, too, and hadn't done as much mileage in testing as had that of the other teams. Ross had played down our competitiveness. He had said he hoped our performance would be 'respectable'.

The flight to Melbourne is a long journey, especially when you feel restless with excitement. I couldn't believe that after the winter of stress, anxiety, frustration and fortitude, we were actually going racing. Paddock insiders didn't know what to expect from us. They knew from testing that we were quick, but I don't think many people really believed we could translate our testing performance into race-winning ability.

We knew we could. We knew we were going to have fun this season.

# The Races

# Australian Grand Prix
## Albert Park, Melbourne
### Friday 27 March – Sunday 29 March

**Number of laps:** 58

**Circuit length:** 5.303 km

**Race distance:** 307.574 km

**Lap record:** 1:24.125
(Michael Schumacher, 2004)

## MY HISTORY AT ALBERT PARK

**2008 (Honda)**
Grid 12; retired (collision)

**2007 (Honda)**
Grid 14; finished 15

**2006 (Honda)**
Grid 1; finished 10

**2005 (BAR-Honda)**
Grid 8; finished 11

**2004 (BAR-Honda)**
Grid 4; finished 6

**2003 (BAR-Honda)**
Grid 8; finished 10

**2002 (Renault)**
Grid 11; retired (collision)

**2001 (Benetton-Renault)**
Grid 16; retired (electrical)

**2000 (Williams-BMW)**
Grid 21; retired (engine)

I am a big fan of Melbourne as a city and as a venue for the first race of the season. The collective excitement of the start of a world championship campaign gives this event a real buzz. After the long winter break, this is the weekend where eve-of-season ambitions start to be realised or are brought back to earth with a bump. The opener is a thrilling technical challenge because none of us knows where we stand until the cars hit the track and race in earnest.

Albert Park provides a beautiful setting – palm trees, water, huge horizon, skyscrapers in the distance – and it is a fast and fun circuit to drive with some technically demanding corners. There are a lot of quick changes of direction. You need a car that dances on its toes. Many of the corners are 90 degrees, and you need a very positive or responsive front end for that. It's bumpy under braking, but I always enjoy driving here – particularly in qualifying when you can get on it and nail a flying lap. I always go well here, even with a poor car.

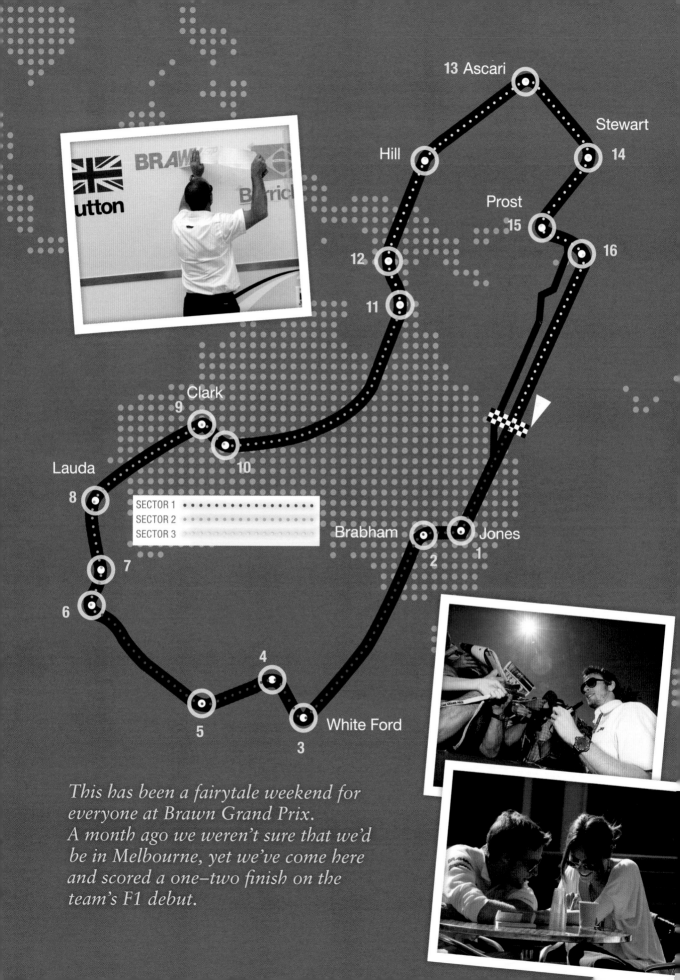

13 Ascari

Stewart

Hill

14

Prost

15

12

16

11

Clark

9

10

Lauda

8

SECTOR 1
SECTOR 2
SECTOR 3

Brabham    Jones

2          1

7

6

4

5

White Ford

3

*This has been a fairytale weekend for
everyone at Brawn Grand Prix.
A month ago we weren't sure that we'd
be in Melbourne, yet we've come here
and scored a one–two finish on the
team's F1 debut.*

# Australia:
## Preparation, practice and qualifying

After the traumatic winter, it's amazing we're here. That moment when a grid full of new cars hits the track in competitive trim is exciting in the extreme, even when you've had a full winter of testing. For us, at Brawn GP, that tension is all the tauter as the BGP 001 car has completed just seven days of pre-season testing. The question everyone is asking is: Can its stunning testing form be carried into the season? We think it can. While the Formula One world was speculating on the team's future, all the guys at the factory were quietly getting on with creating a blinder of a car.

I arrived in Melbourne last Saturday to have a few extra days to acclimatise to the time zone. Walking into the hotel with my bags, I had the biggest grin on my face. It's exciting enough starting the season, even with a bad car, but knowing you are turning up with a car that could win the race is such a buzz. Seeing the other drivers and knowing they are so annoyed that you have this superior car is a great feeling. Honda used to pay for my travel and hotels, but this year I'm paying my own way. Now I realise how much I cost! When I went to Tokyo to see Jessica recently I booked into the Grand Hyatt in Tokyo, and asked for the same room I've always had before, and it was £850 a night. I thought, 'Okay, I am not paying that' – but that was what Honda normally paid for me. Here, I've still checked into the Crown Towers, where I've always stayed. I need to be in a good place mentally, somewhere I feel comfortable. I booked a standard room, but I've been upgraded to a suite, which is amazing.

I am so familiar with the hotel here, I was ready to jump straight onto my bike. The plan was to spend a few days training in the sunshine with my physio Mikey, plus two iron men, one iron woman and some professional cyclists. Talk about a baptism of fire. They set off at a lightning pace to cycle around Melbourne, starting on the coast roads and then going inland. Mikey and I just mouthed 'Oh my God' to each other – and two and a half hours later I'd done one of the fastest rides in my life. These guys tore me to bits, destroyed me, but the weather was stunning, and it was a great way of acclimatising. Otherwise I was going to go mad, sitting around for days thinking about the weekend. With Honda, I'd always stopped en route in Japan for a pre-season visit. This time I'm a free agent.

I also met up with Phil Young, my former physio, who is now based in Australia working with V8 Supercar drivers, so, on a second ride, there were about fourteen of us cycling along the coast having a great time. Jules Kulpinski, my PA, comes from Melbourne and knows some great low-key places to go to in the evening, so it was a fun, relaxed build-up to the race.

### THURSDAY
Every morning I wake up and I can't wait to sit in the car. It's like starting out in Formula One all over again, but better. People don't know what to expect of us – they're in shock about our testing pace, and there's speculation that we tested on low fuel, topping the time sheets to attract the attention of potential sponsors.

We headed in to the circuit. I don't like to get here too early or you run out of things to do, and more and more journalists seem to find you. Brawn GP, as a new team, are in the last garage in the pit lane – the order is allocated according to how the teams finished in the previous year's constructors' championship. But our position at the far end of the paddock has its advantages. It's a lot quieter down here and our garage is well positioned for pit-stop strategy. It's best to be at either end to get an easier entry to or exit from the pits.

A fantastic atmosphere is building up. It was strange walking into the garage and seeing how small it is, and yet our little team still can't fill it. The garages get smaller and smaller as you go down the pit lane. We have 40 people working in that space whereas we had more than 100 people with Honda. So we are 60 per cent down on staff and we don't have many spare parts. Rubens and I have one spare front wing each so if we crash here, that's it, game over. It's a strange position to be in, but working together in such a tight, close-knit unit is like a family and it's very stirring. Here comes the small team charging in to fight the big manufacturers. And destroy them! It reminds me of the good old days of Formula One when small outfits could achieve great things, like Hesketh Racing, with Bubbles Horsley and James Hunt, when the minnows took on the giants and won. The stories in James Hunt's book are amazing, and I feel our team has a bit of that spirit. We've

rocked up to the first race with no sponsors on the car and I wish it could stay like that, but it can't. You need to have sponsors behind the team, but it does remind me of Lord Hesketh's team. Like them, we have a very well-spoken chap in Ross Brawn, we have a British racing driver and our aim is to beat the big outfits! Oh, it's fantastic. It will go down in history as Hesketh Racing did. We just need a cool logo like their teddy bear. I'd like to get hold of some of those Hesketh tops and wear them around the paddock.

Are we worried about the lack of work on different set-ups in the car and on changing set-up in a session? Not as much as people assume we must be. Our team has always managed to wheel out a car for the first time with the set-up almost spot on. It's amazing. We see other teams wheel their cars out, and they're slow, and over a couple of weeks they improve their cars through set-up. But we're always strong immediately. I'm happy with the car. I know we can tweak certain things to find the perfect set-up to suit the conditions and the circuit.

## FRIDAY

It was great to finally fire up an engine and get the season underway! Yep, Brawn Grand Prix made its competitive debut today. To mark the occasion, Rubens and I wore special helmets with a livery to match the team's distinctive yellow, black and white colour scheme. Albert Park is very different to the tracks that we used for our limited pre-season testing programme. The track surface is bumpy, especially in the braking areas, and slippery at the start of the race weekend due to the use of public roads – it takes a while to 'rubber in'.

Driving the first few laps around Albert Park is an incredible feeling. It's special because it's a street circuit, and because March is autumn in the southern hemisphere, leaves are falling off the trees. If you're driving down a straight with a car in front of you, you see a flamboyant rooster tail of leaves fanning up in front of you – because of the way the car floors work. I remember the first time I drove out of the pit lane in 2000 behind Michael Schumacher with that rooster-tail soaring from his Ferrari and I just thought, 'Wow. WOW!'

Today was great, driving out knowing I had an excellent chance of topping every single session. As a driver, you want to win the race, but you also want to be quick all the way through the weekend. Our cars are very strong on pace and we have a lot of fuel on board.

In the first practice session, grip levels were very low, as we expected. I embarked on the Friday programme set out by the engineers – which concentrated on refining the balance of my car and putting as much further mileage on the BGP 001 as possible.

In the second session, conditions improved and we completed a thorough evaluation of the Bridgestone tyre compounds available for this race. So, after today's practice, I feel very positive. The long-run performance of the car looks competitive, particularly on the harder tyre. Tomorrow morning, a priority will be to work on the softer tyre. The annoying thing was that I had traffic on both of my new-tyre runs at the end of the day, which was a shame, as I don't know how quick we are over one lap yet, but I have to say it felt good.

I'm trying to keep everything relaxed. Also, because of the diffuser issue – with other teams now planning to lodge a protest – I don't want to hype up the car. I'm still nervous. I still have a team-mate I want to beat and there are a few other cars up there – Sebastian Vettel's Red Bull, Robert Kubica's BMW and Timo Glock's Toyota.

SATURDAY

*The BGP 001 cars ran at the front of the field throughout qualifying with both drivers vying for position at the top of the timesheets. Rubens took the honours in Q1 and Q2. In the pole position shoot-out, Jenson took pole with a time of 01:26.202 in the dying seconds of the session.*

A great day! Pole position, with Rubens alongside me as Brawn GP lock out the front row of the grid in the team's debut race. To achieve that after the last four months of uncertainty, worry, frustration and intense hard work is a brillliant achievement. The car felt fantastic and I have to give so much credit to Ross, Nick and everyone at the factory at Brackley. To go from a situation where you don't even know if you are going to race in Formula One ever again to achieving pole at the first race of the season weeks later is just incredible.

The car did everything I asked of it. Rubens was very quick throughout qually. I knew I had to get through the first two sessions, and then unleash my quickest lap in Q3, the pole position shoot-out. The experience of being on pole here in 2006 probably gave me extra confidence to really commit. It was a magical moment when I shaved a chunky 0.3s off Rubens' provisional pole time with seconds to go. I think I screamed something like 'Yeee Haaaa' over the team radio. That's all I could say! It was just so emotional. We have to remember what we've been through and enjoy this moment. We've thrown the gauntlet down to the other teams. We've shown our pace. There's no going back. This is where we deserve to be after the tough times. I think we've shocked a lot of the paddock today.

A first pole position for Brawn Grand Prix at our first race. My second pole in Australia... We thought we would celebrate, so all the gang went to a flash restaurant. That's Jessica, Mikey, my manager Richard, the old man and me. Tomorrow is the important day, but we wanted to enjoy the moment. We had some Japanese food and it was such a special moment after the stresses and anxieties we'd been through over the winter. We didn't acknowledge it like that over dinner. We just giggled and looked at each other with big smiles.

*'He must be so delighted. The man who thought his Formula One career was over a month ago is now on pole position!'*
Jonathan Legard, BBC TV

## BRAWN TECHNICAL UPDATES

The car was exactly the same specification as we had run at the Barcelona and Jerez pre-season tests earlier in March. The reliability was impressive for a new car and we knew the pace was good enough to win the race. We just had to make sure we didn't have any silly problems like hoses or pipes rubbing through or wires chafing and causing a short circuit. As it happened, the biggest issue was that my drinks system did not work – not a major concern in Australia, but it could be a more serious problem in the hot and humid conditions of Malaysia.

# Australia:
## The race

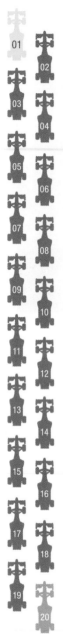

1. **Jenson Button**
2. Rubens Barrichello
3. Sebastian Vettel
4. Robert Kubica
5. Nico Rosberg
6. Felipe Massa
7. Kimi Räikkönen
8. Mark Webber
9. Nick Heidfeld
10. Fernando Alonso
11. Kazuki Nakajima
12. Heikki Kovalainen
13. Sebastien Buemi
14. Nelsinho Piquet
15. Giancarlo Fisichella
16. Adrian Sutil
17. Sebastien Bourdais
18. Lewis Hamilton
19. Timo Glock
20. Jarno Trulli (pit start)

### STRATEGY

Bridgestone brought the Medium and Super Soft dry tyre compounds to Melbourne. From our race weekend work, the Option was the weaker of the two, suffering from graining, and therefore the strategy would be based around running the Super Soft tyre for a shorter stint, at the end of the race, completing most of the race on the Medium compound.

I qualified P1, just ahead of Rubens, on an equal two-stop fuel load – which is the fastest theoretical race. I was brought in under the first safety car, following Nakajima's accident, filling for a long middle stint, minimising the laps on the Option tyre at the end of the race.

*Jenson Button led the Brawn GP team to victory in the season-opening Australian Grand Prix today, achieving his second GP win and capping a stunning debut race weekend for the new British-based team. Team-mate Rubens Barrichello brought his BGP 001 home in second position to achieve the first one–two finish for a new team since Mercedes-Benz in 1954.*

I slept like a baby and woke up looking forward to the race so much. Jules, my PA, had forwarded me some supportive comments by email from Nigel Mansell and John Surtees, both former British world champions. It's amazing how people change their opinions when things go well! Both had made negative comments about me previously. I have saved the emails and the articles with their criticism, but it made me giggle. I've always had a lot of respect for both drivers. It is just the way it goes. And they're not the only ones…

It was a 5pm start local time, to serve European television audiences. The great thing was that I could relax and wake up at 11am. Fantastic. I got up, had brunch and headed for work with all of the gang. Just before we turned in to the circuit I said to them, 'Shall we go for a drink somewhere?' 'Yeah, let's do it' was the resounding response. So we headed down to the beach to a little café we'd been to before and had a cappuccino. It was lovely to chill out before the race, and take it all in. We sat around looking out at the sea, grinning to each other, but not saying too much, because the fight was still to come. But we knew what we had – a great car and a great team behind us and we knew how far we had come already.

My only concern about the race was the early evening start. As the sun gets lower, and shines through the trees, it's very difficult to see on a few of the corners. I would say it made it a bit dangerous – and it had made qualifying tough too. For the 2008 night race in Singapore, which took place under floodlights, Mikey and I had gone on a recce around the streets on a scooter to test a variety of tinted visors. The problem today was that the visor I used had a tint on the outside, but it also had a yellow surround, which was nice because it suited the yellow on the car livery. But when the sun shone, I had the glow inside too.

A luminous yellow dayglo tint inside my helmet. There were some corners where I couldn't see the exit because I was in this bright yellow cloud.

But what an amazing day it turned out to be! A fairytale ending to the first race in the life of Brawn GP. It may have looked like an easy victory, but it wasn't at all. I had a good clean start and maintained my advantage into the first corner, chased by Sebastian Vettel, Robert Kubica, Nico Rosberg's Williams and the two Ferraris of Kimi Räikkönen and Felipe Massa – and went on to build a strong lead over the field. It was a great feeling, racing from the front again after years of mid-grid claustrophobia. I felt I had the race under control. I was leading by 3.9 seconds at the end of the opening lap, and then kept my lead between four and five seconds. I had performance in hand but there were concerns about the reliability, particularly of the gearbox, so it was agreed beforehand I'd go only as fast as I needed to. The guys on the wall were worried about the transmission, with fourth gear having been replaced prior to the race. The Mercedes engine is very different to the Honda so the software is not yet fully developed to reflect that.

You could say the race was a walk in the park because our pace was very good and I was able to pull away from Vettel, but there were also two safety-car periods. Safety cars are a nightmare if you've built up a good lead. They bunch everyone up again and cause a reduction in the tyre temperatures. You have to work to keep heat in your tyres and then as the safety car peels off, you have to be wary because someone will try and jump you. So it was quite a stressful race even though we were leading every lap. Don't get me wrong, though, I was enjoying every minute out in front!

Shov was fantastic on the radio, trying to keep me as calm as possible. This was a position that none of us had been in before. In Hungary, in 2006, when I'd won my sole previous grand prix, it was a completely different situation because we'd started 14th on the grid. Here, we were controlling the race and if nothing went wrong we were going to win. It was a fantastic position to be in. Shov understands how to communicate with me – he doesn't go on a lot, because he knows I don't like it. He gave me the important facts. 'Jenson you don't have to push so hard now, just try and be consistent, save the engine, save the tyres.' I'm able to ask him questions and he gives me the information I need. He is very calming.

I lucked in during the first safety-car period, which was caused by Kazuki Nakajima smashing the nose of his Williams into the wall at the exit of Turn 4 on lap 18. Vettel had already pitted and I wasn't brought in at the end of that lap. Fortunately the safety car wasn't deployed until after I'd made my stop at the end of the following lap. I had a hairy moment at the re-start when I made a break for it from Vettel, but locked a wheel going into the penultimate corner, making me slow through it. However, I managed to get cleanly onto the power in the last part of the turn. I'd flat-spotted the left front, but within a few laps I'd pulled the gap back to four or five seconds. This car is so good.

On lap 46 I made my second stop but it was slow, and I'd stopped in second gear which meant I couldn't select neutral, ready to start in first, so my lead over Vettel was reduced from eight seconds to a mere 1.5 seconds. Then tyres became an issue in the closing laps. I was on deteriorating Super Softs and Kubica, in third behind Vettel, was on harder tyres. Shov came on the radio: 'Kubica's on Prime tyres. He could be a threat.' If Kubica got past Vettel, could he catch me? It was tense, but in attempting to chase me down, Kubica tried to pass Vettel around the outside of Turn 3 on lap 56 and crashed heavily two corners later; Vettel tried to continue on three wheels, earning a $50,000 penalty. Cue another safety car... and the chequered flag. Rubens, the beneficiary of the Vettel–Kubica collision, was second – so Brawn GP had an unbelievable one–two finish.

Ross came on the team radio: 'Sensational job, Jenson, sensational job. Fantastic. You deserve it.'

I said a lot in response, but can't remember my actual words. I think I talked about the winter, how difficult it was for all of us, and how we deserved everything that was going to come to us this season. I ended up with 'Thank you. You're a legend. This is going to be a great year.'

The race was won under safety car-conditions, but so what? Some people asked, 'Is it strange finishing at such slow speed? Is it still exciting?' OF COURSE IT IS. I'd brought the car home to win the first race for the new Brawn GP Formula One team. We qualified on pole, and we won the race, the first of a season we didn't even think we'd be part of. It was totally amazing. There was such emotion on the radio from Shov and from Ross on my slowing-down lap. I have never heard Ross so emotional.

I parked up in parc fermé, and literally jumped for joy. Normally Rubens would not be happy to finish second to his team-mate, but he'd had such a tough race, he was thrilled for us to finish first and second. I bent over him in the cockpit and we shared our amazement at the pace of the car. We just said to each other, 'This is going to be a great season.' A tough season, too, because we both know how competitive we are between ourselves, but we can tell it's not the only time we will be finishing first and second.

I saw Ross and he was speechless. He didn't say a word. He just gave me a bear hug. He's a big guy, Ross, he picks you up and hugs you. Like Bigfoot. Then he put me down and just shook his head. It's a big step for his career. He has won titles with Benetton and Ferrari, but for him to win a race with his name on the side of a car was something new and the best feeling in the world. He is proving straightaway that he is the legend that everyone knows he is. It was an absolutely crazy atmosphere. Emotions were running high with my father and with Jessica. It was the first race that Jessica had attended when I had finished in the points. It was strange for her. She didn't know quite how to react. She was nervous and it was so sweet.

As we were being weighed, Jarno Trulli, who finished third, offered his congratulations: 'I'm really happy for you guys because I wouldn't like to have been in your place two or three months ago.'

On the podium, I was looking for the boys, but they didn't get there in time because our garage was right down the other end of the pit lane. I was celebrating

This is the first time a new entrant in
Formula One has put the car on pole since
Jackie Stewart in 1970 in the Canadian
Grand Prix with Tyrrell Ford, and the
first time since 1954, when Juan Manuel
Fangio did it with Mercedes, that a car
has gone from pole on debut to victory.

everyone appreciated what we'd been through. There was a lot of respect, which is what F1 should be about: one big family sticking together through stressful times.

I enjoyed the moment, and as I said to the journalists in the post-race press conference, we need to enjoy this one because we have endured such tough times to achieve it. It is an amazing story. You don't have to add any Hollywood gloss. I intended to enjoy this victory, forget about the rest of the season until tomorrow, when I will start to think about the next race in Malaysia.

in front of Toyota mechanics. I was a little frustrated that I couldn't spot our boys. They eventually got there, and had to stand to the side, but I could see them all, and I could pick out the old man and Jessica. Ross Brawn came up on the podium with us. Rubens and I decided to aim all the Champagne at him. As Ross always does, he found a way out of the situation. He ended up with the best trophy for deflecting champagne – a big round plate that he wielded like a shield. But we got him! To hear the cheers from our boys was so rewarding, but when they presented Rubens and me with our trophies there was also a cheer from every team, and from the crowd. I think

I went to see the boys in the garage, gave them all a big hug and we had our picture taken together, which we've decided to do every time we win a race. To see the smiles on their faces and to see them so ecstatically happy, ah, it was amazing. I had seen them quite down at the factory, even when they were trying to be positive. It was difficult for them not knowing if they were going to have a job and be competing in elite level racing. Mechanics are so competitive. People

### AUSTRALIAN GRAND PRIX FINAL POSITIONS

| Pos | Driver | Team | Laps | Time |
|-----|--------|------|------|------|
| 1 | Jenson Button | Brawn-Mercedes | 58 | 1:34:15.784 |
| 2 | Rubens Barrichello | Brawn-Mercedes | 58 | +0.8 secs |
| 3 | Jarno Trulli | Toyota | 58 | +1.6 secs |
| 4 | Timo Glock | Toyota | 58 | +4.4 secs |
| 5 | Fernando Alonso | Renault | 58 | +4.8 secs |
| 6 | Nico Rosberg | Williams-Toyota | 58 | +5.7 secs |
| 7 | Sebastien Buemi | STR-Ferrari | 58 | +6.0 secs |
| 8 | Sebastien Bourdais | STR-Ferrari | 58 | +6.2 secs |
| 9 | Adrian Sutil | Force India-Mercedes | 58 | +6.3 secs |
| 10 | Nick Heidfeld | BMW Sauber | 58 | +7.0 secs |
| 11 | Giancarlo Fisichella | Force India-Mercedes | 58 | +7.3 secs |
| 12 | Mark Webber | RBR-Renault | 57 | +1 Lap |
| 13 | Sebastian Vettel | RBR-Renault | 56 | Accident |
| 14 | Robert Kubica | BMW Sauber | 55 | Accident |
| 15 | Kimi Räikkönen | Ferrari | 55 | Differential |
| Ret | Felipe Massa | Ferrari | 45 | Suspension |
| Ret | Nelsinho Piquet | Renault | 24 | Spin |
| Ret | Kazuki Nakajima | Williams-Toyota | 17 | Accident |
| Ret | Heikki Kovalainen | McLaren-Mercedes | 0 | Accident |
| DSQ | Lewis Hamilton | McLaren-Mercedes | 58 | +2.9 secs |

don't realise they are such big team players and when things go well they are on top of the world and, when they don't, they get very angry about certain situations. They work really hard too. To get the car ready for Australia was hard enough but they hardly had time to celebrate on Sunday evening before preparing the car for its journey as air freight to Malaysia.

It was a first race win for Leon, my mechanic who straps me into the cockpit, so he went dancing on Sunday evening… and dislocated his knee. I had left the club earlier, but apparently they'd had to call an ambulance. He was in agony and I don't know when he'll be able to take part in the races again.

Ross, ever practical, commented that operationally the team needs to be sharper. The guys had not done any pit-stop practice. They didn't have a chance. We had two tests and those sessions were all about reliability. We had done a couple of practice stops, but not drilled it. We got to the race and we almost lost the race because our pit-stops were twice as long as they should have been, just because everyone was trying to be careful and cautious. Nobody wanted to make a mistake. The boys also forgot to plug in my drinking bottle, which keeps me hydrated through a race. It did affect me, but at least it was an evening race, and it was in Australia, not the sapping humidity of Malaysia. It's a good sign, though, if you can win races when you still have areas to improve. There was no finger pointing. We all knew the eleventh-hour situation we'd been in. Little mistakes like that won't happen again. This, the first race of the season, was our practice run.

Mum's text was great: 'Yes!!! I am crying so much I cannot see. It has been a very emotional weekend.' You would not believe the amount of texts I'm getting, not just from family but friends and

*'Woo hooo well done bruv, amazing. Looking forward to next weekend in Malaysia. Enjoy your celebrations… You have a very excited niece and nephew. All our love. X x x'*
Natasha, sister

*'Congrats on the race victory!! You deserve this more than anyone, I am so happy for you'*
Seth

*'Mate, absolute legend, so proud of what you've done and so deserved, back where you belong, Ichiban baby! Have a drink for me.'*
Spud, close friend from school

*'Fantastic, watched the race while on holiday, really chuffed for you, keep it going'*
Steve Curtis

people I haven't spoken to in ages. People only text when you win, never in the tough times, but only because they are embarrassed. They don't know what to say when you finish out of the points, or they can't guess what your expectations were. My sisters are all very emotional and I'm glad there are plans for them all to come to races this year. I won't tell you what Richard sent me. Even people from other teams sent me messages.

On the Monday morning, Jessica and I went back to the same little place we'd had coffee before the race. I had fish and chips and a pint of the local beer. It was surreal to see how things had already radically changed in 24 hours. We were sitting in the same spot as the previous day – but this time, there were journalists everywhere, photographers outside. We sat on the beach in the same spot, having won the first grand prix of the year and having walked it basically. There was no challenge. It was a very special feeling…

This win is for me, my family and my team. It's the second grand prix win of my career, but it feels like the first. It's been a traumatic few months and I want to say a massive thank you to them all for being so strong and never losing belief. This weekend we have achieved everything that we deserve for all of our hard work over the past few months. And what's so exciting is that there is so much more to come from myself and from this team. I can't wait to get to Malaysia!

My first win in Hungary in 2006 was very exciting – coming through from 14th when no one expected it was wicked. Today is like another first victory, because it's been so long since the last, and the past two or three years have been very tough and frustrating. The great thing about this win was that it was from pole and I led every lap. To dominate a race weekend is a very satisfying feeling.

You think, racing from the front, it's easy, but it's not. It's great. Take all the points when you can. It wasn't perfect. There's room for improvement. We had an issue getting the temperature in the tyres in the restart and I made a mistake in my second pit stop, but we're going to enjoy it now. I'll enjoy myself tonight, but not too much… Thanks to everyone in the team and their families for putting up with us over the winter because I'm sure we've been very grumpy.

*'Irrespective of whether you want to look at Brawn GP's BGP 001 as a Disneyesque fairytale or the logical end point for a project that combined Honda's resources with the full influence of Ross Brawn's organisational skills, there is no denying that it has gone from near-stillborn to odds-on favourite faster than probably any Formula One car in history.'*
Mark Glendinning, Autosport

*'It's fifteen months' work. We said we were sacrificing last year to concentrate on this car, and what you're seeing is what we said we'd do. So it's perfectly rational in my mind.'*
Ross Brawn

*'I'm delighted for Jenson. When I saw him in Barcelona after he'd had a run in the car for the first time he had a grin from ear to ear. That's an indication a driver knows he's at one with the car.'*
David Coulthard

**OVERALL POINTS**

| | |
|---|---|
| Jenson Button | 10 |
| Rubens Barrichello | 8 |
| Jarno Trulli | 6 |
| Timo Glock | 5 |
| Fernando Alonso | 4 |
| Nico Rosberg | 3 |
| Sebastien Buemi | 2 |
| Sebastien Bourdais | 1 |

2009 FORMULA 1™ ING AUSTRALIAN GRAND PRIX

# Malaysian Grand Prix
## Sepang International Circuit, Kuala Lumpur
## Friday 3 April – Sunday 5 April

**Number of laps:** 56

**Circuit length:** 5.543 km

**Race distance:** 310.408 km

**Lap record:** 1:34.223
(Juan Pablo Montoya, 2004)

### MY HISTORY AT SEPANG

**2008 (Honda)**
Grid 11; finished 10

**2007 (Honda)**
Grid 15; finished 12

**2006 (Honda)**
Grid 2; finished 3

**2005 (BAR-Honda)**
Grid 9; retired (engine)

**2004 (BAR-Honda)**
Grid 6; finished 3

**2003 (BAR-Honda)**
Grid 9; finished 7

**2002 (Renault)**
Grid 8; finished 4

**2001 (Benetton-Renault)**
Grid 17; finished 11

**2000 (Williams-BMW)**
Grid 16; retired (engine)

Malaysia is always a special circuit for me as I achieved my first podium here back in 2004, but the intense humidity makes it the toughest race on the calendar. You can feel sleepy and extremely uncomfortable because you get so sweaty, so you have to work hard to acclimatise. Even though there are long straights, you're taking in hot air through your helmet, which makes it difficult to breathe, and you can feel quite claustrophobic. A couple of years ago, my water bottle didn't work and I started to shiver during the last twenty laps as a result. My vision started to go, too, so it was pretty scary. Dehydration is a potential problem. Even when your water bottle is working, it's the temperature of tea after about three laps, which is pretty grim.

The circuit poses a technical challenge with its demanding corners, long straights and bumpy asphalt. It's hard to find a good balance, and it's a difficult circuit to get the tyres to work well for the whole lap. If you get the soft tyres working in the first sector, they're normally damaged by the time you get to the last sector. So it's a bit of a juggling act.

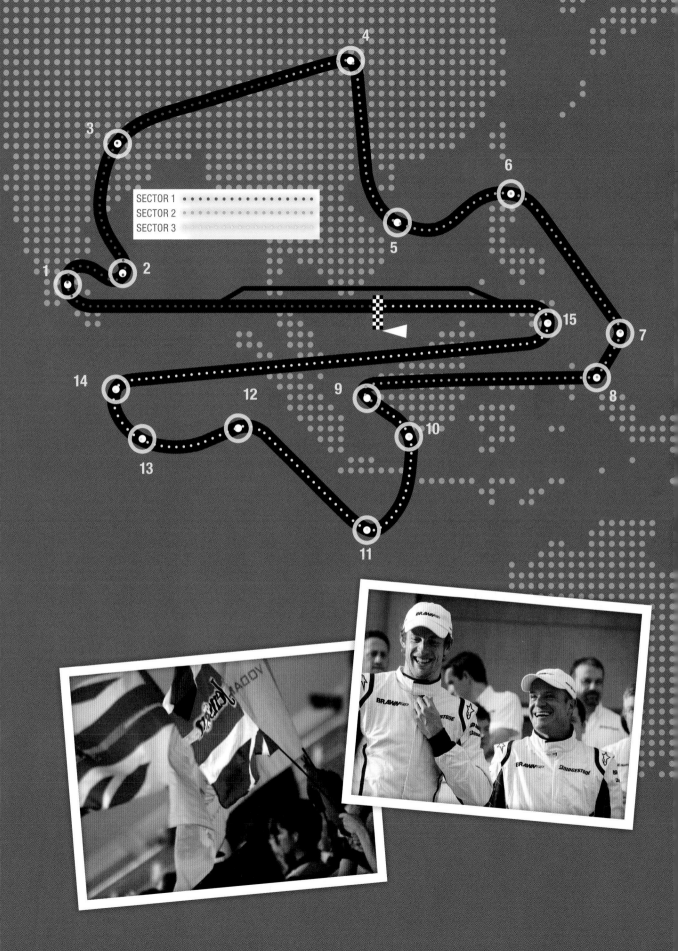

SECTOR 1
SECTOR 2
SECTOR 3

# Malaysia:
## Preparation, practice and qualifying

Normally I'd get to Malaysia as soon as possible to acclimatise, but I stayed on in Australia for a couple of days to train in the hotel sauna and steam room instead. Mikey had devised a challenging programme. We did twenty minutes on the running machine, then headed into the sauna for the rest of the session: two minutes heating up, then 25 press-ups, another minute's rest, then 25 press-ups. We repeated that seven or eight times to try and get the body used to working in humidity.

It would have felt like torture if Mikey had been standing there barking orders, but he never just watches me, he does every bit of fitness training with me whenever I'm travelling. When I have longer stretches free in my schedule in Europe, I have my trainer John to push my fitness level with triathlon, and ensure I remain injury-free. Mikey does the day-to-day maintenance work when we're travelling as well as the massage, nutrition and hydration preparation. And he always has a banana on hand for me after I've been in the car. It is a great relationship and we're really good friends as well. He pushes me hard. We are roughly the same size. Working with weights, I can't keep up with him, but in cardiovascular work we're very close. He is a big part of Team Button. Now I can't afford to fly my PA Jules to all the races, Mikey is doing more than merely physio. He keeps my schedule calm, sorts out little logistical problems, and he's also Security when I need it! He's doing a great job. I can't see that there's ever been a family around me like we are in 2009. I am very lucky to have my little team. No other driver has the same environment. The only pity is that I can't afford to fly everyone around the world to all the races. It costs about £80,000 per person. When you've got your manager, your physio and you've got your family coming to quite a few races, it's amazing how it adds up. And I don't want to fly economy on long-haul trips because I have to start work when I get there.

Mikey keeps our work varied. He might have me sitting on a Swiss ball visualising possible race scenarios. I really value the way he talks to me when I'm on the massage bench just before I get into the car for each session. He asks what I want from practice, from qualifying, from the weekend. He's putting it into perspective as it's happening. He is not trying to talk me up, saying anything like 'You're the best!', because he knows I won't take that. It is good to talk things through, good to think about your aims stage by stage. He asks questions that make me focus on the important things about each session. We have good little chats, always with our music on. We go through different types from dance to R&B or rap. Or we might play Queen's *Greatest Hits* – the anthems, and songs like Fat-Bottomed Girls! Music is important before a race. It can get you wound up, get the adrenalin pumping through the veins. After the massage he puts a couple of bandages on to prevent me getting rubbing marks from the seat, then I'm straight into the garage and into the car. But not before I've downed a last-minute espresso.

In Malaysia I stay in a place called Cyber View Lodge. I booked the smallest room and I am upgraded to this massive room. Again! I also booked economy flights and got upgraded. It's wicked! Cyber View Lodge is a fantastic resort, fifteen or twenty minutes from the circuit. A lot of people stay in the airport hotel, which is right next to the circuit, but I find that depressing. Rubens is also at Cyber View Lodge, plus the Red Bull guys Mark Webber and Sebastian Vettel. Jessica is here, too, with a friend from Japan, which is great because it meant I could leave her here on Thursday – which is not the most exciting day in a grand prix paddock – and she drank Champagne by the pool. It's so sweet because the Lodge gives each guest this dude who looks after you, a sort of butler I guess. My guy is called Arasu. He looked after me last year, too. He is my friend on Facebook and he's somehow even found out my mobile phone number. He looks after us exceptionally well. He is a big, big fan of F1, and our new little team. It was great to be reunited with him because he was here last year when things were tough, and on top of the frustration with the bad 2008 car, I got a big flake of carbon in my eye. He sorted out the car to take me to hospital to get it removed. He's put little teddy bears on our pillows. I've decided I'm going to take my Cyber View teddy bear everywhere with me this season. I've named him Arasu.

*I enjoy this circuit. It is very fast flowing and I think it will suit our car pretty well. There are some very low speed corners which I think will suit us. Also, mechanically our car is strong. I am looking forward to getting out on the circuit tomorrow. Weather-wise it is going to be a lot trickier this weekend than in Melbourne.*

## FRIDAY

It's incredibly hot today – 33°C and 71 per cent humidity. I headed in to the circuit determined to capitalise this weekend on our stunning start – especially before our small team's potential lack of finances allows others to catch up.

We completed some useful running today to work on improving the balance of the car and making tyre evaluations with the soft and hard compound Bridgestone Potenza tyres allocated for this weekend. My biggest problem is that we are locking the tyres and brakes very easily so we need to have a good look at this. The car isn't performing quite as well as in Australia last weekend. We're not quite there yet but we are going in the right direction and I'm confident we will achieve the optimum set-up ready for qualifying tomorrow. No doubt the weather is going to play its part. Huge rainclouds gathered dramatically overhead, but conditions remained dry.

## SATURDAY

*Jenson Button took his second successive pole position today in qualifying for the Malaysian Grand Prix at the Sepang International Circuit. The Brawn-Mercedes drivers topped the times in all three qualifying sessions with Jenson posting the fastest lap of Q2 and taking pole in a time of 01:35.181.*

Qualifying went fantastically well. Achieving pole position today in Malaysia in an incredibly close session is possibly even more special than in Australia. It's not easy to get one pole, but two successive poles is just fantastic and a first for me in my Formula One career. It's a great feeling and proves that our car works well on different types of circuit. We were struggling with the balance yesterday and I had lot of rear locking. However, we made some changes to the car overnight which really improved it for today and it felt good throughout qualifying. It's a massive turnaround and I have to say thank you to the team for their hard work in such tough conditions. They did a fantastic job.

The competition is a lot closer – Jarno Trulli and Toyota look a big threat, as well as the Red Bulls of Sebastian Vettel and Mark Webber. It's interesting how the new F1 world order is shaping up with Felipe Massa's Ferrari dropping out in Q1 and Lewis Hamilton's McLaren in Q2. Q3 was such an exciting session as we exchanged fastest times with Jarno and Sebastian.

Like qualifying today, the race is a 5pm start again. Somehow, someone forgot to tell the organisers that it always rains in Malaysia at about five o'clock. You get such humidity, which builds throughout the day under the scorching sun and leads to a downpour in the late afternoon. Always. Every day I've been here. But still, they choose to schedule the race to suit European television viewers. We are hoping the rain stays away tomorrow but we'll also be working hard tonight to make sure we are prepared for all eventualities.

*'Well done! Lap looked great on TV. Best wishes Nick & Kate'*
Nick Fry

*'Get in there! Congratulations you little star'*
Samantha, sister

*'Yes! Way to go! Bring home that 2nd win. Very best of luck tomorrow'*
Stuart Dyble

*'Well done again! Little bruv I don't think my nerves can stand it all season. It's fantastic to see your face light up, big kiss'*
Tanya, sister

## BRAWN TECHNICAL UPDATES

As the races were only separated by a week we didn't have any changes planned. The car was running well so it was just a case of inspecting everything closely after the Melbourne race and making sure there were no signs of any problems. It rained on lap 22 and this was the first time we'd run the car in wet conditions. You need a different car balance in the wet and we had to guess where to set the front wing for the race.

Luckily we were not far off and so we were able to run with good pace. The conditions were extreme and we found a number of areas where the car was filling with water and causing some electrical problems – fortunately nothing serious enough to stop it running. We're not expecting rain in Bahrain but have some fairly major waterproofing to do before the next event.

01
02
03
04
05
06
07
08
09
10

1. **Jenson Button**
2. **Jarno Trulli**
3. **Timo Glock**
4. **Nico Rosberg**
5. **Mark Webber**
6. **Robert Kubica**
7. **Kimi Räikkönen**
8. **Rubens Barrichello (gearbox penalty)**
9. **Fernando Alonso**
10. **Nick Heidfeld**
11. **Kazuki Nakajima**
12. **Lewis Hamilton**
13. **Sebastian Vettel (10-place penalty)**
14. **Heikki Kovalainen**
15. **Sebastien Bourdais**
16. **Felipe Massa**
17. **Nelsinho Piquet**
18. **Giancarlo Fisichella**
19. **Adrian Sutil**
20. **Sebastien Buemi**

11
12
13
14
15
16
17
18
19
20

### STRATEGY

Bridgestone brought the Hard and Soft dry tyre compounds to Sepang. The Soft tyre worked well, and was chosen as the primary dry tyre.

The fastest dry strategy was a two-stop, due to low degradation on the Soft tyre and the long pit lane. I qualified P1, on an optimum two-stop fuel load, but was jumped at the start by Trulli and Rosberg, who were both fuelled shorter and stayed ahead until they stopped. I had two laps in free air to make the gap required to both cars, which I did comfortably. At the stop a fresh set of Soft tyres was fitted, fuelling for a reasonable middle stint, with the expectation of rain coming soon.

The rain was forecast to be very heavy, and started to fall on lap 22. I pitted and was fitted with the Bridgestone Wet tyre compound, made for heavy rain and aquaplaning conditions. I stayed out for seven laps and pitted again on lap 29 for the Bridgestone Intermediate tyre, when the rain was lighter than originally expected, with the Intermediate working better in those conditions. I was able to remain ahead of the field and crossed the line on lap 31, ultimately to take the race win.

*Brawn GP's Jenson Button continued his perfect start to the 2009 Formula One season as he took his second successive grand prix victory today when the Malaysian Grand Prix was stopped after 31 laps following a torrential downpour. Team-mate Rubens Barrichello also had a strong race to bring his Brawn-Mercedes car home in fifth position.*

Another late race start so I got up leisurely at 11am and Jessica and I did the coffee trick. We went to the bar area outside the pool and had our cappuccino before heading in to the circuit. Already the skies were darkening and lowering. It rained between 1pm and 2pm, then dried out for the start of the race. I was very excited lining up on pole, because if we had a clean start, I knew we'd have a very good race. But the start wasn't great. I lost out to Nico Rosberg in the Williams from the start down to Turn 1. I tried to hog the outside line, but he ran wide and pushed me wider so I ended up on the dirty part of the circuit. I went in deep at Turn 1 and got a big snap of oversteer, ran wide and lost out to Jarno Trulli and Fernando Alonso, which dropped me to fourth. It was so frustrating. I knew I was stopping longer than Rosberg and Trulli but I knew also that Alonso was fuelled for 28 laps and if I ended up stuck behind him, when he has the boost benefit of KERS technology, the lead two would pull away and I wouldn't see them again. I had to fight my way past Alonso, which I did neatly on Turn 13 at the end of lap 1.

I was up to third, then I had to chase down the two leaders. I thought that as long as Rosberg didn't pull away from Trulli too much I should be fine and come out in the lead after the first stop. Rosberg pitted. Trulli pitted. Ross came on the team radio to say: 'Two fast laps please, Jenson.' And I kicked in. The time screens went purple, purple, purple – the two fastest laps of the race – and then we pitted and I came out in the lead. I love that final push before a stop. It's such a buzz when you know you've got a great car and it's just about pushing that car to the limit. You don't need to look after the tyres because you're coming in. You're on the edge, it's just two qualifying laps.

The gap I pulled was massive, more than enough. There was no holding back and the guys did a magnificent job on the pit-stops. After the slowish

ones in Australia, the team had drilled pit-stop practice. I came out four seconds in front of Rosberg, so far in the lead. I pulled away another five seconds and then, on lap 20, it started spitting with rain and it was like, 'Oh no! Are you kidding me?' I've just got the lead and everything should be quite easy from here as long as I keep my head. And then the rain! I did almost a full lap on slicks in the rain. I pulled almost nine seconds on Rosberg – on dry tyres in the wet, which was fun – and that made a big difference.

I came into the pits, put the X Wets on, the tyre with the deep grooves so you can go through deep water because when it rains in Malaysia, it chucks down. But the weird thing was the rain didn't get heavier. It stayed spitting. The other front runners were on the same tyres as me, so it was just about not damaging them too much, but because it didn't chuck it down, we were on the wrong tyre for the conditions and you had people like Glock flying around on the intermediate tyre, catching us about eight seconds a lap. So we had to pit again. I came in, put on the Intermediates and came out just behind Glock, so I was in second place. I knew that our pace was good, and that we should be good in the wet. Not that we knew, because we'd never driven our car in the wet at all. His tyres were getting old and he lost speed, so I was able to get past him to re-take the lead. He pitted

for tyres. I did one more lap, pulled out a big enough advantage, and then it did start to chuck it down. Lap 30, and we were on the wrong tyre again.

It was a crazy race. It was the worst conditions I've experienced in Formula One. The sky was as dark as night, lit up by great forks of lightning. I had half a lap to go with rivers streaming across the circuit. It was all about getting round, getting into the pits and trying to get out in front of Glock, which I did, having put on the X Wet again. We sit so low down in the car, it was like swimming in an F1 car. You could not see the circuit. The droplets of rain were massive. If you study pictures, it looks like the cars were in about three inches of water, you can't see underneath the front wing. I was leading, with Glock and Heidfeld behind me. The team said the safety car was out, and I thought 'Thank God for that,' but the problem was I couldn't keep up with the safety car. The water was so forceful people were spinning off. I went through Turn 6 in second gear, taking it easy, and I hit a lake and the car started sliding off the circuit. I just kept it on and I glimpsed Glock behind me do exactly the same. From then on it was about driving around at snail's pace trying to get to the start because we realised the race was going to get red-flagged. I could have walked more quickly. Even the pace car was sliding off the circuit and that's twelve inches off the ground.

The problem is when you're going that slow, you're getting wet too. Inside the cockpit, I was drenched. Three inches of water was sloshing around inside the car. The problem you then face is that all the electrical boxes can suffer water damage. This season our front wings are adjustable, like an aeroplane's wing flaps, operated by little electric motors on the wing. But we hadn't anticipated it raining that hard... and the water screwed the motors.

I pulled up at the start/finish line. I couldn't see the other cars through the rain. Half the grid had already spun off. We were hoping that it wouldn't be restarted for the further ten laps required to make the 75 per cent distance for full championship points. I knew it would only be five points for the win because we hadn't completed half distance, but I would rather that than race again and risk spinning off and getting nothing. By now the rain was torrential. The grandstand was struck three times by lightning. It must have been terrifying for the spectators. I sat in the car on the starting grid, with Mikey holding an umbrella above me. I took my gloves, balaclava and helmet off and swapped them over for a dry set. I was trying to dry out the cockpit. Webber was running about telling everyone to get out, it was too dangerous to race. Kimi Räikkönen had already got out of the car, changed into shorts and T-shirt, had an ice cream and wasn't even considering getting back into the car because it was so dangerous. They ended up red-flagging the race and it was game over, after just 32 of the scheduled 56 laps.

So I won another race without crossing the line at speed. In fact, this time I won the race while stationary! I got out of the car when I was told I had won. It was fun because all the mechanics were there by the car and we had a big hug. Normally you can't get to the mechanics until after the podium ceremony. All the drivers were offering congratulations as I walked up the pit lane, waving at the grandstand and fans – a great feeling. Shov, my engineer, ran up and said, 'I am coming with you. Ross said I could come on the podium'. It was brilliant to be up there with him, because we're so close during a race. He's literally air-traffic-controlling the state of my race strategy over the radio and normally I don't see him until after all the interviews when I'm tired, and the moment's gone a little bit. He came up on the podium and it was so sweet because he wears glasses and I forgot Nick Heidfeld and Timo Glock on the podium and just started spraying Shov with Champagne and he was shouting, 'Stop it, stop it, I can't see.' I was like, 'Shov, you're on the podium, you've just won the race. Just enjoy the moment for ten seconds.' A typical engineer!

Two wins out of two now – unbelievable!

> '2 out of 2. Can you make it a hat trick? Looking forward to having a beer with the world's best driver! Sweet.'
>
> Ben Payne

### MALAYSIAN GRAND PRIX FINAL POSITIONS

| Pos | Driver | Team | Laps | Time |
|---|---|---|---|---|
| 1 | Jenson Button | Brawn-Mercedes | 31 | 55:30.622 |
| 2 | Nick Heidfeld | BMW Sauber | 31 | +22.7 secs |
| 3 | Timo Glock | Toyota | 31 | +23.5 secs |
| 4 | Jarno Trulli | Toyota | 31 | +46.1 secs |
| 5 | Rubens Barrichello | Brawn-Mercedes | 31 | +47.3 secs |
| 6 | Mark Webber | RBR-Renault | 31 | +52.3 secs |
| 7 | Lewis Hamilton | McLaren-Mercedes | 31 | +60.7 secs |
| 8 | Nico Rosberg | Williams-Toyota | 31 | +71.5 secs |
| 9 | Felipe Massa | Ferrari | 31 | +76.9 secs |
| 10 | Sebastien Bourdais | STR-Ferrari | 31 | +102.164 secs |
| 11 | Fernando Alonso | Renault | 31 | +109.422 secs |
| 12 | Kazuki Nakajima | Williams-Toyota | 31 | +116.130 secs |
| 13 | Nelsinho Piquet | Renault | 31 | +116.713 secs |
| 14 | Kimi Räikkönen | Ferrari | 31 | +142.841 secs |
| 15 | Sebastian Vettel | RBR-Renault | 30 | Spin |
| 16 | Sebastien Buemi | STR-Ferrari | 30 | Spin |
| 17 | Adrian Sutil | Force India-Mercedes | 30 | +1 Lap |
| 18 | Giancarlo Fisichella | Force India-Mercedes | 29 | Spin |
| Ret | Robert Kubica | BMW Sauber | 1 | Engine |
| Ret | Heikki Kovalainen | McLaren-Mercedes | 0 | Spin |

'Hey Jenson congratulations on your 1st 2 races... It's your time this year. Hope you're well and keep up the good work... All the best'
Craig David, singer

2009 FORMULA 1® PETRONAS MALAYSIAN GRAND PRIX

Last weekend we said that we'd had the fairytale start to the season and I am so proud that has continued here. Two poles and two victories – can't ask more than that!

This was a fantastic result under very difficult conditions. We made all the right decisions about tyres in crazy conditions. People assume because we're top drivers it's easy. We're going at 60kph, but just having to drive around and keep it out of the barrier was horrendous.'

*Love that feeling! Winner JB xx'*
Richard Goddard, manager

*'Go go gadget trophies! Congrats fella, incredible stuff'*
James Williamson, Team Button

*'WOO HOO!! You beauty, yee ha! Another one in the bag!'*
Jules, PA

*'Well done son, great laps before your stop. Cool in the wet. All the best DC'*

*'Great work again today mate, We have got off to a fully deserved flyer! Have a great holiday and see you in China'*
Mikey Collier, physio

**OVERALL POINTS**

| | |
|---|---|
| Jenson Button | 15 |
| Rubens Barrichello | 10 |
| Jarno Trulli | 8.5 |
| Timo Glock | 8 |
| Nick Heidfeld | 4 |
| Fernando Alonso | 4 |
| Nico Rosberg | 3.5 |
| Sebastien Buemi | 2 |
| Mark Webber | 1.5 |
| Lewis Hamilton | 1 |
| Sebastien Bourdais | 1 |

# Chinese Grand Prix
# Shanghai International Circuit
## Friday 17 April – Sunday 19 April

**Number of laps:** 56

**Circuit length:** 5.451 km

**Race distance:** 305.066 km

**Lap record:** 1:32.238
(Michael Schumacher, 2004)

### MY HISTORY AT SHANGHAI

**2008 (Honda)**
Grid 18; finished 16

**2007 (Honda)**
Grid 11; finished 5

**2006 (Honda)**
Grid 4; finished 4

**2005 (BAR-Honda)**
Grid 4; finished 8

**2004 (BAR-Honda)**
Grid 3; finished 2

Two races, two wins, what a great position to be in returning to Shanghai. It's a track which always produces interesting races and one I've always enjoyed with some technically challenging corners which are really fun. In the inaugural race here in 2004, Rubens won for Ferrari and I came second for BAR Honda – so we both know our way to the podium.

The track is laid out following the shape of the Chinese character 'shang', which translates into a combination of straights (including a long 1.1km back straight) and a range of differing speed corners from the long and tightening turns 1 to 3 to the fast left-right chicane at turns 7 and 8. It's a great track for racing because there are plenty of opportunities for overtaking here, which, combined with unpredictable weather – and perhaps cooler conditions because the 2009 race is scheduled six months earlier than usual – often creates exciting action.

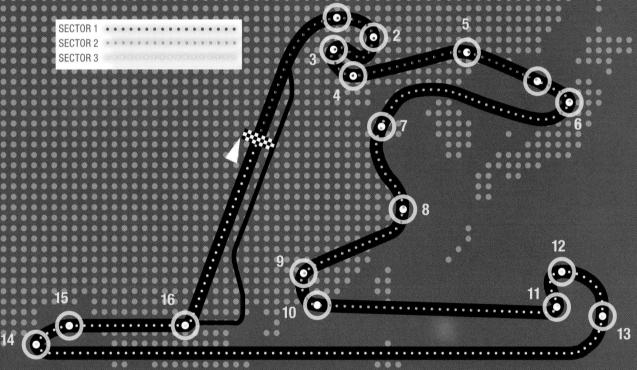

SECTOR 1 ● ● ● ● ● ● ● ● ● ● ● ● ● ● ● ● ●
SECTOR 2 ● ● ● ● ● ● ● ● ● ● ● ● ● ● ● ● ●
SECTOR 3 ● ● ● ● ● ● ● ● ● ● ● ● ● ● ● ● ●

1
2
3
4
5
6
7
8
9
10
11
12
13
14
15
16

# China:
## Preparation, practice and qualifying

After Malaysia I went to the Four Seasons in Langkawi with Jessica. It was the first time we'd had a little holiday, just the two of us. We spent almost a week chilling out, relaxing, kayaking, doing a bit of training. We had a villa on the beach and it was perfect for getting used to a humid climate in preparation for China, because it can be hot there too. We were together for five nights, and then I flew to Japan to drop Jessica home on my way to the race.

After the back-to-back races in Australia and Malaysia, we've had a two-week break which has given us the chance to relax and reflect on our team's achievements in the opening races of the season. In the background, I was aware of the controversy involving Lewis Hamilton and McLaren and the stewards in Malaysia, but I wasn't interested. Drivers are blinkered and my mind was only on winning the next race. I guess Lewis's position and mine so far in 2009 serve to emphasise the topsy-turvy fortunes of a life in Formula One. But it's funny how Mercedes are still at the top. They won the world championship as partners of McLaren last year, and they're winning races as our engine supplier this season. Norbert Haug, the Vice President of Mercedes-Benz, is a great guy, and obviously has an interest in what we're doing. He's so into his racing. He oversees all the motorsport activity associated with Mercedes. You see him at Formula One, but he's also at DTM, German touring cars which is pretty much Mercedes v Audi. He's a big fan of what we're doing in our little team.

I was looking forward to Shanghai. I settled into a hotel, not with the team, but with my gang. We're in a great position, but I am aware that we are only two races in and our competitors will not stand still. Red Bull and Toyota are just behind us. We fully expect a tough fight from here if we want to continue our early successes. The great thing is our car has gone well at two very different race tracks.

### FRIDAY
We headed in to the circuit for a straightforward session working on the balance of the car and fine-tuning the set-up. Here, you need to have a very good aerodynamic balance combined with a stable car and good straight-line speed to take advantage of the long straights. The team concentrated on evaluating the Super Soft and Medium tyre compounds available for this race. We topped the timesheets after 35 laps. The balance of the car really improved over the last couple of runs after we'd been struggling a little to find the right set-up early on. We completed a great deal of work with the two very different tyre compounds to establish what condition they would be in after longer runs. A useful first day. And interesting to note how strong the Red Bulls are at high speed. At low speed, we have an advantage. But I still think we can beat them.

### SATURDAY
*Brawn GP's Rubens Barrichello and Jenson Button qualified in fourth and fifth positions for Sunday's Chinese Grand Prix after a closely fought qualifying hour at the Shanghai International Circuit today.*

Qualifying didn't go quite as well as I'd hoped. Our car feels good around here but there were a few cars quicker than we expected. The Red Bulls of Sebastien Vettel and Mark Webber were very strong in high-speed corners, as we predicted, and we knew by the end of Q2 that we had a fight on our hands. On my final run, I experienced too much understeer and so will line up in fifth. The worst thing was being outqualified by Rubens because we are on a similar strategy. Alonso qualified P2 but is due to pit early. The Red Bulls are stopping five laps before us, and we know we could beat them in the dry easily if everything goes to plan. It will be interesting to see how the different strategies work out in the race. We will give it our best shot. Congratulations to Red Bull on their first pole position.

## BRAWN TECHNICAL UPDATES

We had no significant updates for this race although it was clear that a number of our competitors were improving their cars and we no longer had the performance margin that we enjoyed in the first two events.

The car was working well, particularly on the Super Soft tyre, so we were confident that our pace in dry conditions would still be good enough to win. However, Sunday was a complete wash-out and our lack of running in wet conditions is beginning to show. We simply didn't have the pace of the Red Bull cars and had to settle for third place. Our main issue was aquaplaning in the deep puddles.

# China:
## The race

1. Sebastian Vettel
2. Fernando Alonso
3. Mark Webber
4. Rubens Barrichello
5. **Jenson Button**
6. Jarno Trulli
7. Nico Rosberg
8. Kimi Räikkönen
9. Lewis Hamilton
10. Sebastien Buemi
11. Nick Heidfeld
12. Heikki Kovalainen
13. Felipe Massa
14. Kazuki Nakajima
15. Sebastien Bourdais
16. Nelsinho Piquet
17. Robert Kubica (pit start)
18. Adrian Sutil
19. Timo Glock (gearbox penalty/pit start)
20. Giancarlo Fisichella

## STRATEGY

Same tyre combination as Melbourne (Medium and Super Soft) for the race. From our pre-event and Friday running the Medium compound was going to be the primary race tyre, with the Super Soft again struggling with graining issues.

The dry strategy was a two-stop, with a slightly shorter first stint to ensure a good qualifying position, and a longer middle stint to minimise the laps on the weaker Super Soft tyre. With the Medium tyre being very consistent, and again with a long pit lane, three stops would not have been the correct strategy.

I qualified P3, with both Red Bulls on significantly less fuel taking the front row. The race was wet all the way through, with the Bridgestone Wet tyre being the only choice. We stopped the car twice, both times as planned, for fuel and fresh Wet tyres.

*Brawn GP's Jenson Button took his third consecutive podium of the 2009 Formula One season at the end of a rain-soaked Chinese Grand Prix at the Shanghai International Circuit today. Team-mate Rubens Barrichello finished in fourth position to secure further valuable points for the team's championship challenge.*

I woke up and it was raining, and it rained hard all morning. I have started races under safety-car conditions many times, often at Fuji in Japan. It's always wet there. So, inevitably, we started this third race of the season in the wet behind the safety car, with all drivers starting on wet tyres. The visibility was appalling and I was really struggling to get the brakes up to temperature. It wasn't a time for heroics. I was fifth, and just driving behind the safety car was difficult enough because there was so much water on the circuit. In a few places, there were rivers running across the track. With these cars being so low, if the floor of the car touches the water it just aquaplanes over the surface. You have no grip. The race got properly under way on lap 9 with me lying fourth behind the Red Bulls and Rubens. Alonso had pitted already. As normal in the wet, you cannot see a thing. I almost went off at Turn 1, but just held it together. Rubens had suffered a brake warm-up issue and I was pushing him quite hard. On lap 11 he ran wide and I moved up to third place. Then really it was about trying to keep the gap to the Red Bulls in very tricky conditions. They'd pulled a big gap already, especially Vettel. I could still see Webber but Vettel was a long way in front. We looked at the times and they were destroying us even with the fuel difference, they were so much quicker.

*We always thought it would be raining today, but it's amazing the amount of water build-up considering it hasn't been raining that hard.*

Then another safety car came out and brought us all back together. Mark made a mistake and I was able to dive past inside of him. Then I made a mistake, and he got back past me, and then he made a small mistake and I passed him, and then I made a mistake and he got past me again, so it was a good little fight we had. Our pace was not good enough. On average they were one second a lap quicker than us. It wasn't that we were slow, we were quicker than the rest of the field, but they were a second quicker than us. Later we discovered why we had lost so much downforce. It's quite complicated and to do with the aerodynamics and taking downforce off the front wing. The problem in the wet is you always end up with too much front grip. So we adjusted the front wing, and it took some front grip away but it also took a lot of rear grip away, so we had lost a second's worth of downforce. We hadn't just got understeer, we had oversteer and I couldn't get enough heat into the tyres.

'Well done. That looked like an exhausting race. Leading the championship by 6 points!! Stunning'
Samantha, sister

Third was as good as I could do in the race. Every lap I did I felt I was going to put the car in the barriers because it was so, so slippery. Every so often Shov would ask me over the radio if I could push any harder. I'd try, rescue the car from a 'big moment' and shout back 'No!' We did the best we could. I decided it was best to maximise what was possible to build on my championship lead. I kept the car on the track and negotiated two pit-stops and a further safety-car period to cross the line in third, ahead of Rubens and the rest of the pack. It was as good as we could have got. I hadn't won the race, which was disappointing, but I finished the race. To get to the end of that race was an achievement in itself – and I finished on the podium.

Initially we were worried about our times in the wet, even though the car seems unbeatable in the dry, but the guys resolved that issue and looking ahead there are no worries about performance in the wet.

The old boy sent me a text message. It said, 'I know you might think I'm a bit mad, but you need to realise I've been a fan of F1 since Stirling Moss back in the 1950s. This is what I love, it's not just because you're here.' He gets worried that I think he's a bit crazy. To see his little boy, as I'm sure he still thinks of me, leading the world championship. It's all a big dream to him. I'm sure he wakes up every morning, opens his eyes, and then has the biggest smile on his face. My family all sent me crazy messages. They were so emotional, I think because it was a tough race. For a person close to a driver to watch that race must have been difficult, because it was so dangerous, and I think they got quite emotional that we'd achieved such a good result from it.

I headed back to Europe after the race and went straight to the factory. It was the first time I've been back to Brackley since 300 people had lost their jobs. It must have been a tricky atmosphere while that process was ongoing, but I found everyone so positive. Everyone was asking questions. Why had I qualified fifth in Shanghai? Why had we not won in Shanghai? We soon came up with the reasons and we soon solved them. We'd obviously done well in the first two races, but no one dwelt on that. We only talked about the third race and how we can improve in the wet. And how we were looking forward to Bahrain – a hot, dry race on the sort of circuit where our car should do well with the stop-start corners and not so much high speed. Aerodynamically we are very strong. Our downforce works well in slow and mid-speed corners, but not so well at high speed. So we are looking forward to the next race. I can't wait to get out there. When things are going well, you want to race every single day. It's so enjoyable.

## CHINESE GRAND PRIX FINAL POSITIONS

| Pos | Driver | Team | Laps | Time |
| --- | --- | --- | --- | --- |
| 1 | Sebastian Vettel | RBR-Renault | 56 | 1:57:43.485 |
| 2 | Mark Webber | RBR-Renault | 56 | +10.9 secs |
| 3 | Jenson Button | Brawn-Mercedes | 56 | +44.9 secs |
| 4 | Rubens Barrichello | Brawn-Mercedes | 56 | +63.7 secs |
| 5 | Heikki Kovalainen | McLaren-Mercedes | 56 | +65.1 secs |
| 6 | Lewis Hamilton | McLaren-Mercedes | 56 | +71.8 secs |
| 7 | Timo Glock | Toyota | 56 | +74.4 secs |
| 8 | Sebastien Buemi | STR-Ferrari | 56 | +76.4 secs |
| 9 | Fernando Alonso | Renault | 56 | +84.3 secs |
| 10 | Kimi Räikkönen | Ferrari | 56 | +91.7 secs |
| 11 | Sebastien Bourdais | STR-Ferrari | 56 | +94.1 secs |
| 12 | Nick Heidfeld | BMW Sauber | 56 | +95.8 secs |
| 13 | Robert Kubica | BMW Sauber | 56 | + 106.8 secs |
| 14 | Giancarlo Fisichella | Force India-Mercedes | 55 | +1 Lap |
| 15 | Nico Rosberg | Williams-Toyota | 55 | +1 Lap |
| 16 | Nelsinho Piquet | Renault | 53 | +2 Laps |
| 17 | Adrian Sutil | Force India-Mercedes | 50 | Accident |
| Ret | Kazuki Nakajima | Williams-Toyota | 43 | Transmission |
| Ret | Felipe Massa | Ferrari | 20 | Electrical |
| Ret | Jarno Trulli | Toyota | 18 | Accident damage |

'You deserve the championship
just for finishing that boat
race in P3! Splendid son.'
Nav Sidhu, former colleague at Williams

A very difficult race and I am so pleased that we got both cars to the end of 56 laps and scored as many points as possible. I was on the third step down but it's a pleasing result because it was so easy in those conditions to throw it off. The conditions were pretty crazy with rivers of water all over the circuit which changed every time you encountered them. The last turn particularly was like a lake and you just couldn't brake for the corner. I struggled with the car aquaplaning and the tyres shuddering as we couldn't get the temperature high enough to make them work properly. Every lap I thought I was going to throw the car off. The Red Bulls were consistently 1.5 to 2 seconds per lap quicker. Mark Webber and I had a good fight for a few laps but I just couldn't stay with him. We couldn't have beaten the Red Bulls. They were too fast for us today.

*'Well done honey! Great job, Still leading the world championship. Chu chu (kiss)'*
Jessica, girlfriend

**OVERALL POINTS**

| | |
|---|---|
| Jenson Button | 21 |
| Rubens Barrichello | 15 |
| Sebastian Vettel | 10 |
| Timo Glock | 10 |
| Mark Webber | 9.5 |
| Jarno Trulli | 8.5 |
| Nick Heidfeld | 4 |
| Fernando Alonso | 4 |
| Heikki Kovalainen | 4 |
| Lewis Hamilton | 4 |
| Nico Rosberg | 3.5 |
| Sebastien Buemi | 3 |
| Sebastien Bourdais | 1 |

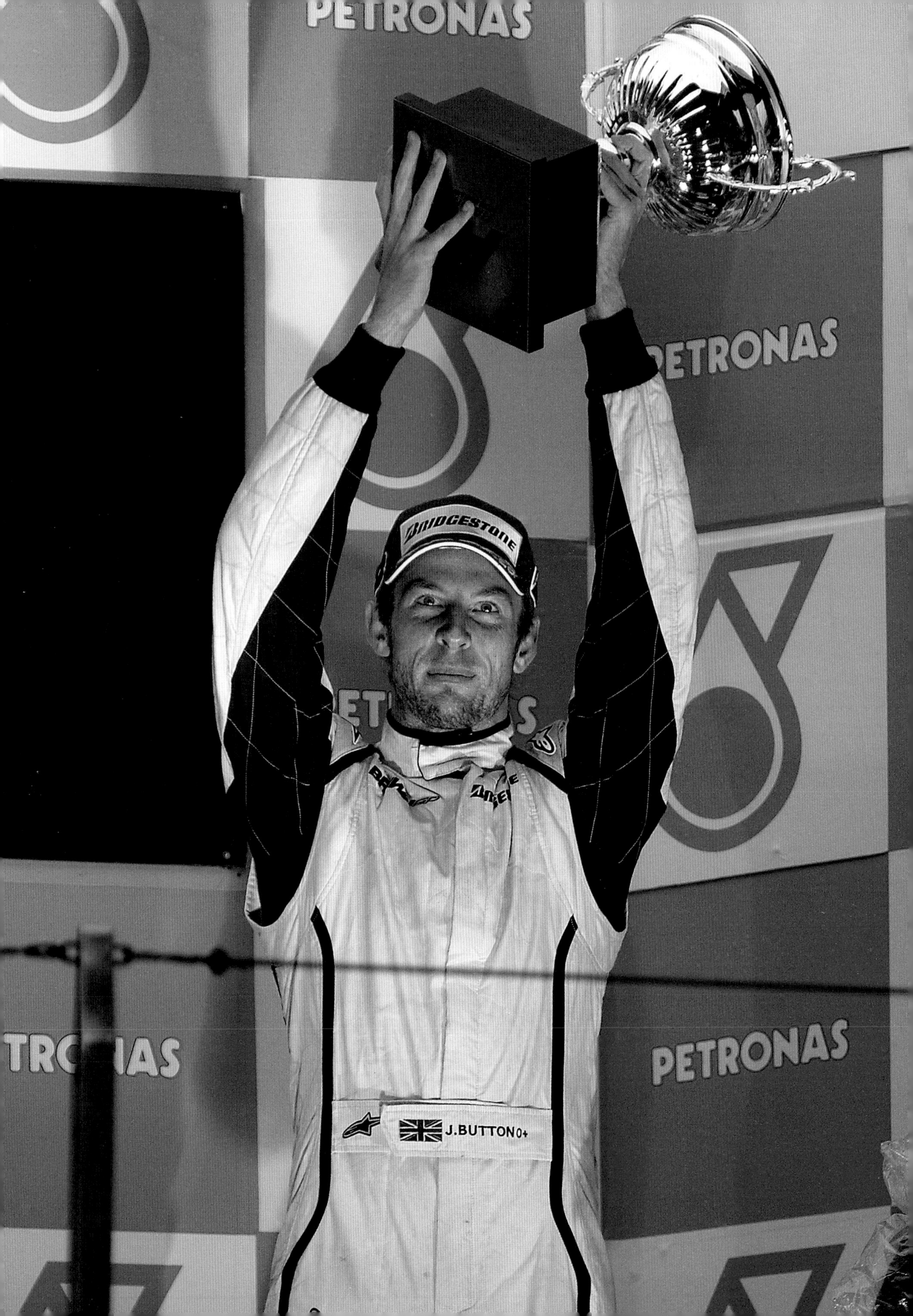
PETRONAS
PETRONAS
BRIDGESTONE
PETRONAS
J.BUTTON

# Bahrain Grand Prix
# Bahrain International Circuit, Sakhir
## Friday 24 April – Sunday 26 April

**Number of laps:** 57

**Circuit length:** 5.412 km

**Race distance:** 308.238 km

**Lap record:** 1:30.252
(Michael Schumacher, 2004)

### MY HISTORY AT BAHRAIN

**2008 (Honda)**
Grid 9; retired (accident damage)

**2007 (Honda)**
Grid 16; retired (accident damage)

**2006 (Honda)**
Grid 3; finished 4

**2005 (BAR-Honda)**
Grid 11; retired (clutch)

**2004 (BAR-Honda)**
Grid 6; finished 3

This is one of my favourite races. I love the circuit with its great, fast-flowing sections which allow you to push the car to its limits. Braking and traction are crucial. You need good straight-line speed to maximise the long straights. It's a good circuit for overtaking, particularly at Turn 1 after the long straight where you brake very hard from over 300kph in seventh gear, coming all the way down to first gear. Confidence under braking is the key to a quick lap. People tend to brake surprisingly early here so you can make up crucial ground if you are brave. You have to believe in the car's performance and have faith in being able to stop it effectively.

The desert location with high ambient temperatures presents an interesting challenge for the teams as sand blown onto the track surface in the frequently breezy conditions can vary grip levels dramatically. But after the monsoons in Malaysia and China, I like the idea of a dry race – especially as the track characteristics suit our car and my driving style.

*This was a tough race for us. You might say I was leading for most of it but we didn't have the pace we had in the first three races. I don't know where it has gone...*

4

13

5

6

12

7

9

8

3

10

11

2

14

1

15

SECTOR 1
SECTOR 2
SECTOR 3

# Bahrain:
## Preparation, practice and qualifying

Formula One drivers must have one of the noisiest jobs going, so we tend to crave peace and quiet. Three years ago, I commissioned a house to be built in Bahrain. The kingdom has a similar policy towards the paparazzi to Monaco. Not only can you have a stylish house with your own little stretch of beach in front, but you're not bothered here at all. It's just about finished, and I'll be staying there next year. For 2009, I'm back in the Ritz, where all the drivers stay.

Heat is a big issue – both for drivers and for engines. To keep me cool, Mikey introduced an ice vest – for Malaysia initially, but we discovered it has great benefits here, too. It's basically an insulator vest that you put in the freezer – like a wine-bottle cooler sleeve – and I wear it on the grid just before getting into the car. It keeps my body temperature constant so my heart-rate doesn't become elevated. It's another tiny detail that helps give me the edge on my competitors. It's a secret weapon but, unfortunately, it's visible so several guys have asked me what it is. I tell them, but don't let on where you get them from!

The diffuser protest is long over, but the latest talking point is a rival team's attempt to prevent Brawn GP from getting a share of the TV money shared between all the teams at the end of the season. Their team boss's stance is another indication of how competitive Formula One is. When you're ahead on the track, other teams will try to fight you off it in any way they can. Each team is rewarded with a share of the sport's profits after three years, and part of getting Brawn GP off the ground was an agreement signed by all the Formula One Teams Association (FOTA) members to declare they considered Brawn GP to hold the same legal entity as Honda. It may be the talk of the Sakhir paddock – as people sip cardamom tea and Arabic coffee on benches around palm trees – but I'm just concentrating on my job.

## FRIDAY

A pretty standard programme for me today on what has been a scorching hot Friday. Mikey is on hand with litres and litres of fluids to keep me hydrated. We have successfully completed our scheduled test items and evaluated a number of set-up options to find the best balance for my car around this track. We're familiar with the Super Soft and Medium tyre compounds that we are using, but the unique conditions here mean that they are working in a different temperature range so we focused our efforts on understanding the behaviour of the tyres.

The heat is intense, and we've had concerns over cooling issues for engines and brakes. However, we are well prepared for this now and can't wait for the novelty of a dry race weekend. The pace looks good from our initial evaluations and I am sure it will be a closely fought battle in qualifying tomorrow. The Red Bulls are surprisingly quick. I didn't expect them to be quite so competitive. And the Toyotas have good pace. We know it's going to be a tight fight. KERS has a big effect in Bahrain so Lewis was quick today in his McLaren. I am excited at the prospect of the race, but I can't predict how it's going to go at all.

**The Red Bulls are surprisingly quick. I didn't expect them to be quite so competitive.**

## SATURDAY

*In an intense qualifying hour at the heat-soaked Bahrain International Circuit, the Brawn GP team's Jenson Button and Rubens Barrichello qualified in fourth and sixth positions respectively for Sunday's 57-lap Bahrain Grand Prix.*

I was aiming for pole position today, but it wasn't my best qualifying session of the season and the pace just wasn't there. The track temperatures exceeded 50°C and we are learning all the time how to make the tyres and chassis work in such extreme conditions. I didn't have a great lap on my final run in Q3. I was struggling for grip on the corner exits and locking tyres through the session. I was surprised by our lack of pace and the speed of our competitors today; they have obviously made advances and caught up quickly. The Toyotas of Jarno Trulli and Timo Glock pulled it out of the bag from nowhere. I don't know where their times came from, and they have ended up first and second on the grid. Sebastian Vettel is third and I am fourth. I'm disappointed because I thought we had a good chance of getting on the front row. It's going to be a tough race tomorrow. However, our long-run pace with heavy fuel was competitive in practice yesterday so that will stand us in good stead if I can get a clean start. Vettel is fuelled for one lap longer, so he is the man to beat. I think we can happily deal with the Toyotas in the stops.

## BRAWN TECHNICAL UPDATES

We had some new rear dampers to improve the ride quality of the car, although this was only a small performance gain. Other competitors are making significant steps, on top of which a number of the other teams had spent two weeks testing at the track earlier in the year. Toyota, in particular, were looking very impressive. This was the first time that we have run the Mercedes engine in really hot conditions – we were seeing air temperatures over 40ºC and track temperatures well in excess of 50ºC. This gave us real cause for concern as even on maximum cooling, we are right on the limit of safe engine temperature.

I spent the first stint in traffic, which wasn't helping, but after the first stops we were able to get the car in free air, cooling the engine down and giving us a little bit of margin. We've now done two tests and four races on more or less the same set of parts and by now the bodywork is looking very tired. This doesn't just look scruffy; the damage to wings and the underbody causes a measurable loss of aerodynamic performance. On getting back to Europe, the car will be stripped back to the carbon and completely repainted in time for Barcelona.

# Bahrain:
## The race

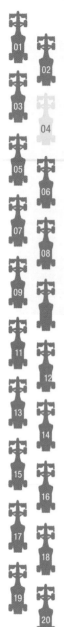

1. **Jarno Trulli**
2. **Timo Glock**
3. **Sebastian Vettel**
4. **Jenson Button**
5. **Lewis Hamilton**
6. **Rubens Barrichello**
7. **Fernando Alonso**
8. **Felipe Massa**
9. **Nico Rosberg**
10. **Kimi Räikkönen**
11. **Heikki Kovalainen**
12. **Kazuki Nakajima**
13. **Robert Kubica**
14. **Nick Heidfeld**
15. **Nelsinho Piquet**
16. **Sebastien Buemi**
17. **Giancarlo Fisichella**
18. **Mark Webber**
19. **Adrian Sutil (3-place penalty)**
20. **Sebastien Bourdais**

## STRATEGY

Bridgestone brought the Medium and Super Soft combination for the race. From our pre-event work and Friday running, the Super Soft was going to be the primary race tyre, with Bahrain's layout and surface working well with that tyre compound. The dry race plan was to run the Medium tyre, which was slower, at the end of the race.

The pit lane is fairly long at Bahrain, but with the Super Soft as the main tyre, a two-stop and three-stop strategy were very close. I qualified P4 on a short two-stop fuel load, behind both Toyotas and Vettel, who was slightly longer on fuel. I had a good start, and passed Vettel on lap 1 and Hamilton (who had jumped both me and Vettel) on lap 2 of the race into Turn 1. I then closed the gap to the two Toyotas ahead, again saving the tyres and fuel while building a gap to the pack behind, who were held behind Hamilton.

Both Toyotas stopped first, choosing to fit the Medium tyre, resulting in very poor performance relative to the pack. When I stopped, we fitted the faster Super Soft tyre, allowing me to build a significant gap over the field behind, who were held up by Trulli struggling on the Medium compound.

*Brawn GP's Jenson Button achieved his third victory of the 2009 Formula One season today at the end of an exciting Bahrain Grand Prix. Team-mate Rubens Barrichello brought his Brawn-Mercedes car home in fifth position to score valuable points and consolidate the team's lead in the Constructors' Championship after the opening four rounds.*

The old boy thinks this is my best race ever. It was very emotional for him. When I saw him afterwards, he was crying his eyes out. He got me into cars, buying me a kart for Christmas just before my eighth birthday, so Formula One is his life as much as mine. But he's not the sort of guy who has ever pushed me. He's at the races because he loves racing; he's never telling me what to do.

I said to him on the journey to the circuit this morning, 'It's all about the first lap today.' The engine had been drastically overheating all weekend and after the first lap I was going to have to drop the power down to get air into the engine. So I knew this was going to be a tough race. I knew I had to go out and grab it by the scruff of the neck. It was crucial I got past Vettel early and then caught the two Toyotas of Trulli and Glock at the pit-stops.

Ah, but I had a poor start. We've had problems with our clutch and that was one of the worst moments. Lewis got ahead of me, but I was lucky that more of the field didn't fly past. I dived down the outside at Turn 1 – Lewis was on the inside, Vettel was in the middle, I was on the outside – and we both went around Vettel, which put me back up to fourth. The only way for me to beat Vettel in the long run was to get past Lewis on lap 1. I knew I wouldn't get past him on any other lap because he has KERS (which can mean three tenths of a second advantage over a lap of the Bahrain circuit) and he can just push the boost button when you get close. He was in a combative mood. I tried three times on lap 1, and it didn't happen, but it put him off line coming onto the straight for the second lap so I towed up behind him on the straight. He pushed

his KERS button and pulled away a bit. We had one car length between us, but I thought I had to make the move. I zipped out and outbraked him at Turn 1 on lap 2 – quite an enjoyable move – threw the car up the inside. He made it reasonably difficult, as you would, but I got past him and was up to third.

Then it was about chasing the two Toyotas. I caught them up even though they were on a much lighter fuel load. They pitted. I had three or four laps to put in some quick times, which I did. I pitted and came out in front of both of them – a very nice position to be in. Vettel, with his one more lap of fuel, pitted and came out stuck behind Trulli. So I was able to pull away and build up a gap, but the whole time I knew that if Vettel broke free of Trulli, he would chase me down. When he did break free, his lap times were very similar to mine. There was a tenth between us on every lap. In the end I crossed the line and won the race seven seconds ahead of Vettel. Cue more euphoria inside my helmet!

'Oh my god oh my god you're amazing! Best birthday present ever! Well done little bruv, love u loads'
Tanya, sister

Ross came on the team radio and said: 'You won it on the first lap. Great overtaking.'

What a fantastic feeling. We won the race today on the perfect strategy – and it was the first victory I had achieved without seeing the chequered flag from behind a safety car! It was the sweetest victory. If I hadn't fought my way past Vettel and Lewis on the first lap we wouldn't have won the race, because we were battling the heat all the way through. Had I been stuck behind Lewis, I would have been in trouble. But I managed to work my way into clean air. Even then the temperature was on the limit. When you are behind a car you don't get the cooling effect, because the air is disrupted by the downforce created by the car in front, and the air doesn't get into the side pods. We were on the limit and we lost our advantage a bit because of the cooling problems with the engine, lost a few horsepower. So for me, this is the most exciting and fulfilling win – and for the whole team, too.

I pulled a good advantage on my main rivals in the championship, including Rubens, so it was a very important race in my quest. We enjoyed it in our normal fashion, posing for a big picture with every team member. Unfortunately, Rubens was saying things like 'Jenson is getting the luck, like Michael used to.' He was using the word 'luck' ironically, in a reference to his previous situation at Ferrari as Michael Schumacher's team-mate. Maybe sometimes I do get the luck. I'm not the only one. You have to position yourself correctly and make your own luck. The win was no fluke. I won because I worked hard and fought my way through on the first two laps, and made it count when I needed to.

That evening we headed to a party at the house of His Highness Crown Prince Sheikh Salman bin Hamad Al Khalifa, which was amazingly colourful. The Crown Prince has the full-flowing robe and headgear on by day, but when we rocked up at his place on the beach in the evening, there he was in jeans, T-shirt and flip-flops. His party was a great way to celebrate a fantastic race, though I left pretty early. I'd got very, very hot in the race and it just got to me a bit.

> 'Congratulations honey... I knew you were gonna win again! I really wish I was there with you to celebrate your win! Biggest chu.'
> Jessica

I flew out of Bahrain with a fresh perspective. Now we know that the Red Bulls are quick, and they will be our main competition going forward. They have certainly found some performance, and we no longer have the advantage we enjoyed at the first race. However, going into Europe with three wins out of four – it's unbelievable!

I keep being asked if it's frustrating to have had to wait until relatively late in my career for a competitive car. I can only say that, if I'd had this car in 2001, I might have had a chance of winning the championship, but I wouldn't have been a complete driver. Now I'm 29 – I'm just five years older than the guy who won last year's world championship, but I have ten years' experience. It's the best position to be in.

Arriving home in Monaco, I found an email from Jimmie Johnson of NASCAR fame: 'Hey man, I wanted to send you a note to congratulate you on your success. I truly enjoy watching good people receive good things and I couldn't be happier for you. If you ever travel to the States and want to see some NASCAR action, let me know. Keep up the good work!'

## BAHRAIN GRAND PRIX FINAL POSITIONS

| Pos | Driver | Team | Laps | Time |
|---|---|---|---|---|
| 1 | Jenson Button | Brawn-Mercedes | 57 | 1:31:48.182 |
| 2 | Sebastian Vettel | RBR-Renault | 57 | +7.1 secs |
| 3 | Jarno Trulli | Toyota | 57 | +9.1 secs |
| 4 | Lewis Hamilton | McLaren-Mercedes | 57 | +22.0 secs |
| 5 | Rubens Barrichello | Brawn-Mercedes | 57 | +37.7 secs |
| 6 | Kimi Räikkönen | Ferrari | 57 | +42.0 secs |
| 7 | Timo Glock | Toyota | 57 | +42.8 secs |
| 8 | Fernando Alonso | Renault | 57 | +52.7 secs |
| 9 | Nico Rosberg | Williams-Toyota | 57 | +58.1 secs |
| 10 | Nelsinho Piquet | Renault | 57 | +65.1 secs |
| 11 | Mark Webber | RBR-Renault | 57 | +67.6 secs |
| 12 | Heikki Kovalainen | McLaren-Mercedes | 57 | +77.8 secs |
| 13 | Sebastien Bourdais | STR-Ferrari | 57 | +78.8 secs |
| 14 | Felipe Massa | Ferrari | 56 | +1 Lap |
| 15 | Giancarlo Fisichella | Force India-Mercedes | 56 | +1 Lap |
| 16 | Adrian Sutil | Force India-Mercedes | 56 | +1 Lap |
| 17 | Sebastien Buemi | STR-Ferrari | 56 | +1 Lap |
| 18 | Robert Kubica | BMW Sauber | 56 | +1 Lap |
| 19 | Nick Heidfeld | BMW Sauber | 56 | +1 Lap |
| Ret | Kazuki Nakajima | Williams-Toyota | 48 | Oil pressure |

'That was a magnificent drive. Last year, even with the car we had, I saw some flashes of something exceptional. The guys on the team were always telling me he really was a bit special but I hadn't been privileged enough to see it regularly. With the car we've got now he is able to show what he can do. You cannot see him at work in the car, it's quite extraordinary. He's so smooth, looks after the car so well, keeps the tyres in perfect shape.' Ross Brawn

It was a great race today and I'm so happy to have seen the chequered flag without a safety car or red light in front of me. To achieve my third victory of the season is amazing and we are going back to Europe now after an intense five-week, four-race period with a strong lead in both championships. I couldn't wish for anything more.

It's been a tough weekend for the team, which makes this win even more rewarding as we didn't have the pace that we expected. I was really happy with my first lap. I knew that I had to overtake Sebastian quickly and got him round the outside on Turn 1. I had a couple of attempts at Lewis round the first lap and almost got him at the last corner. I knew that he would pull away from me on the straight so I dropped in behind and used the tow to overtake him at Turn 1. It wasn't easy from there but getting up to third on the first lap was crucial for me.

This race asked a lot from me – with our compromised grid position, concerns about the engine in the intense heat, the need to nail the fast laps to leapfrog the Toyotas at the first stops – and I delivered.

**OVERALL POINTS**

| | |
|---|---|
| Jenson Button | 31 |
| Rubens Barrichello | 19 |
| Sebastian Vettel | 18 |
| Jarno Trulli | 14.5 |
| Timo Glock | 12 |
| Mark Webber | 9.5 |
| Lewis Hamilton | 9 |
| Fernando Alonso | 5 |
| Nick Heidfeld | 4 |
| Heikki Kovalainen | 4 |
| Nico Rosberg | 3.5 |
| Kimi Räikkönen | 3 |
| Sebastien Buemi | 3 |
| Sebastien Bourdais | 1 |

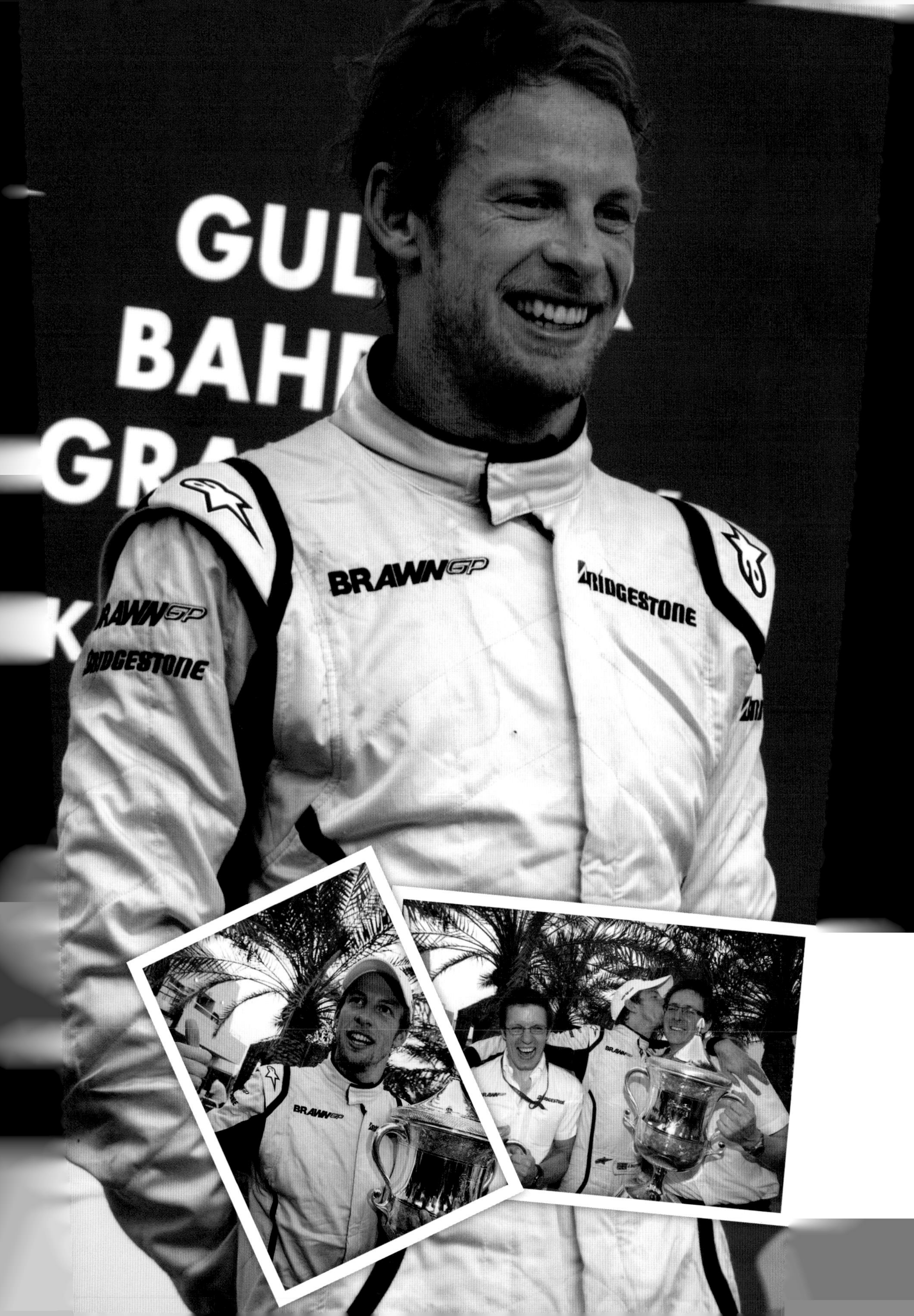
BRAWN GP
BRIDGESTONE

# Spanish Grand Prix
## Circuit de Catalunya, Barcelona
### Friday 8 May – Sunday 10 May

**Number of laps:** 66

**Circuit length:** 4.655 km

**Race distance:** 307.104 km

**Lap record:** 1:21.670
(Kimi Räikkönen, 2008)

### MY HISTORY AT CATALUNYA

**2008 (Honda)**
Grid 13; finished 6

**2007 (Honda)**
Grid 14; finished 12

**2006 (Honda)**
Grid 8; finished 6

**2004 (BAR-Honda)**
Grid 14; finished 8

**2003 (BAR-Honda)**
Grid 5; finished 9

**2002 (Renault)**
Grid 6; finished 12

**2001 (Benetton-Renault)**
Grid 21; finished 15

**2000 (Williams-BMW)**
Grid 10; finished 17

The Circuit de Catalunya is like a home circuit because we test so much here, and the grand prix weekend always feels familiar. The key to a quick lap is good downforce – and we're lucky our car behaves predictably, which enables you to feel completely confident when committing to high-speed corners. The new chicane can be tricky as it's extremely slippery and therefore very slow. A mistake there costs you a lot of time. Most of sector three is slow. So you also need the car working well in the slow stuff to be able to establish a good rhythm.

Overtaking can be a challenge, but one of the best opportunities is going into the first corner. You can squeeze by there once the race has settled down, but it's very difficult. The track is no longer the high-speed challenge it once was, but it's still interesting.

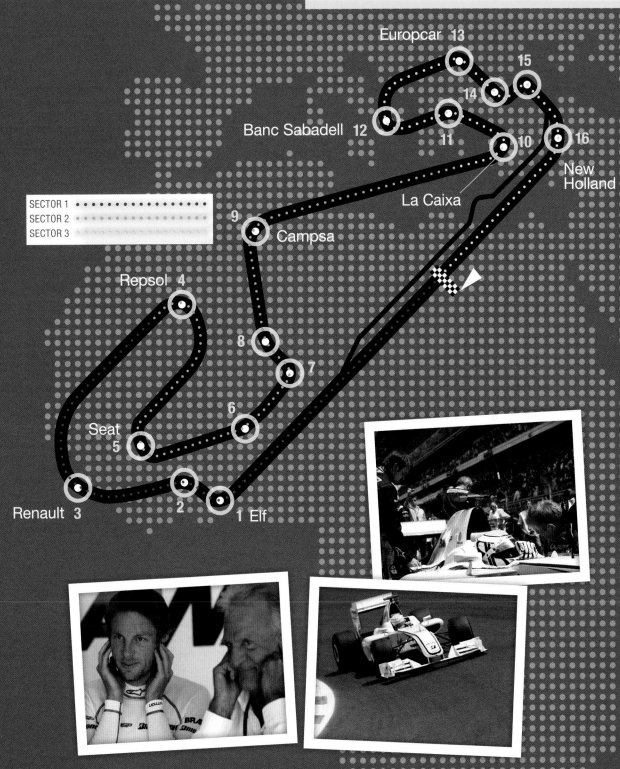

*They all mean a lot obviously but coming back to Europe and winning in Barcelona, a circuit that I've always found a little bit tough... it's a good feeling and gives me a lot of confidence for the rest of the season.*

Europcar **13**

**15**

**14**

Banc Sabadell **12**

**11**

**10**

La Caixa

New Holland **16**

| SECTOR 1 |
| SECTOR 2 |
| SECTOR 3 |

**9** Campsa

Repsol **4**

**8**

**7**

**6**

Seat **5**

Renault **3**

**2**

**1** Elf

# Spain:
## Preparation, practice and qualifying

After Bahrain, we had a two-week break between the first four fly-away races and the start of the European season in Spain. I popped back to the factory for a small celebration of our successes so far and to catch up on the progress of our latest developments. I toured all the departments to thank the guys for their hard work, and to look forward collectively to consolidating our achievements in the forthcoming thirteen races.

Then I flew to Nice to spend time at home in Monaco with John, my trainer. John, who runs a triathlon training company, has changed the approach to my fitness this season. The aim is to maintain my base level of fitness, but without risk of injury. Whereas before I'd do short, intense, 90-minute, knackering sessions based on triathlon, John has introduced 'maintenance' programmes of lower intensity work for longer periods of time. When we started working together in November 2008, he had to rein me back. My instinct was to do everything at 100mph. He's shown me that we can do four hours at lower intensity and still achieve the same levels of fatigue as a flat-out 90 minutes. When we do the short, sharp stuff, it's quality work.

John took me up into the mountains above Monaco to get away from it all for a while. Obviously I was still thinking about racing, but it's refreshing to take your mind away from that environment. When I'm winning I'm just longing to be back in the car again, and time spent 'not racing' drives me crazy. I need to keep busy. We cycle up into the mountains on a 90km, half iron man route, which has three big climbs. It is beautiful up there and cooler than down by the sea. Mark Webber, Sebastian Vettel and Fernando Alonso cycle a lot, too, but I never come across them while I'm out training. I've met Lance Armstrong locally a few times. He has asked me to cycle with him and I'm like, 'Not today, Lance!' One day I'll be close enough in fitness to him so he wouldn't consider it a waste of time.

The Spanish Grand Prix marks a shift in attitude. It is rarely a dramatic race, because you can't overtake, but it's the first race of the European season, and a technical race where observers are assessing raw performance. It's a big aero circuit and everyone has their first big update kit since wheeling the new cars out at the start of the season. Is our position at the top of the points table under threat? With the no-testing rule, it is a huge risk to introduce a big upgrade, but all the teams are in the same boat, and so, yes, this weekend will give a significant indication of the new world order in Formula One.

We're only four races into a seventeen-race season. I'm not getting comfortable as championship leader. We are intensely aware of the level of performance we have to sustain if we are serious about challenging for the title this year. Our team started working on our car months ago when it was obvious the 2008 car was not worth wasting time and energy on. We started the 2009 season with a head start, but are now braced for the manufacturers, with their big budgets, to start making inroads in developing their cars and update packages. The field has compressed considerably just four races in and the performance margins at the front are now very tight. But Ross Brawn is the master of shrewd thinking and while we have been away racing over the past few weeks, the factory has been working extremely hard on a big upgrade package of developments, including new wings, floor and side-pod. This is the first time we will have something new on the car since Australia, plus we can explain how we lost some of our initial advantage. We were struggling with the adjustable front wing after Malaysia, because of water damage to the electrics. That hurt me quite substantially because I use the adjustment a lot around a lap to give myself more front wing in the high-speed corners.

I travelled to Barcelona on Thursday and settled into my motorhome, which, along with other drivers' motorhomes, is parked in a field behind the race track. I love my motorhome, literally an apartment on wheels. Instead of living out of a suitcase, in dozens of different hotels, it means I have a home from home at most of the European tracks. It's a home, think-tank, exercise studio and chill-out zone all rolled into one. Several drivers have them and it makes such sense. Mine is driven around and looked after by a guy called Topsy. He's great, an ex military boy. He gets very emotional about the racing, he's one of the team for sure.

## FRIDAY

The paddock atmosphere feels very bustling and business-like compared to the vast paddock at Shanghai or the palm-tree adorned one in Bahrain. I'm very aware the media are scrutinising our potential as title favourites. Although we've had some great races, some commentators are saying, 'This is the race where we'll see who is quick' – as if they haven't noticed we've been quick. We've won three out of four races, and haven't been off the podium. It is an important race for us to continue the winning momentum.

The paddock is full of the news that Ferrari have threatened to quit Formula One. The war between the Formula One Teams Association (FOTA) and the Max Mosley-led FIA has reached boiling point with talk of budget caps, two-tier championships and alternative series. As a driver, my role is to keep my blinkers on and focus on what I have to do in the car, and today I struggled. We arrived with our aerodynamic upgrades and ran a programme to evaluate them, but I couldn't get a balance with the new kit. I experienced oversteer in the car on low fuel and I've been struggling for grip, which was frustrating but we believe that we have identified the reasons. Our little team worked well together with Rubens collecting some good baseline data which we can study overnight and resolve my problems.

> 'Button pulled a beautiful lap out, especially through the last few corners. He will be thoroughly, thoroughly satisfied with that effort.'
> Martin Brundle, BBC TV

## SATURDAY

*Brawn GP's Jenson Button secured his third pole position of the season at the Circuit de Catalunya in Barcelona today. After crossing the line for his final flying lap in Q3 with just two seconds to spare, Jenson put in a fantastic lap on his race fuel load to snatch pole position from Sebastian Vettel. Team-mate Rubens Barrichello put his Brawn-Mercedes car on the second row of the grid after a closely fought qualifying hour and will start from third place.*

I struggled this morning, but got my act together in qualifying. We made a few adjustments to change the balance of the car and it worked. I crossed the line to start my flying lap with just two seconds to go. It could have gone very, very wrong. We didn't think we were going to make it, but then, perhaps with the adrenalin coursing through me, I did by far the best lap I've had here this weekend. In every session Rubens has been tremendous. I found it very difficult to hang onto him on the low fuel, but I got the lap on the high – race-load – fuel. It was a bit of a surprise when I heard Shov's voice when I crossed the finishing line saying I'd got pole. I could tell he and the team were surprised, too, as was my team-mate. After dominating the weekend, Rubens was not happy to miss out on pole, but he realised mine was a good lap and congratulated me.

It's probably my most satisfying pole of the season because it is unexpected. This is such a low-grip track you have to throw the car around a bit and that's not my style. I was able to benefit from looking at Rubens's set-up to overcome some of the issues that we faced yesterday. The upgrades on the car are performing well and it's certainly a good step forward, although we haven't got the most out of the package yet.

I'm looking forward to the race. For the last ten years, the winner has started from the front row, but I am concerned about the long drag down to Turn 1. We know our starts are good, but I'm sat out in front with everyone behind ready to try to jump me.

## BRAWN TECHNICAL UPDATES

We arrived in Barcelona with our first major upgrade, which consisted of a new floor and diffuser. The field has closed up significantly since Melbourne and teams that started the year with basic diffusers are starting to introduce more complicated twin-deck designs after the FIA clarified that they were entirely legal.

Barcelona is a track we tested on for four days in early March and we were quick and consistent. However, the circuit is always lower grip during the race weekend and temperatures are generally a lot higher. We had a decent balance for most of the lap, but were struggling with understeer in the very fast turns 3 and 9 and it was in these corners that the Red Bulls were gaining on us.

*'An amazing performance. He came out of nowhere. He's been struggling to understand the upgrade all weekend. Rubens had the edge on him. He's just dug deep, used that experience. He's been through remarkable highs and lows in his F1 career already.'* David Coulthard, BBC TV

# Spain:
## The race

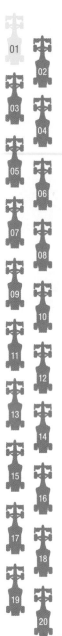

1. **Jenson Button**
2. Sebastian Vettel
3. Rubens Barrichello
4. Felipe Massa
5. Mark Webber
6. Timo Glock
7. Jarno Trulli
8. Fernando Alonso
9. Nico Rosberg
10. Robert Kubica
11. Kazuki Nakajima
12. Nelsinho Piquet
13. Nick Heidfeld
14. Lewis Hamilton
15. Sebastien Buemi
16. Kimi Räikkönen
17. Sebastien Bourdais
18. Heikki Kovalainen
19. Adrian Sutil
20. Giancarlo Fisichella

## STRATEGY

Barcelona is slightly harder on tyres than Shanghai and Bahrain, and therefore we were back to the same tyres as Sepang (Hard and Soft). Similar to Sepang, the Soft tyre worked well, and would be the primary race tyre, leaving the Hard tyre until the end of the race, for a shorter stint.

The strategy calculations showed a three-stop to be slightly better than a two-stop strategy, due to a short pit lane and reasonable drop on the Soft tyres over a stint. I qualified P1, just ahead of Vettel, who was on slightly more fuel. Rubens had a good start from P3, and managed to jump Vettel off the line and pass me into Turn 1 on lap 1 of the race. Rubens was kept on the planned three-stop. However, I would not have been able to jump Rosberg at his stop if I'd stayed on a three-stop, so was converted to a long middle stint two-stop. I drove a good race on heavy fuel, and Rubens was unable to maintain the strategic lead, finishing P2 behind me.

*Brawn GP achieved the team's second one–two result of the 2009 F1 season with Jenson Button taking his fourth victory of the year and team-mate Rubens Barrichello securing second position.*

I had the all-important good start from pole, but Rubens, starting from third, had an absolute flier. He got the jump on Sebastian Vettel. Felipe Massa also got the jump on Vettel. I pulled to the inside to block that side of the track, but Rubens had a good run and was able to get past me into Turn 1, so I was stuck behind him – annoyingly, because I sensed that I was quicker. A collision triggered by Nico Rosberg's Williams, which resulted in Jarno Trulli's Toyota then spinning into both the Torro Rossos and Adrian Sutil's Force India, brought out the safety car for the first four laps.

When the race was under way again on lap 5, Rubens and I were told to push as hard as possible to build a lead over the chasing pack. Having lost the lead to Rubens, and with the prospect of being caught behind Nico Rosberg, we made the decision to switch from a three-stop to a two-stop strategy when I came in for my first stop on lap 18. A three-stop would have destroyed my race, but I needed to make the two-stop work. I needed to be in clean air. The car felt so heavy with the fuel on board after my first stop, but I persisted on my final two stints to make the strategy work for me. My engineer was on the radio saying 'You've got to put in the laps now,' and at this point Rubens was still three seconds ahead on predicted timing.

I'd damaged the tyres quite a bit by pushing so hard on a heavy fuel load, but I found I could still get the time out of the car by being aggressive with it. It's not normally my style but it's necessary here, and something I've learnt over the weekend from watching Rubens. Every lap at this point was flat-out. I've never driven in that way and I'm sure it looks messy, but it was the best way. The team said, 'Right, you are this far behind Rubens in the race. If you keep going like this you will have a chance of beating him, because he's struggling with the tyres on his third stint.' So I kept pushing and after his last stop Rubens came out behind me and I was able to pull away from him.

I know Rubens wasn't very happy because he thought he should have switched to a two-stop, but I'd edged ahead of him by adapting strategy to my own race circumstances and making it work. Our strategy specialist said a three-stop was quicker. Full stop. And that was what we'd both fuelled for. The problem was that Rubens didn't make the three-stop work, and so it looked like the team put me on a better strategy in order to beat him. But Rubens just wasn't quick enough. He lost his eight-second advantage, plus more. We're all here to win. Today it went my way. That's just the way it is. I made it work and I won the race.

What I said over the team radio says it all: 'Start was a nightmare. Great strategy. Sorry for Rubens.' Shov replied: 'Fantastic Jenson, you really looked like you wanted to win that.'

Rubens is Latin, as we all know, and he can let his emotions run wild, but initially he seemed fairly resigned to the order of our Brawn one–two finish. While we were being weighed before the podium ceremony, we sat down next to each other and Rubens said: 'I don't know how the hell I lost the race, man. From the third set of tyres on, the car was pphhh…' And I said, 'I'm pleased I won the race but I feel for you, man.'

Then I had to try to find the way to the podium. I know the Circuit de Catalunya inside out, but I didn't know the way to the podium!

In the press conference, emotions seemed to get the better of Rubens, which turned 'team orders' into a media issue. It just made it difficult for the team and for myself being bombarded by questions, but the fact remains a three-stop was the quickest strategy and Rubens didn't make it work for him.

The frustrating thing for me was I had such a good race. Two laps from home I lapped Lewis Hamilton, the defending world champion. I pushed so hard, and I was on the limit at every corner I came to, so for me this win was the best win, and so enjoyable. My mother was here for the first race she'd ever seen me win and my sister Natasha, too, and it was great celebrating with them. The sad thing was I kept being distracted from whole-heartedly enjoying my victory because of the negative media attention.

**SPANISH GRAND PRIX FINAL POSITIONS**

| Pos | Driver | Team | Laps | Time |
| --- | --- | --- | --- | --- |
| 1 | Jenson Button | Brawn-Mercedes | 66 | 1:37:19.202 |
| 2 | Rubens Barrichello | Brawn-Mercedes | 66 | +13.0 secs |
| 3 | Mark Webber | RBR-Renault | 66 | +13.9 secs |
| 4 | Sebastian Vettel | RBR-Renault | 66 | +18.9 secs |
| 5 | Fernando Alonso | Renault | 66 | +43.1 secs |
| 6 | Felipe Massa | Ferrari | 66 | +50.8 secs |
| 7 | Nick Heidfeld | BMW Sauber | 66 | +52.3 secs |
| 8 | Nico Rosberg | Williams-Toyota | 66 | +65.2 secs |
| 9 | Lewis Hamilton | McLaren-Mercedes | 65 | +1 Lap |
| 10 | Timo Glock | Toyota | 65 | +1 Lap |
| 11 | Robert Kubica | BMW Sauber | 65 | +1 Lap |
| 12 | Nelsinho Piquet | Renault | 65 | +1 Lap |
| 13 | Kazuki Nakajima | Williams-Toyota | 65 | +1 Lap |
| 14 | Giancarlo Fisichella | Force India-Mercedes | 65 | +1 Lap |
| Ret | Kimi Räikkönen | Ferrari | 17 | Hydraulics |
| Ret | Heikki Kovalainen | McLaren-Mercedes | 7 | Gearbox |
| Ret | Jarno Trulli | Toyota | 0 | Accident |
| Ret | Sebastien Buemi | STR-Ferrari | 0 | Accident |
| Ret | Sebastien Bourdais | STR-Ferrari | 0 | Accident |
| Ret | Adrian Sutil | Force India-Mercedes | 0 | Accident |

'If you come out at Barcelona, which is a damned good test of a car, with a 1–2 finish, you've got to start believing in yourselves as title favourites.' Pat Symonds, Renault director of engineering

I don't ever want to go down the avenue of talking about team orders, because it's so far removed from the situation in our team. To come away with the win is a little unexpected, but it means so much to continue our run of success. Obviously Rubens is disappointed not to have got the win today and he has been a huge help over the weekend in me overcoming the issues that I faced on Friday. His turn will certainly come. There's a great feeling within our team and I am very proud of them for producing such a great car. Today is a fantastic result after a great deal of hard work to maximise the performance of our new developments.

*'Awesome mate. Well done! Stunning qualifying!'*
Ed Lawson Johnson, friend

*'Blimey that was a stunner! Congratulations bro. Hugs'*
Samantha, sister

*'Simply the best, better than all the rest'*
Tanya, sister

*'You fiend well done man, you had a stormer again! I'm so happy for you dude'*
Ainsley

*'Mate, perfect weekend again and another brilliant drive!! Have a belter in Barcelona tonight. I bet this one feels good'*
Mark Hynes

## OVERALL POINTS

| | |
|---|---|
| Jenson Button | 41 |
| Rubens Barrichello | 27 |
| Sebastian Vettel | 23 |
| Mark Webber | 15.5 |
| Jarno Trulli | 14.5 |
| Timo Glock | 12 |
| Lewis Hamilton | 9 |
| Fernando Alonso | 9 |
| Nick Heidfeld | 6 |
| Nico Rosberg | 4.5 |
| Heikki Kovalainen | 4 |
| Felipe Massa | 3 |
| Kimi Räikkönen | 3 |
| Sebastien Buemi | 3 |
| Sebastien Bourdais | 1 |

# Monaco Grand Prix
## Street Circuit, Monte Carlo
## Thursday 21 May – Sunday 24 May

**Number of laps:** 78

**Circuit length:** 3.340 km

**Race distance:** 260.520 km

**Lap record:** 1:14.439
(Michael Schumacher, 2004)

### MY HISTORY AT MONACO

**2008 (Honda)**
Grid 11; finished 11

**2007 (Honda)**
Grid 10; finished 11

**2006 (Honda)**
Grid 13; finished 11

**2004 (BAR-Honda)**
Grid 2; finished 2

**2002 (Renault)**
Grid 8; retired (collision)

**2001 (Benetton-Renault)**
Grid 17; finished 7

**2000 (Williams-BMW)**
Grid 14; retired (engine)

The Monaco Grand Prix is a special race weekend – a showcase for the sport with the mega yachts in the harbour, the roar of V8 engines echoing back from condominium buildings and the mountainous backdrop, the parties, fun and glamour. There is a belief that the demands of this circuit divide drivers into those who flourish here and those who don't. I've been on the podium once, but I have never felt I've got on well here, which is all the more incentive to make it happen for our little team. Victory in Monaco is the achievement everyone – drivers, mechanics, management, sponsors, fans – wants to gild their CV.

As a resident of the principality, this will be my first 'home' race of the season, with the British Grand Prix at Silverstone following next month. The streets of Monaco present a very different circuit. It's very, very tight and twisty. Nelson Piquet once said it's like riding a bike around your sitting room – and Monaco apartments have small sitting rooms! The good thing is that there's been some recent re-surfacing work, so it's not as bumpy as it used to be. It's a maximum downforce circuit and it's quite slow compared to most tracks we visit, but it feels twice the speed of most circuits because you are hemmed in by the barriers and tall buildings.

My usual driving style is very smooth, but I will have to adapt to get the best out of the car. You have to be aggressive, and wring the car's neck, but within limits. You can't let the barriers intimidate you, while obviously paying them due respect. Every time you take to the track, it's a non-stop challenge which requires you to maintain absolute focus, concentration and precision.

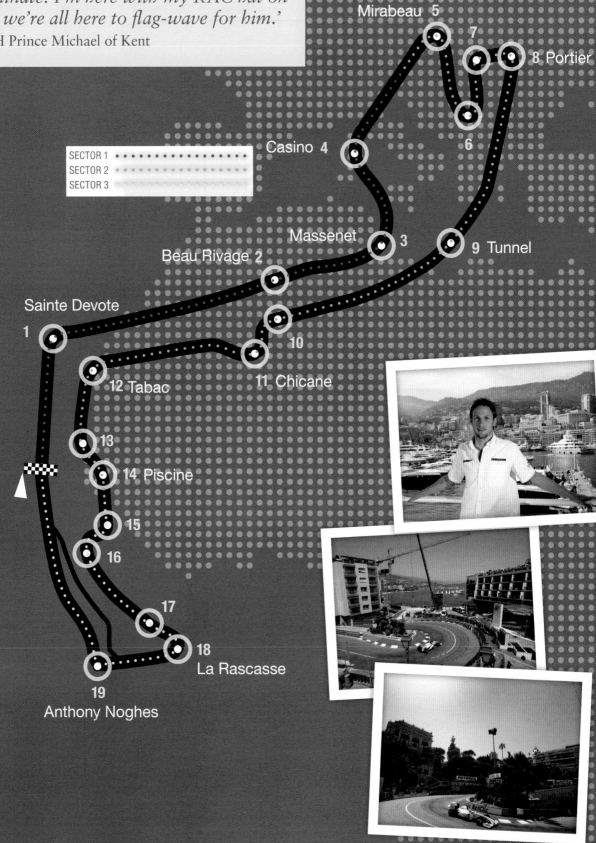

'This brilliant young driver has come through from the dark days of last autumn and now he's beginning to dominate. I'm here with my RAC hat on and we're all here to flag-wave for him.'
HRH Prince Michael of Kent

Mirabeau 5

7

8 Portier

6

SECTOR 1
SECTOR 2
SECTOR 3

Casino 4

Massenet

3

9 Tunnel

Beau Rivage 2

Sainte Devote

1

10

12 Tabac

11 Chicane

13

14 Piscine

15

16

17

18
La Rascasse

19
Anthony Noghes

# Monaco:
## Preparation, practice and qualifying

This is not a race I have to travel to – as I live through the tunnel in the rock to the west of the Monaco harbour in Fontvieille. I've been training hard, chilling out and relaxing because it's always a frenetically busy weekend with family and friends coming to cheer me on.

I'm certainly not in a comfort zone going into this race as championship leader. The Red Bulls are still our main challenge, but the Ferraris made a notable leap in improvement in Barcelona. I'm confident that the car will be fantastic round the slow-and-twisty circuit because of its superior mechanical grip, but it's on my mind that I've always struggled here against Rubens. Practice is on Thursday – to allow for the traditional Friday 'day off', which makes it a longer event for spectators, and logistically hectic for the team people involved.

It's not helped by the fact that the FOTA versus FIA saga has escalated. I'd rather not be distracted by the politics and I think it's best for drivers not to get too involved. As a collective, the GPDA (Grand Prix Drivers' Association), we drivers can probably make a difference. We are an important element in the Formula One show and we have become involved in that we've said we support FOTA, which we do, and we've supported every direction they have taken so far. But some of the drivers are employed by teams who are not part of FOTA, such as Williams and Force India. I hope it will sort itself out soon because it's an irritating distraction when we all want to concentrate on racing.

## THURSDAY
The aim is to secure pole on Saturday because it's almost impossible to overtake once the race is underway. Ah, at the moment that looks a distant dream. I struggled today. I could not get a balance. I was so far off the pace of Rubens – six tenths to eight tenths slower than him over one lap. It's important to get into a rhythm, so we focused on longer runs and tyre evaluations. This morning proved challenging for me: I had rear locking in the low-speed corners and understeer in the high-speed corners and didn't

feel at one with the car. However, we made some significant set-up changes this afternoon and my last runs on the softer tyres were much better. We finished the day knowing we're going in the right direction for qualifying.

## FRIDAY
The traditional rest day in Monaco. For spectators it's all about Champagne lunches on boats, parties, sunbathing, 'racing' your road car around the grand prix circuit when it opens again for public use (which, in reality, means crawling around at snail's pace as everyone has the same idea).

'He's done his apprenticeship now. He knows how hard it's been, how easy for other people. He's not going to let this opportunity go. Adversity builds character.'

Nigel Mansell

Jessica is here, and I'm seeing my family and mates, but I'm not joining in the partying. I was planning to take my little rib boat out – because it's so peaceful out at sea – but I thought being out on the water for a long period is not a good idea on a race weekend because of the rocking sensation you carry back with you. Besides, I've waited nine years for a car this good and I'm determined to make the most of this opportunity. I've become a bit boring, because what I really like doing is studying the data, looking at the technical feedback, thinking about how to improve, asking the engineers stuff. I'm definitely not letting my hair down in the middle of a race weekend.

## SATURDAY
*Brawn GP's Jenson Button secured his fourth pole of the season and his best qualifying position ever for the Monaco Grand Prix around the iconic street circuit. Team-mate Rubens Barrichello put his Brawn-Mercedes car on the second row of the grid for tomorrow's 78-lap race with an excellent third position.*

Three facts: 1) Monaco is the most stressful race weekend for team personnel because of the logistics of the working environment. 2) Grid position is crucial here. 3) Qualifying is the most stressful hour of any grand prix weekend. Add those three elements together and Monaco qualifying is combustibly exciting! Make that mentally challenging, too. To reach the pit lane

'Jenson's getting into the habit of saving the best to last! He wasn't happy in Q2, made some little changes. He just knew that was the lap where he had to produce, and he's driving exceptionally well at the moment.'
Ross Brawn

and garages from the paddock, you have to cross the track, going up and down in little lifts on either side of the bridge, so you are 'on view' to the exuberant fans camping out on the rocky hillside above Rascasse at a time when you are usually gathering your thoughts, trying to stay in a zone.

Every detail has to be right. We improved the balance overnight and I approached qualifying very happy with our pace. We have such a strong and responsive car. I was aware the main threat came from the Ferraris, not so much the Red Bulls. In Q1, amazingly, Lewis Hamilton and Jarno Trulli (two Monaco winners) went out as well as Robert Kubica and Timo Glock. In Q2, I struggled with understeer and a lack of front grip, and finished the session in eighth place. It was quite hairy – at one stage I was tenth, on the edge of falling into the drop-out zone. I tried to change my style to be more aggressive, then reverted back to my smooth style. The team were working on reverting the set-up throughout qually and we put it all together for the final lap.

In Q3, I knew I had to win, but I didn't know where any extra performance could come from. I was up against Rubens, the two Ferraris, two Red Bulls, two Williams, Fernando Alonso's Renault and Heikki Kovalainen's McLaren. It was so intense. I just gave it my all. Everything just fell into place and I found that extra little bit with the car that you get when you go into this zone. It's like you are watching it on replay, it's really strange. You're rubbing the barriers, feeling the barriers every time you go through a corner. They are working with you. You have to respect the barriers. If you don't, you will damage the car. Crossing the line at the end of the lap I knew it was pole position before anyone said anything. And it was! I'd snatched it from Kimi Räikkönen in the dying seconds of the session.

Shov came on the radio and went absolutely crazy. We know how important pole is for the race in Monaco. We all want to win it. It comes with a lot of history. Unreal!

De-briefing with the engineers after a session like that, when the team is firing on all cylinders, just passes in a flash. We were all on cloud nine. Later on Saturday night the team and I had a few PR duties on our schedule. Brawn GP had some special guests, including HRH Prince Michael of Kent, who is President of the Royal Automobile Club and of the Motor Sports Association, and a voluble supporter of British drivers. I was amazed when he congratulated me on the season so far and said he'd been glued to every race.

**BRAWN TECHNICAL UPDATES**

Monaco is a unique track but we had a good feeling that the car would work well on the bumpy and tight circuit. We had an aero package to take us to maximum downforce, and did a lot of work at the factory tuning the damper settings to improve the ride quality.

Monaco is one of the hardest tracks to set up a car for, as the window where you have the right balance is so narrow and can come and go over the course of a session or a race. You need good front grip to position the car accurately, but good rear grip so that the rear is stable in the heavy braking areas. We needed to launch the car off the kerbs, so it had to land well allowing us to get back on the power and make time on exit. More than anything, I needed confidence that the car would do exactly what I asked of it.

*'This means everything to Jenson Button. He was talking about how you've got to go for broke, and he's done it! He almost came under the radar, there. He timed it to perfection.'*
Jonathan Legard, BBC TV

# Monaco:
## The race

## STRATEGY

Monaco is a unique circuit, and Bridgestone moved away from the standard two steps between tyre compounds for this event, resulting in the Soft and Super Soft being brought. Historically the circuit evolves towards the softest tyre, with Thursday's running only acting as a guide to the race on Sunday.

Monaco has traditionally been either a one-stop or two-stop strategy circuit, due to the high probability of safety cars, and very low tyre degradation. We chose a two-stop strategy with a short first stint, allowing us to start the race on the Super Soft compound. Vettel also started on the Super Soft, however he suffered significant graining by lap 4 of the race, holding the pack up behind him. I looked after my tyres well, and pulled a gap on Rubens behind. At the stop we fitted the Soft compound and ran the two-stop race to plan.

*Brawn GP dominated the Monaco Grand Prix weekend as Jenson Button led from the front to secure his fifth win of the 2009 F1 season with team-mate Rubens Barrichello taking second place for the team's third one–two finish of the season.*

I woke up on a gloriously sunny morning, but feeling a bit of pressure. I put a lot of pressure on myself, and there is no escaping the unpredictability of a Monaco Grand Prix. Still, starting from pole is obviously the best position. I knew I had to get off the line cleanly. I had a KERS car starting next to me, Kimi's Ferrari. I had Rubens behind me. He was disappointed about qualifying as he'd been the strongest for most of the weekend, but he also acknowledged it was probably the best lap of my life. He said afterwards: 'I left nothing in that lap, so I don't know how Jenson went faster.'

We debated at length which tyres to take, the Soft or the Super Soft. In the end we went for the Super Soft, and along with Vettel, we were the only ones to make that choice. I got away cleanly to lead into Turn 1. Rubens jumped Kimi, which was impressive. I knew he couldn't overtake me around Monaco so I made sure I looked after the rear tyres because we were damaging them very easily in practice. About six laps in, I started pushing the tyres a little bit more and I saw Rubens dropping away from me. I was quite surprised because I wasn't pushing that hard. The team came on the radio and said: 'Rubens has damaged his tyres.' From then on I took it reasonably easy with the tyres, but I was able to put 1.5 to 2 seconds a lap on Rubens. I was able to build up a 16-second lead. The team also came on and said: 'Vettel's backing everyone up. He's four seconds a lap slower than you. He's destroyed his tyres.'

It was such a great position to be in. I had a 16-second lead before the first pit-stop. We pitted a lap earlier than planned to ensure the tyres didn't suddenly deteriorate. The pit stop was gloriously relaxed. We had the lead. They got me out just in front of Massa who was very annoyed, because he was fighting for a podium finish. I had to be consistent, not make a mistake. Rubens began to catch me, but I wasn't worried. Just before my second stop, I pushed for five laps and pulled out a 16-second lead again. Rubens

started closing so it was a matter of protecting the gap, staying focused. Lose concentration in Monaco and you're in the wall, game over. I'm sitting lower in the car this season, and with the big front wings, it felt precariously easy to scrape a barrier. Precision is key.

It's surreal, leading at Monaco. It's so tough mentally. Your surroundings seem to close in on you. The barriers get closer and closer, like you're going around in ever-decreasing circles, faster and faster. The race felt like it went on forever. I was praying, 'Oh God, please get me to the end of the race.' I was also looking after the engine, which is a priority this season under the new regulations. I was finding it tough. Shov came on the radio a little, but he could sense I didn't need any external distraction. He said: 'I'll leave you alone now to concentrate.' About ten laps from the end, he came on again and said: 'Take it easy, you've got a 14-second lead from Rubens. Just back it off a bit. And I did. I crossed the line six seconds in the lead.

'You've done it, man. Great job, the one we all wanted. Well done. Awesome,' Shov screamed in my earpiece.

I went pretty crazy on the radio: 'YEAH BABY, we've won Monaco.' Five out of six wins, and Monaco! It was a stunning moment for everyone in the team.

I was so excited I didn't hear when Shov said 'Go straight to the grid', and I parked up in parc fermé instead of the start–finish line. I realised I was in the wrong place and thought: 'Oh no, how embarrassing.' Everyone was like, 'What are you doing?' An official told me to wait for a car to drive me to the start line, but I had an overwhelming impulse to enjoy the moment. I had the most uplifting – and probably illegal – run all the way down the start–finish straight to the podium. Wow! It was a great mistake to park in the wrong place. When you're driving around in the

> *'He's been faultless all weekend. This man is clearly world class and if he doesn't end up world champion at the end of this year, I'll be amazed.'*
> David Coulthard

car, you don't hear the cheers from the grandstand. You see flags waving and hands clapping, but it's mute, because you're cocooned in your helmet. On the run uphill to the podium, I could drink in the ecstatic atmosphere. Mechanics were high-fiving me all the way down – even Red Bull guys. It was the perfect way to end an unbelievable day.

I eventually got there – I can tell you, it's a very long way! Nick Fry gave me a big hug, and I ran straight up to the podium in the Royal Box. I didn't feel out of breath at all. It must have been the adrenalin pumping still. I jumped onto the podium and apologised to Prince Albert for being late. He laughed and said: 'Very nice entrance.'

I shook his hand and received my trophy. I said goodbye to everyone on the podium, to Princess Caroline's children, Charlotte, Pierre and the gang. As I was walking off the podium, Prince Michael of Kent came up and shook my hand and said: 'What an amazing job. I'll be supporting you at Silverstone also. Thank you so much for this and congratulations!'

Then I grabbed my bottle of Champagne and sprayed everyone to celebrate our hat-trick of one–two finishes. It was quadruply special to have Jessica and my family here – the old boy, of course, plus my mum, Simone, and my sister Samantha, witnessing the high point of what is turning into an exceptionally fun season.

On a beautiful, balmy evening we celebrated at Prince Albert's Grand Prix Ball. He invited Nick Fry and his fiancée Kate, Ross Brawn and his wife Jean, myself and Jessica. We all went to this black-tie event and had the honour of sitting on the top table with Prince Albert, Charlene his girlfriend, who is a former South African swimmer, and the rest of the Grimaldis. I had Charlotte next to me and Pierre across the table with their other halves. Jacky Ickx, the Belgian former Formula One racer and six-time Le Mans winner, was also on the main table. It was tremendously enjoyable and a real accolade – only the winning team are invited to the palace ball. I live in Monaco so I had my black tie, but Ross and Nick had been too superstitious to come prepared with their dinner jackets so they turned up in borrowed clothes. Prince Albert is fascinating company. He was interested in our season, and the race, and touched by the amazing story of Brawn GP.

I gave a little speech on the stage and there followed a bit of dancing. I knew all my gang were at Amber Lounge, the temporary VIP nightclub that is set up at four of the grands prix each year, organised by Sonia Irvine, sister of former Ferrari racer Eddie. Later on, I asked Prince Albert if he wanted to come to Amber Lounge. He suggested I ask Charlene, and she was keen, so the royals came along with us, Ross, Jean, Nick and Kate, and we all rocked up at Amber Lounge together, which seemed a fitting way to celebrate a Monaco GP victory!

The next day, I thought it would be great to go for a nice little romantic lunch with Jessica on the beach. So we did, and after a couple of glasses of wine we thought, hmm, shall we invite the boys down for a couple of drinks, and then all head off home and have a quiet night? We called the boys and they came down and ordered two Jeroboams of rosé, which went down a treat. One of our friends from Zenos, a restaurant-bar-club, called to say he had a bottle of Champagne waiting, so why not come up. We sat down on the outside terrace, looking out at the sea, just beautiful, and he walks up with a nine-litre bottle of Champagne (technically called a Salmanazar). So we finished that off, the twelve of us, then at 9.30pm he brings out a six-litre bottle of Champagne (a Methuselah), and plonks it on the table, and we have a go at that, but we just could not finish it. It was the biggest day of drinking I've ever had, but it felt richly deserved.

> 'As one Hollywood studio man said to me last week, "We'd never dare write a script like this."'
> Jonathan Legard, BBC TV

### MONACO GRAND PRIX FINAL POSITIONS

| Pos | Driver | Team | Laps | Time |
| --- | --- | --- | --- | --- |
| 1 | Jenson Button | Brawn-Mercedes | 78 | 1:40:44.282 |
| 2 | Rubens Barrichello | Brawn-Mercedes | 78 | +7.6 secs |
| 3 | Kimi Räikkönen | Ferrari | 78 | +13.4 secs |
| 4 | Felipe Massa | Ferrari | 78 | +15.1 secs |
| 5 | Mark Webber | RBR-Renault | 78 | +15.7 secs |
| 6 | Nico Rosberg | Williams-Toyota | 78 | +33.5 secs |
| 7 | Fernando Alonso | Renault | 78 | +37.8 secs |
| 8 | Sebastien Bourdais | STR-Ferrari | 78 | +63.1 secs |
| 9 | Giancarlo Fisichella | Force India-Mercedes | 78 | +65.0 secs |
| 10 | Timo Glock | Toyota | 77 | +1 Lap |
| 11 | Nick Heidfeld | BMW Sauber | 77 | +1 Lap |
| 12 | Lewis Hamilton | McLaren-Mercedes | 77 | +1 Lap |
| 13 | Jarno Trulli | Toyota | 77 | +1 Lap |
| 14 | Adrian Sutil | Force India-Mercedes | 77 | +1 Lap |
| 15 | Kazuki Nakajima | Williams-Toyota | 76 | +2 Laps |
| Ret | Heikki Kovalainen | McLaren-Mercedes | 51 | Accident |
| Ret | Robert Kubica | BMW Sauber | 28 | Brakes |
| Ret | Sebastian Vettel | RBR-Renault | 15 | Accident |
| Ret | Nelsinho Piquet | Renault | 10 | Accident damage |
| Ret | Adrian Sutil | Force India-Mercedes | 0 | Accident |

'If someone had said at the start of the season that Jenson Button would win five of the first six races, they'd have been certified. It just wasn't even thinkable. It's such a magical fairytale.'
Eddie Jordan, BBC TV

'It's only ten points like all the rest but this is the big one. He's delighted with that. He didn't put a foot wrong all afternoon. Took the lead from the start. Today the world championship becomes a reality for him. He'll be thinking about that now.'
David Coulthard

Wow. Winning the Monaco Grand Prix is something that you dream about as a child and as a racing driver. The reality of taking victory just feels awesome. To win here is a truly special feeling. With Rubens taking a superb second place, a one–two finish for the team, it's fantastic. This result is massive for us.

*'Sublime drive mon ami, beautiful job mate, wish I was there to tug your little beard with congratulations'*
Alex Woof, friend

*'Dear Jenson, my sincere congratulations to another pole and another fantastic win from you, 5 out of 6, 3 in a row, all of them with the same engine, you are writing history my friend'*
Norbert Haug, Vice President, Mercedes-Benz

*'As you said on the team radio, MONACO YEAH BABY... Fantastic drive'*
David Coulthard

*This was the third victory in a row using a single Mercedes-Benz engine – a record for modern-day F1.*

**OVERALL POINTS**

| | |
|---|---|
| Jenson Button | 51 |
| Rubens Barrichello | 35 |
| Sebastian Vettel | 23 |
| Mark Webber | 19.5 |
| Jarno Trulli | 14.5 |
| Timo Glock | 12 |
| Fernando Alonso | 11 |
| Kimi Räikkönen | 9 |
| Lewis Hamilton | 9 |
| Felipe Massa | 8 |
| Nico Rosberg | 7.5 |
| Nick Heidfeld | 6 |
| Heikki Kovalainen | 4 |
| Sebastien Buemi | 3 |
| Sebastien Bourdais | 2 |

'Monaco, it hit me. I was very emotional after he took
the chequered flag, the eyes were a bit watery. He'd
parked the car in the pit lane and had to run up the
hill to the podium ceremony. I was wondering where
he was, then I saw the big screens in the harbour
showing him as he ran up the track and all the guys
from the other teams at the back of their garages were
high-fiving him all the way up the straight. Amazing.'
John Button, father

# Turkish Grand Prix
# Istanbul Park
# Friday 5 June – Sunday 7 June

**Number of laps:** 58

**Circuit length:** 5.338 km

**Race distance:** 309.396 km

**Lap record:** 1:24.770
(Juan Pablo Montoya, 2005)

## MY HISTORY AT ISTANBUL PARK

**2008 (Honda)**
Grid 13; finished 11

**2007 (Honda)**
Grid 21; finished 13

**2006 (Honda)**
Grid 6; finished 4

**2005 (BAR-Honda)**
Grid 13; finished 5

The Istanbul Park circuit, surrounded by forest and fields, is located 90 kilometres from Istanbul on the Asian side of the Bosphorus channel. I enjoy driving here and I've been quite competitive in the past. Hermann Tilke – the German Formula One architect who has also designed the circuits in Malaysia, Shanghai, Bahrain, Valencia and Abu Dhabi, where we will race for the first time this season – did a great job with the layout. The changes in gradient are great fun and challenging.

The most notable characteristic is that it is an anti-clockwise track, one of only four on the F1 calendar (Singapore, Brazil and Abu Dhabi are the others). I've experienced excellent racing here with good overtaking opportunities at turns 1 and 3. You can also pass down the hill into Turn 9 and at turns 12 and 13, if you brake late enough and get it just right. Turn 8 is the corner that everyone talks about – probably the longest corner I've ever driven around. It's seven seconds of constant turning at 270kph, no braking, with 5Gs. Seven seconds of that level of gravitational force apparently adds up to more force on the body than is endured in a shuttle's blast-off. It puts a lot of stress on your neck, particularly on the side of your neck you normally don't use. You have to be as smooth as possible through the triple apex and if you get it right and take it flat, then it is one of those corners where you exit with a huge smile having made up a lot of time.

Stand-out features of the lap are the fast changes of direction at the start, the long triple-apex Turn 8 and a slower section through the last three turns, all of which combine to make car set-up an intriguing challenge.

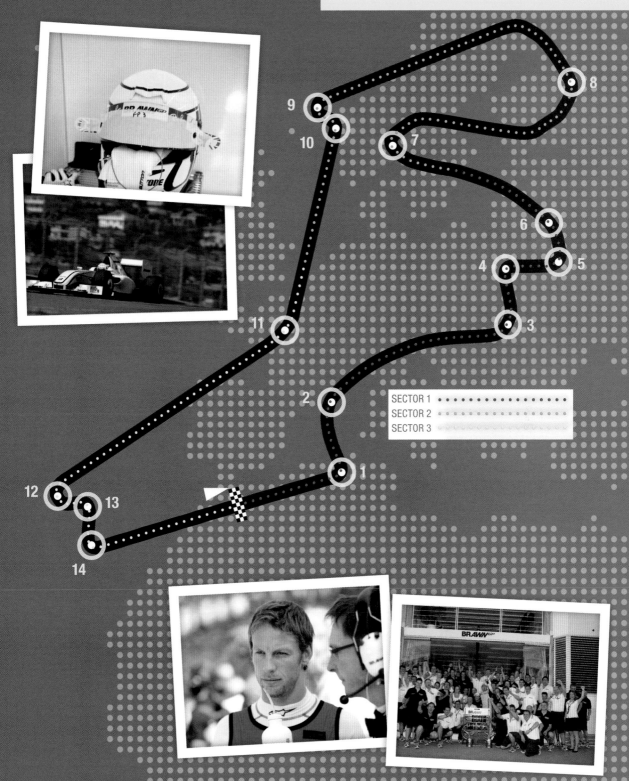

*This is the first race really where the car has just been absolutely perfect for me. We have had very good pace in other races but I have still found it difficult to drive. But here the car has been fantastic...*

9
10
8
7
6
4 5
3
11

SECTOR 1
SECTOR 2
SECTOR 3

2
1
12
13
14

# Turkey:
## Preparation, practice and qualifying

I flew to Turkey on Easyjet with the boys. We travelled out a few days early on Tuesday to fit in some training and catch a bit of sun. It's too far for the motorhome to travel (when it's not at races, it lives in Andover), so we stayed in a new hotel close to the circuit called The Titanic – a cool beach resort shaped like an ocean liner. I learnt from the first race here in 2005 not to stay in Istanbul itself. That was a big mistake because the traffic jams on the Bosphorus Bridge meant it took us two and a half hours to get back to the hotel each evening.

Neck-muscle training is standard for all racing drivers. That's why we all have such impressive bullnecks! But we didn't do any specific preparation for Turn 8. I know it is going to hurt, but I can take the pain. I don't put a sissy pad on the headrest on the side of the car, like a lot of the boys do. They do! Then they can lean their head against it when they go through Turn 8. I've never done that and never will, even though it does hurt.

After Monaco, I can't describe how much I'm looking forward to getting back in the car. I know it's going to be hot, which suits our car, but I'm also on red alert for the Red Bull challenge. Sebastian and Mark have been closing in on us in recent races. For different reasons, they haven't won races, but their car has been as quick as ours. They've done an impressive job as a team.

> 'Lewis Hamilton. Remember him? He's the guy who was winning everything when people had forgotten about the similarly gifted Jenson Button.'
> Autosport

### FRIDAY

It's been a tough first day of practice. Yet again I'm struggling on a Friday. I just couldn't find a balance and actually ran off the circuit for the first time this year. A well-balanced car is essential around here – with fourteen turns, undulating tarmac and a variety of corner speeds and grip levels. We tried many different set-up options over the course of the two sessions, but unfortunately we couldn't get the car to where I want it to be and I struggled with a lack of grip on both the Hard and Soft tyres. I ended up 12th after 53 laps and climbed out of the car wondering why we don't look competitive.

I was happier after our regular debrief. We reviewed a great deal of information in the engineering meeting and we've reached some understanding of what is causing the problem. Friday evenings are crucial. We sit around a table inside the team motorhome with a large circuit map and give our comments on every single corner. We run through all the evaluations and info garnered from the day's practice – what we think works, what doesn't, what we should try the next day. It's a process of sifting the positives and negatives from the day's on-track action. We have headphones connected to the factory at Brackley, so the specialists there can offer their view. It is always a busy night. I normally leave a circuit late, at about ten o'clock. I like to be part of the team effort, though most drivers leave earlier. The mechanics finish by midnight.

> 'We all know what we've been through. For the team to produce the car in the circumstances, it's incredible, but it's always this mix, this marriage of car and driver. The guys in the team told me Jenson was exceptional. I didn't see a lot of it last year. Now I believe them.' Ross Brawn

## SATURDAY

*Brawn GP's Jenson Button and Rubens Barrichello qualified their Brawn-Mercedes cars in second and third positions today ahead of tomorrow's 58-lap Turkish Grand Prix at the Istanbul Park Circuit.*

It was an amazing team effort to achieve a front-row grid position! Thanks to intense, hard work overnight from the team, both here and at the factory in Brackley, we resolved the issues we faced yesterday and found the pace that we needed to compete at the front in qualifying. We think my Friday problems, which were in danger of becoming a pattern, are something to do with the gearbox I use on the Fridays. So we won't be using it again. And there's a front wing issue, too, which the guys have sorted.

Qualifying demonstrated how close the fight at the front has become. Suddenly everyone seems to have made a big step forward. With the changes to the set-up that we made overnight, the car felt much better, but getting through to Q3 was nail-biting stuff. Rubens was three hundredths of a second away from being pushed out in Q2. It was tricky to choose between the tyres as their performance was quite similar. The Prime was a little twitchy for my liking so I continued to run the Option tyre for Q3, which had a more gradual and rolling feel.

I was very happy to be lining up on the front row, although of course I would prefer to be on pole. Vettel did a good job, but he was running less fuel. When we are 'fuel corrected', I am on pole. The only snag is I am on the dirty side of the circuit, which can make things difficult getting a clean start.

I went back to the hotel and had a relaxed dinner in the roof restaurant with the gang. I'm looking forward to a great race tomorrow as I relish racing on this circuit. You can overtake here so the spectators should witness some good battles out on the track. We will be trying very hard to change the statistic that everyone who has started from pole here has won the race! And the statistic that has so far seen Vettel win every race he's started from pole…

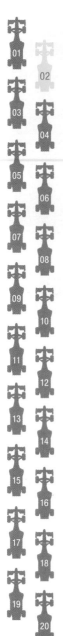

1. Sebastian Vettel
2. **Jenson Button**
3. Rubens Barrichello
4. Mark Webber
5. Jarno Trulli
6. Kimi Räikkönen
7. Felipe Massa
8. Fernando Alonso
9. Nico Rosberg
10. Robert Kubica
11. Nick Heidfeld
12. Kazuki Nakajima
13. Timo Glock
14. Heikki Kovalainen
15. Adrian Sutil
16. Lewis Hamilton
17. Nelsinho Piquet
18. Sebastien Buemi
19. Giancarlo Fisichella
20. Sebastien Bourdais

## STRATEGY

We were back to the Sepang and Barcelona compound options for Istanbul (Hard and Soft). The Friday running work showed the Soft tyre to be fastest initially, but dropping significant lap-time to the Hard tyre over a long run, so the Hard tyre was the primary race tyre, with again a short stint at the end of the race on the Soft tyre.

It was again close between a two-stop and three-stop strategy around Istanbul. However, with the Hard tyres' low laptime degradation over a run, a two-stop was favoured. Vettel chose to go with a three-stop strategy, qualifying just ahead of me on the grid as a result. On lap 1 of the race, however, Vettel made a mistake into Turn 9/Turn 10, allowing me to take the lead. The two-stop strategy went to plan, with Webber behind doing a similar race. Vettel chose to stay with his three-stop strategy, however, and after losing significant time behind me on the middle stint of the race, was unable to make the gap to his team-mate, finishing P3.

*Brawn GP's Jenson Button dominated the Turkish Grand Prix at the Istanbul Circuit today, taking the lead on the first lap and driving a superb race to bring his Brawn-Mercedes car home for his sixth victory of the 2009 F1 Season. Team-mate Rubens Barrichello had a more eventful race as he suffered the team's first retirement of the season.*

Today was sweltering, even hotter than yesterday. I travelled to the circuit thinking through my tactics. Rubens and I had a meeting with Ross in the morning. We both knew we were free to race each other, but after Rubens's comments in Spain, it was important the situation was clarified by Ross to restore a good atmosphere.

I had a good start from the dirty side of the grid, with my car pointed towards Sebastian's side of the track. Rubens was in third, on the grippier side and fuelled a few kilogrammes lighter, so I needed to protect myself. It was crucial I maintained second position off the line and into the first corner, which I did (Rubens triggered his anti-stall, ruining his start). I knew that if I got off the line second behind Vettel I had a good chance of beating him because our first stop was scheduled after his. Vettel was surprisingly aggressive on the first lap. He was putting wheels off the circuit everywhere and he made the inevitable mistake at Turn 9. He went wide. I got past him. Brilliant! From there, we could control the race.

I knew, because of the heat, that I had to look after the rear tyres, but I was still pulling away four tenths a lap on Vettel. Amazing, such a great position to be in. The car felt fantastic. Everything felt so easy. It was just how I like a car: it had rear stability and carried a lot of speed into corners. It reacted as I wanted it to. Once we knew Vettel was on a three-stop strategy, we filled the car up at my first stop to make ours a two-stop strategy and I just tried to be as consistent as possible to keep him behind me. It's not terribly relaxing to see a car catching you so quickly, even when you know he is on low fuel. I had a five-second lead on Vettel going into the pits. He came out and caught me up because he was on a lot less fuel, but he couldn't pass me. I just had to look after the tyres, keep him behind me until he pitted again and then give it the beans. So he pitted for his second stop, and I pushed hard. I had three

'I'm beginning to run out of superlatives to describe our season. Jenson drove an outstanding race today and demonstrated the level of talent and composure that we have come to expect.' Ross Brawn

laps to go before I had to pit. I was gaining a second on my previous lap times, which was enough. He never got that close to me again. I exited the pits in front of him and he still had one more pit-stop to go. I had a smile on my face for pretty much every lap to the chequered flag. The car felt that good, and after building up a twenty-second lead I was able to back off in the last stint to conserve the engine and take it easy for the final few laps and cross the line ahead of both Red Bulls. That brought my tally of wins to a superb six out of seven. Rubens didn't score any points, which gave me a ten-point advantage over him, and took my lead in the drivers' table to 26 points.

I vented my emotions out on the team radio: 'What can I say? What can I say, guys? You have built me an absolute monster of a car. You're all absolute legends.'

Vettel ended up being beaten by Webber, which he was fuming about during the weigh-in and podium ceremony. I had Peter 'Bono' Bonington, my assistant race engineer, alongside me on the podium and the celebration was a full-on team event. We've made such a step forward with the balance and the aero of the car. Even ten to fifteen laps in, I wanted to radio the team and say, 'This car is just outrageous'. It was tempting fate a bit, so I left the superlatives until the end of the race. It means so much to the team to see just how good this car, their creation, is.

In the evening, we headed into Istanbul for the first time this weekend. We went to a Japanese restaurant called Zuma, which overlooks the Bosphorus, and lingered outside, just chilling out and enjoying yet another euphoric occasion. To be heading next to Silverstone for our home race, leading the world championship, is a wonderful feeling.

| Pos | Driver | Team | Laps | Time |
| --- | --- | --- | --- | --- |
| 1 | Jenson Button | Brawn-Mercedes | 58 | 1:26:24.848 |
| 2 | Mark Webber | RBR-Renault | 58 | +6.7 secs |
| 3 | Sebastian Vettel | RBR-Renault | 58 | +7.4 secs |
| 4 | Jarno Trulli | Toyota | 58 | +27.8 secs |
| 5 | Nico Rosberg | Williams-Toyota | 58 | +31.5 secs |
| 6 | Felipe Massa | Ferrari | 58 | +39.9 secs |
| 7 | Robert Kubica | BMW Sauber | 58 | +46.2 secs |
| 8 | Timo Glock | Toyota | 58 | +46.9 secs |
| 9 | Kimi Räikkönen | Ferrari | 58 | +50.2 secs |
| 10 | Fernando Alonso | Renault | 58 | +62.4 secs |
| 11 | Nick Heidfeld | BMW Sauber | 58 | +64.3 secs |
| 12 | Kazuki Nakajima | Williams-Toyota | 58 | +66.3 secs |
| 13 | Lewis Hamilton | McLaren-Mercedes | 58 | +80.4 secs |
| 14 | Heikki Kovalainen | McLaren-Mercedes | 57 | +1 Lap |
| 15 | Sebastien Buemi | STR-Ferrari | 57 | +1 Lap |
| 16 | Nelsinho Piquet | Renault | 57 | +1 Lap |
| 17 | Adrian Sutil | Force India-Mercedes | 57 | +1 Lap |
| 18 | Sebastien Bourdais | STR-Ferrari | 57 | +1 Lap |
| Ret | Rubens Barrichello | Brawn-Mercedes | 47 | Gearbox |
| Ret | Giancarlo Fisichella | Force India-Mercedes | 4 | Brakes |

**TURKISH GRAND PRIX FINAL POSITIONS**

I wish I could have had the whole team up there on the podium with me today. This was definitely a victory for us all, everyone at the track, back at the factory in Brackley and at Mercedes-Benz High Performance engines in Brixworth. Today we really showed what this car and engine can do, and to beat our closest competitors fair and square is a great feeling. This is the first time the car has been absolutely perfect for me and it means so much to the team to see just how good this car is, but we know we have to keep pushing to maintain our advantage.

*'What an amazing job, true superstar drive with a superstar start! Well done, wish I was there'* Richard Goddard

*'Well done honey, great job! You did it again! Just like you said you would... I'm loving seeing you win! Xx'* Jessica

*'Congratulations Jenson, another great victory which makes it 6 out of 7! Unbelievable!! You are in a league of your own. Enjoy it'* Norbert Haug

*'JB... You are doing a fantastic job, Perfect, many congrats'* Gil de Ferran, racing driver

**OVERALL POINTS**

| | |
|---|---|
| Jenson Button | 61 |
| Rubens Barrichello | 35 |
| Sebastian Vettel | 29 |
| Mark Webber | 27.5 |
| Jarno Trulli | 19.5 |
| Timo Glock | 13 |
| Nico Rosberg | 11.5 |
| Felipe Massa | 11 |
| Fernando Alonso | 11 |
| Kimi Räikkönen | 9 |
| Lewis Hamilton | 9 |
| Nick Heidfeld | 6 |
| Heikki Kovalainen | 4 |
| Sebastien Buemi | 3 |
| Robert Kubica | 2 |
| Sebastien Bourdais | 2 |

# British Grand Prix
## Silverstone
### Friday 19 June – Sunday 21 June

**Number of laps:** 60

**Circuit length:** 5.141 km

**Race distance:** 308.355 km

**Lap record:** 1:18.739
(Michael Schumacher, 2004)

### MY HISTORY AT SILVERSTONE

**2008 (Honda)**
Grid 17; spun off

**2007 (Honda)**
Grid 17; finished 10

**2006 (Honda)**
Grid 19; retired (oil leak)

**2005 (BAR-Honda)**
Grid 2; finished 5

**2004 (BAR-Honda)**
Grid 3; finished 4

**2003 (BAR-Honda)**
Grid 20; finished 8

**2002 (Renault)**
Grid 12; finished 12

**2001 (Benetton-Renault)**
Grid 18; finished 15

**2000 (Williams-BMW)**
Grid 6; finished 5

I'm 29, and this is my tenth British Grand Prix. It is also exactly twenty years since I first raced here in go-karts. Silverstone has been a big part of my life. Along with Suzuka and Spa, it's one of the classic racing tracks. It has an amazing sixty-year history and it's a thrill to compete here knowing that all the greats have raced round this former World War II airfield.

The track requires high downforce and an emphasis on aerodynamic efficiency. Every driver loves it as it's so fast and you can push the car to its limits. It's also a great circuit for the fans as you can see just how amazing the cars are from the speed, the change of direction and the braking. I particularly love the section of track around Becketts, which is one of the best complexes in Formula One and a great place to watch the race. I have so many memories of Silverstone going right back to Nigel Mansell's win in 1987 and my first F1 race in 2000 when David Coulthard won and I finished fifth.

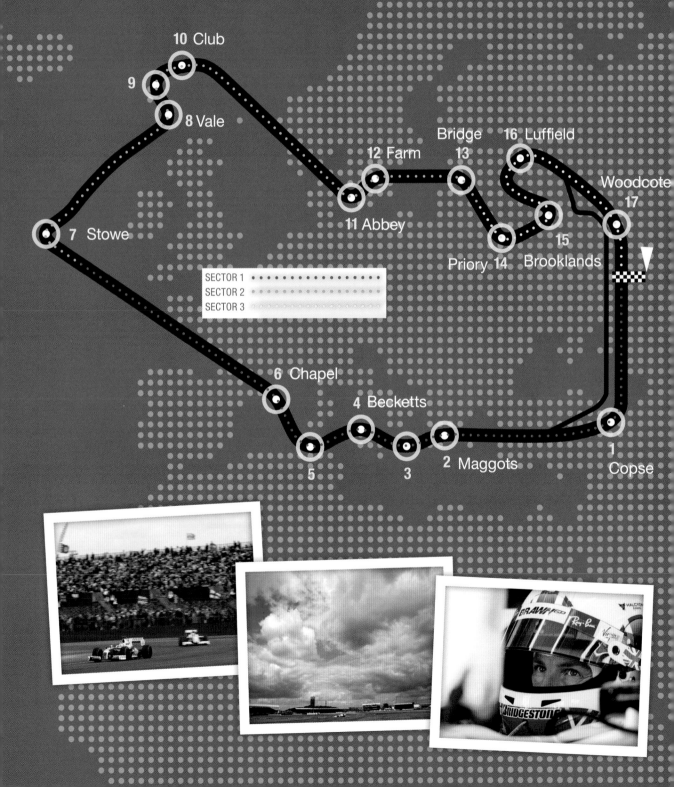

'Yes fella sew it up this weekend. Glad you are able to see how much support there is for you in the UK. It is not just because you are winning but the fact you seem to enjoy and appreciate it. I shall be shouting at the TV!!'

Nick Scott, close friend

10 Club

9

8 Vale

Bridge 16 Luffield

12 Farm 13

Woodcote 17

7 Stowe

11 Abbey

Priory 14

15 Brooklands

SECTOR 1
SECTOR 2
SECTOR 3

6 Chapel

4 Becketts

5

3

2 Maggots

1 Copse

# Great Britain:
## Preparation, practice and qualifying

To arrive here, at my home grand prix, leading the world championship is something that I've never experienced before and it puts a smile on my face every time I think about it. I've raced at Silverstone from some fairly tough positions in the past, and the fans have always been so encouraging. I'd love to give them a performance that they can enjoy this weekend, but the reality is we know it's going to be a tough few days for Brawn.

The Red Bulls will be quick, because Silverstone has a lot of fast changes of direction, plus they have a big aero update. It's forecast to remain cold, 15–16°C, and we just don't get tyre temperature in the cold. I suffer more than Rubens because his aggressive driving style puts more heat through the rubber. We can't even expect to be quick in the last sector, with its slow corners, because we'll have lost too much tyre temperature in the first two sectors.

Knowing that, I found the media build-up of my expectations at Silverstone way over the top. I never want to disappoint the fans by hyping unrealistic goals. I was being asked loaded questions to try to get dramatic headlines and I saw my words twisted to say things like: 'It would be a disaster if I didn't win my home grand prix.' I didn't say anything like that, because I wasn't thinking about the race in that context. My main aim is to win the world championship. Each race is a stepping stone on the way to achieving that goal – and this one was always going to be challenging.

The atmosphere carries you on a tide of optimism. It was the biggest crowd I've ever seen at Silverstone. The debate about the FOTA breakaway threat was bubbling away in paddock conversations amid much mud-slinging and reports of endless meetings. It managed to overshadow even the Bernie/British GP saga, but sell-out crowds every single day show how much the British public love and support Formula One. It makes a mockery of the talk of removing the British Grand Prix from the calendar. Somehow, I can't believe this will be our last race at Silverstone.

It's the first event of the year when the atmosphere feels 3-D: seas of fans and waving banners, the Red Arrows, the buzz from the campsites. Brawn GP managed to get some last-minute merchandise here – just! – and I had flags and caps as well. They sold a helluva lot of stuff. It was so touching. Everywhere you went you saw a Brawn hat. So many people came up to me said our team story had re-ignited their interest in Formula One. To see new names at the front – Brawn cars battling with Red Bulls, not grandees like McLaren, Ferrari or Renault – was a great boost to audiences.

My motorhome was parked in the drivers' enclave at the BRDC farm, which is such a great atmosphere – as if a host of British drivers past and present and their families have all gone on holiday together!

*Your home grand prix is always going to be very special. But also the British fans are fantastic. There are so many fans in Britain for Formula One. Last year was a sell-out crowd and I am guessing it will be the same this year and you don't get that in many circuits around the world. It's also great to have so many of my family here to support me. Hopefully we can put a good show on for everyone this weekend.*

## SATURDAY

*Brawn GP's Rubens Barrichello delivered an excellent performance in qualifying for the British Grand Prix at Silverstone today to put his Brawn-Mercedes car on the front of the grid for the race tomorrow. Jenson Button brought his car home in sixth position and will start his home race from the third row of the grid after struggling with the balance of his car.*

Ah... just as we expected, we struggled to get our tyres up to temperature. We tried everything but we could never get the tyres into their working range in the cool conditions. Our car is easy on the tyres and the Red Bulls are not, and that is the difference. I finished Q1 in fifth. In Q2 I was really under pressure. At one point I was down in 11th and hovering in the drop-out zone, but managed a quicker lap to get through to the pole position shoot-out. In Q3, despite some adjustments for the final run, the balance of my car was not right and I struggled massively with understeer in the high-speed corners and then had oversteer at low speed. When you're not happy with the balance, you can't take the car to the limit.

Qualifying sixth was pretty much as good as it would get. The annoying thing was that I had another lap to go, and I was a bit quicker, which would have put me P5 for the race. However, my engineer Shov made the first mistake he's ever made, and told me to come in a lap early to save fuel for the race. I would have been P5, which would have made the race so much simpler.

While qualifying in sixth is by no means a bad result, of course I'm hugely disappointed not to be starting my home grand prix from further up the grid. It was the first debrief session when I had genuine frustration to convey. On the one hand, I sort of accepted that our car/tyre combination wasn't going to work well here; on the other hand, you always think, come the race, it will be different.

The day ended with the annual BRDC black-tie dinner, in the clubhouse, and I was invited on stage to give a little speech. Obviously I was disappointed after qualifying, but I was on stage for fifteen minutes and received big cheers from every corner of the room. That was a tremendous boost.

## BRAWN TECHNICAL UPDATES

We'd dominated the race in Istanbul when the track temperature was over 50°C and some of this was down to our ability to stop the tyres from overheating. Bridgestone had brought the same two compounds to Silverstone where the track was only 20°C and we expected that we'd have some difficulties getting the tyres into their working range.

This is a circuit that we knew would suit the Red Bull car because of the high-speed corners and lack of braking. To make matters worse for us, they have a major aero upgrade to their car. We struggled to generate tyre temperature all weekend, which meant we couldn't get the car to balance. There were stages in the race where the tyres would suddenly come in and the lap times and balance would improve, but, basically, we just weren't quick enough.

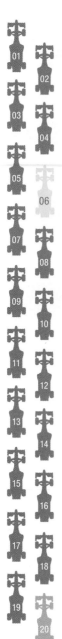

1. Sebastian Vettel
2. Rubens Barrichello
3. Mark Webber
4. Jarno Trulli
5. Kazuki Nakajima
6. **Jenson Button**
7. Nico Rosberg
8. Timo Glock
9. Kimi Räikkönen
10. Fernando Alonso
11. Felipe Massa
12. Robert Kubica
13. Heikki Kovalainen
14. Nelsinho Piquet
15. Nick Heidfeld
16. Giancarlo Fisichella
17. Sebastien Bourdais
18. Lewis Hamilton
19. Sebastien Buemi
20. Adrian Sutil (pit start)

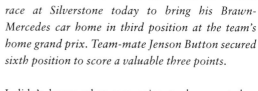

*Brawn GP's Rubens Barrichello drove an assured race at Silverstone today to bring his Brawn-Mercedes car home in third position at the team's home grand prix. Team-mate Jenson Button secured sixth position to score a valuable three points.*

I didn't know what was going to happen today. Starting from sixth, I began the race with the aim to get as many points as possible. As Ross says, 'Strike when you've got the tools and consolidate when you haven't. That's what a championship is built on.'

If anyone caught me straight after the race, they'd have got an adrenalin-fuelled torrent of phrases like: 'Couldn't get tyre temperature, plus you can't overtake here and I got a terrible start... frustrating because we had good pace on the Soft tyre... on the Hard tyre, the car just didn't work.'

I had a bad start because, in front of me, Jarno Trulli got a really slow getaway, as the Toyotas normally do, and I had nowhere to go. I tried the inside, but the space wasn't there, and the outside was full, so I was stuck, boxed in, and everyone just shot by on the outside. From ninth place it was never going to be an easy race. On the first stint I slowed up a little bit behind Trulli and then accelerated just to see what times I could do and I was between eight tenths and one second quicker than him. But I was

## STRATEGY

Bridgestone brought the Hard and Soft tyres to Silverstone, required due to the demanding layout of the track and loading through the high-speed corners. The Soft tyre worked well on shorter stints on Friday. However, the Hard tyre was slightly better over a very long run than the Soft tyre. In races previously there tended to be a 'weaker' tyre which was run at the end of the race. However, at Silverstone both the Hard and Soft tyres could be used, depending on the length of the stint.

The temperatures during the British GP were significantly colder than at any previous event in the 2009 season, and the tyres were struggling to get up to temperature correctly.

I struggled in qualifying, putting the car P6, relative to Rubens who was P2. Silverstone again has a reasonable pit-lane time, and a two-stop was the only option around here. I had a good start, but was blocked by Trulli, eventually resulting in me coming around P9 at the end of lap 1. I passed Massa on lap 2, but was held up behind Trulli until he stopped on lap 18. We chose to complete a very long middle stint of the race, on Prime tyres, since it would have been difficult to jump Trulli during the stop alone, and to beat Nakajima/Räikkönen, who were also fighting me. I was able to maintain my gap to Trulli and Räikkönen during the second stint, allowing me to put in some fast laps when Trulli, Räikkönen and Nakajima all stopped ahead. We then went for the Soft tyre again on the last stint of the race to finish P6.

trapped behind him, losing so much time, which was unbelievably frustrating as the car felt good on the softer tyre. The team heard my exasperation over the radio at this point... I eventually jumped him at a pit stop, and pulled out 22 seconds on him in nine laps.

We then had a long middle stint on the harder tyre and both Rubens and I struggled to get the tyres into their working range in the cool conditions with a heavy fuel load. With so little braking on this circuit and, therefore, little brake energy going into the tyres, we couldn't get their temperature up. On the softer rubber at the end of the race, I was able to close right up to Nico Rosberg in the Williams and Felipe Massa's Ferrari very easily, which proves the pace of the car was actually pretty good. At least it gave the spectators something to cheer! However, it is so difficult to overtake that I couldn't make any improvement on sixth position with only a few laps left.

Vettel, my main rival, gained seven points on me, which is obviously not very good, but I've collected three points on a weekend when we were underperforming. We need to understand why our car doesn't work so well at low temperatures – this was evident at Shanghai earlier this year, too. I am confident we can improve it a bit, but the problem is integral with the design of the car and the way it works. Different cars work the tyres in different ways according to their weight distribution, suspension geometries and aerodynamic loadings. Our car is supernaturally easy on them and it hurts us in places like England and Germany where the temperature is so low. I hope, at least, the Nürburgring is warmer than here because the Red Bulls are going to be very quick, though I don't think their advantage is as big as it looked today.

Ah, such a tough weekend. I lost points to Rubens, to Mark, and to Sebastian at my home grand prix. I went on the stage after the race, in front of more than 10,000 fans, and oh my God the cheer they gave me was amazing. I spoke about the race, explained how

*On the softer rubber at the end of the race, I was able to close right up to Nico Rosberg and Felipe Massa, which proves the pace of the car was actually pretty good.*

difficult it was for us to get tyre temperature and I still left the grand prix with a 23-point lead.

The problem I faced was three weeks off! I knew I'd just mull over Silverstone. When you have a bad race, you dwell on every detail of it, during the day and every night when you go to bed – what could have been, what could now happen, et cetera. I flew to Japan to see Jessica to take my mind off the disappointment and then Jessica came back to Europe with me for a few days. I took part in a triathlon at Dorney Lake, Eton College's rowing facility, a beautiful place. There were over 1,200 triathletes taking part and I finished third in my age group, and 26th overall, so at least that gave me some sporting satisfaction – and it's good practice for the London Triathlon that I've entered with Shov and Bono in August.

The next day I went to the Cotswolds for Nick Fry's wedding. Ross, who was sitting on the table behind me at the wedding breakfast, tapped me on the shoulder and said, 'Can I have a word? When are you leaving?'

I said: 'I have to leave soon, heading for Goodwood.'

'I just want to have a word and make sure you're feeling okay, that you're still positive and confident.'

I said: 'Yeah, of course I am.'

And he replied: 'Because a lot of drivers are very insecure, even people who nobody would guess were insecure...'

But I said: 'Don't worry about me. I'm leading the championship by 23 points. I'm not going to get down after one race.'

| **BRITISH GRAND PRIX FINAL POSITIONS** | | | | |
|------|--------|------|------|------|
| Pos | Driver | Team | Laps | Time |
| 1 | Sebastian Vettel | RBR-Renault | 60 | 1:22:49.328 |
| 2 | Mark Webber | RBR-Renault | 60 | +15.1 secs |
| 3 | Rubens Barrichello | Brawn-Mercedes | 60 | +41.1 secs |
| 4 | Felipe Massa | Ferrari | 60 | +45.0 secs |
| 5 | Nico Rosberg | Williams-Toyota | 60 | +45.9 secs |
| 6 | Jenson Button | Brawn-Mercedes | 60 | +46.2 secs |
| 7 | Jarno Trulli | Toyota | 60 | +68.3 secs |
| 8 | Kimi Räikkönen | Ferrari | 60 | +69.6 secs |
| 9 | Timo Glock | Toyota | 60 | +69.8 secs |
| 10 | Giancarlo Fisichella | Force India-Mercedes | 60 | +71.5 secs |
| 11 | Kazuki Nakajima | Williams-Toyota | 60 | +74.0 secs |
| 12 | Nelsinho Piquet | Renault | 59 | +1 Lap |
| 13 | Robert Kubica | BMW Sauber | 59 | +1 Lap |
| 14 | Fernando Alonso | Renault | 59 | +1 Lap |
| 15 | Nick Heidfeld | BMW Sauber | 59 | +1 Lap |
| 16 | Lewis Hamilton | McLaren-Mercedes | 59 | +1 Lap |
| 17 | Adrian Sutil | Force India-Mercedes | 59 | +1 Lap |
| 18 | Sebastien Buemi | STR-Ferrari | 59 | +1 Lap |
| Ret | Sebastien Bourdais | STR-Ferrari | 37 | Accident damage |
| Ret | Heikki Kovalainen | McLaren-Mercedes | 36 | Retired |

'Did the bubble burst for Button in Britain? No. He has won six races and I think this is just a glitch, providing Brawn have some performance updates in the pipeline.' Martin Brundle, BBC TV

All points are important at this stage of the season and to come away with three from this weekend is therefore okay, but it's been a very frustrating home grand prix for us. I had a bad start as Trulli was slow off the line in front of me which left me nowhere to go… From ninth place it was always going to be an uphill struggle. The balance of the car and the pace we showed in the last few laps of the race are encouraging and we will be taking a close look at the issues that we experienced with the tyres to see what countermeasures can be taken. Congratulations to Red Bull on their superb one–two finish today.'

**OVERALL POINTS**

| | |
|---|---|
| Jenson Button | 64 |
| Rubens Barrichello | 41 |
| Sebastian Vettel | 39 |
| Mark Webber | 35.5 |
| Jarno Trulli | 21.5 |
| Felipe Massa | 16 |
| Nico Rosberg | 15.5 |
| Timo Glock | 13 |
| Fernando Alonso | 11 |
| Kimi Räikkönen | 10 |
| Lewis Hamilton | 9 |
| Nick Heidfeld | 6 |
| Heikki Kovalainen | 4 |
| Sebastien Buemi | 3 |
| Robert Kubica | 2 |
| Sebastien Bourdais | 2 |

*'Well done bruv, another 3 points to add to your championship lead. big hugs'*
Natasha, sister

*'I suppose it wouldn't be fair to win them all would it. I'm sure the car will be back to its best for Germany.'*
Andy Mcpherson, family friend

'Inevitably the seemingly
invincible Brawn team had to
falter some time and it happened
on their home ground.'
Murray Walker, BBC online

# German Grand Prix
# Nürburgring
# Friday 10 July – Sunday 12 July

**Number of laps:** 60

**Circuit length:** 5.148 km

**Race distance:** 308.863 km

**Lap record:** 1:29.498
(Michael Schumacher, 2004)

## MY HISTORY AT THE NÜRBURGRING

**2007 (Honda)**
Grid 17; spun off

**2006 (Honda)**
Grid 6; retired (engine)

**2005 (BAR-Honda)**
Grid 13; finished 10

**2004 (BAR-Honda)**
Grid 5; finished 3

**2003 (BAR-Honda)**
Grid 12; finished 7

**2002 (Renault)**
Grid 8; finished 5

**2001 (Benetton-Renault)**
Grid 20; finished 13

**2000 (Williams-BMW)**
Grid 11; finished 10

The Nürburgring is a circuit that I really like. We haven't driven here since 2007, because the German Grand Prix is alternated between here and Hockenheim, but it's a really fun track with a good range of low- to high-speed corners. A lot of the corners are cambered – both positively and negatively – which is unusual. It's a great challenge because it's a tricky circuit and can be quite hot even though it is situated in the Eifel Mountains. This year, though, it looks like it will be a bit cooler. So not perfect for us, which is a pity as it's also the home race for Brawn GP's engine partner Mercedes-Benz. There are good overtaking chances into Turn 1 and the chicane, and you can even have a shot at getting up the inside through the Mercedes Arena.

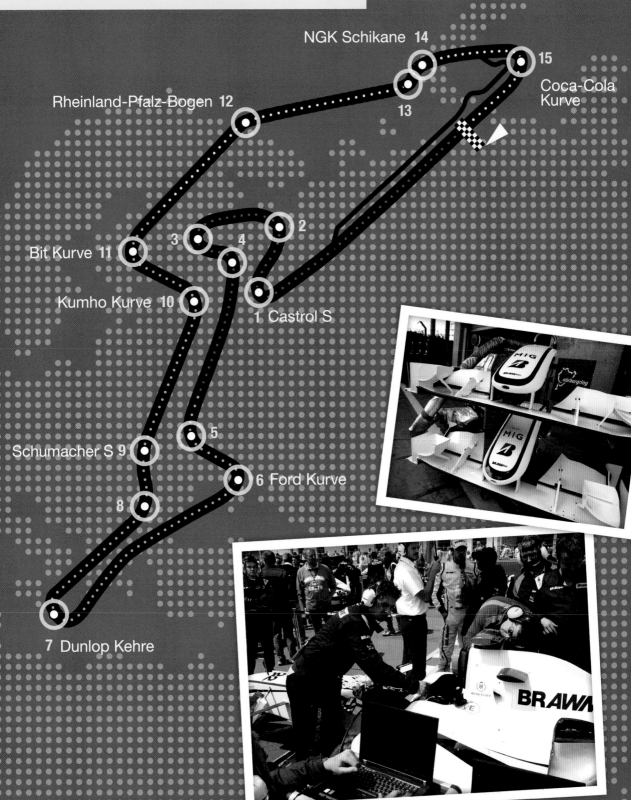

*It is going to be a tough race. So much can happen with the weather here. Twelve degrees in mid July, this is worse than England. Who says English weather is bad?*

SECTOR 1
SECTOR 2
SECTOR 3

NGK Schikane **14**

Rheinland-Pfalz-Bogen **12**

**15**

Coca-Cola Kurve

**13**

**2**

**3**

**4**

Bit Kurve **11**

Kumho Kurve **10**

**1** Castrol S

Schumacher S **9**

**5**

**6** Ford Kurve

**8**

**7** Dunlop Kehre

# Germany:
## Preparation, practice and qualifying

Before travelling to the Nürburgring, I was at Goodwood for a pretty hectic few days at the Festival of Speed. I had the incredible experience of driving the W25 Mercedes-Benz from 1934 – the first Silver Arrow to win a race. It's a beautiful four-litre-engine, 750-kilogramme, 350-horsepower work of art. The strangest thing about it, though, is that the throttle pedal is in the middle between the clutch and the brake. So I drove up the famous hill, aware that if I had to slam on my brakes, and instinct took over, I'd be in trouble. The Goodwood faithful give drivers a fantastic reception: you're mobbed wherever you walk. I loved driving a classic car in that amazing setting in the South Downs.

Then it was time to prepare for Germany. We knew it would be another tough race, but we expected it to be easier than Silverstone. The Nürburgring suits our car better, being a relatively slow circuit with a lot of medium-speed corners, and an overall heavy braking requirement. And we assumed it would be warmer.

When I first jumped into the car, it was 11°C, and it remained 11°C for all of Friday and Saturday. You are joking! We needed at least another 10°C – and it never came. I knew we had to start beating the Red Bulls, but you can't do that any other way than by taking it race by race, and trying to win every single race we compete in.

After Silverstone I started to look at the calendar and think about which circuits favour which cars. Nürburgring, no. But Hungary, yes. The Hungaroring is a circuit where our car should be competitive... And so on.

### FRIDAY

We had a reasonable day and were able to make good progress on the set-up of the car. We are still lacking in a few areas that we needed to look at overnight and make improvements. But overall today was a pretty good start. As ever – and there's nothing I'd like more than to stop looking at thermometers – the main problem is the cold conditions. The air temperature was almost what you'd expect in winter testing and the low track temperatures are causing problems with the harder Prime tyre. We will struggle with that tyre if it stays like this. The problem, when you're working with the car on tyre temperature, is that all you are doing is trying to get tyre temperature, you're not working on balance or trying to improve the car.

### SATURDAY

*Brawn GP's Rubens Barrichello and Jenson Button fought their way through a thrilling qualifying hour at the Nürburgring today to secure second and third positions on the grid for Sunday's 60-lap German Grand Prix.*

The weather ensured an intense and chaotic qualifying hour. Rain looked imminent so we were quick out on the softer Option tyres to complete two runs and progress safely into Q2. Then it was madness! Light rain suddenly became heavier and we had to dash back to the pits after a few laps to replace slicks with intermediates. Rubens made an inspired call to dive back in and switch to slicks and immediately became the quickest car on the circuit. I was called in to swap tyres and got out with just enough time for one timed lap which was quite stressful as it began to rain again. Q3, by comparison, was calm, though on my actual qualifying lap, I was weaving the car from side to side along the straights to get some heat into the tyres.

However, to qualify third was a respectable job. I felt reasonably happy. Rubens was second, but I was on the clean side so I thought I could squeeze past him in Turn 1. We were stopping earlier than the Red Bulls – at 13 and 14 laps while Vettel and Webber were stopping on laps 19 and 20 – that's a hell of a lot longer, so to beat them will be difficult.

## BRAWN TECHNICAL UPDATES

Having struggled with the cold at Silverstone, we were hoping for a heatwave in Germany. To our dismay, it was even colder! Only 10°C when we arrived. We had a reasonable aero upgrade with changes to the wheel covers and winglets around the front wheels. We also have new front and rear wings.

Nürburgring is a heavy braking circuit with a lot of low-speed corners. We were definitely in better shape than at Silverstone but we were struggling in every session for tyre temperature. Bridgestone's data showed that we had the coldest tyres of any team. Like at Silverstone, we were off the pace and struggling to balance the car.

*'Well done honey and good luck for tomorrow!!! Fingers crossed, GANBATTE!!! XXX'* Jessica (GANBATTE means 'good luck' in Japanese)

*'Good Luck for the race tomorrow Jenson!! Love and Big Hugs from a Very Proud Mum XXX'*

1. Mark Webber
2. Rubens Barrichello
3. **Jenson Button**
4. Sebastian Vettel
5. Lewis Hamilton
6. Heikki Kovalainen
7. Adrian Sutil
8. Felipe Massa
9. Kimi Räikkönen
10. Nelsinho Piquet
11. Nick Heidfeld
12. Fernando Alonso
13. Kazuki Nakajima
14. Jarno Trulli
15. Nico Rosberg
16. Robert Kubica
17. Sebastien Buemi
18. Giancarlo Fisichella
19. Sebastien Bourdais
20. Timo Glock (3-place penalty)

### STRATEGY

Bridgestone brought the Medium and Super Soft tyres to the Nürburgring (the same compounds as Bahrain), with the track layout and surface being a little kinder on tyres here than in the last two rounds. The Friday running tyre results showed a clear trend of the Prime tyre being just too hard in the cool conditions, with the Option tyres being quicker, but degrading significantly faster. On Friday we were struggling to generate sensible tyre temperatures in the cool conditions, similar to Silverstone.

A two-stop and three-stop strategy were again close on time, and for this event we calculated, from Friday running, that Red Bull had a race performance advantage over us in the cold ambient conditions. This pushed us towards the more aggressive strategy; getting either ahead, or in between the RBR drivers in qualifying, creating a buffer to the KERS cars behind for the start. Nürburgring has a very large start advantage for KERS cars, with a long run to T1, so grid positions are more powerful than the overall fuel load for this event.

*Brawn GP endured a disappointing race at the German Grand Prix today despite Jenson Button and Rubens Barrichello bringing their cars home in points-scoring fifth and sixth positions respectively.*

We thought it would rain on Sunday, but it didn't. It got a bit warmer, for about fifteen minutes, but only by another five or six degrees. Not enough. The worry off of the start were the KERS cars: there were two McLarens right behind me on the grid and two Ferraris right behind them. From the information we had, we thought the KERS cars would make up 15 to 16 metres from the start to Turn 1. We can't compete with that.

I got a reasonably good, immediate start, then had to hold back a bit as Rubens pulled alongside Mark Webber. And then the KERS cars came. I had a McLaren rocket past either side of me. And then the Ferraris came alongside as if in escort. Sebastian Vettel had started fourth, which was a good thing for me, but when I braked for Turn 1, with the Ferraris sandwiching me, they both seemed to be coming towards me, and there was not enough room. In that split second, I was afraid I would break my front wing and it wasn't worth the risk, so I lifted off the power and lost a place to Vettel.

Unbelievably, I was back to eighth going into Turn 2. Lewis Hamilton ran wide with a puncture, so I got

I dropped to P5 on lap 1 of the race, held up behind Kovalainen, who had a good start with KERS, but who was also significantly slower than Rubens and Webber ahead. We opted to stay on a three-stop strategy, to allow me to fight my way back up to the front. I dropped out behind Buemi and Kubica, but passed them both by lap 19 of the race, fighting back through the pack ahead, eventually closing up to the back of Webber, who had just stopped for fuel and tyres. I was on the Super Soft tyres, which started to grain, and as a result I was unable to keep up with Webber despite the lighter fuel load. We decided to switch to the Medium tyres, and I was up behind Rubens on track after our stops. I was able to save sufficient fuel behind Rubens to go one more lap beating him for P5.

past him. I went around the outside of Kimi Räikkönen on Turn 3, and then Vettel on Turn 4, and I was up to fifth. Then I sneaked through on Massa into Turn 1 so I was up to fourth.

By this stage, Rubens had got the lead, Webber was second and Heikki Kovalainen third. Heikki was fuelled quite long, and he was quite slow, and I was a second a lap down on the leaders. I pitted on lap 13, and we did a three-stop while all the other teams were on two-stops. I came out of the pits and caught up with Sebastien Buemi and got past him. I caught up with Nick Heidfeld and got past him at Turn 1. They still hadn't stopped. So I was flying along, and our pace was good. Webber came out just in front of me, because he'd had a drive-through penalty for something, and I had no chance of getting past him. That lost me a bit of time in the second stint. I was catching Rubens all the time because he was stuck behind Massa, who was also yet to stop. Then Massa stopped. Rubens stopped and I stopped, but when Rubens stopped the team had a fuel-rig problem, which forced the guys to switch rigs, and lost him

about four seconds. He came out only four seconds in front of me.

At this point the sun suddenly sank behind clouds and it started to get really cold. The only way I could achieve good lap times was by weaving to preserve some heat in the tyres, so I started weaving from side to side. I was catching Rubens by about a second a lap. I caught up with him, but couldn't get past. He couldn't get as much heat in his tyres. I was radioing the team to get Rubens to push because we were going to lose out to Massa and Rosberg. I was stuck behind him for eight or nine laps. He pitted and I had one lap to push to make the gap to get past him. On that lap I went 1.3 seconds quicker than my previous best, just because I had been stuck behind him, which was frustrating. I had got past him, but I was now behind Rosberg and Massa...

At the finish it was Webber, Vettel, Massa and Rosberg. It was annoying because I thought we could have had Massa and Rosberg – but Webber and Vettel? No way.

It should have been an easy P3 or P4, but it did not happen. When we're not as quick as the Red Bulls we should be getting third or fourth, but we didn't do a good enough job. You cannot be perfect every race. We have to make sure we don't make mistakes again.

I had a fun race because I'd overtaken a lot of cars, but I lost points to Webber and Vettel. Rubens was incensed and, in the heat of the post-race moment, made out that the team had lost him the race on purpose. It was all a bit aggressive and public. But he calmed down after we'd talked about it. The problem is, when he fires off like that, it makes us all look bad and it's not deserved. The team had a problem with the fuel rig, but it screwed my race, too, because I was stuck for ten laps behind him. It lost me so many points. But let's hope we've now got the two most difficult races out of the way. We have to start beating the Red Bulls, and it's going to take the whole team working together to do that. We can't have fighting within the ranks. Every single person must pull their weight otherwise we won't be competitive and we won't be fighting for the constructors' or the drivers' championships.

I understand it was difficult for Rubens – he was leading the race at one point. But, as Ross said in an interview, Rubens posted the 11th quickest race lap. You're never going to win a race with the 11th quickest race lap. Rubens has been quick all year and very competitive. He just hasn't found himself in a position when he can win a race yet, and I've won six. But he's a very quick driver and he's really good at working with the team when he's in the right mood. He does get emotional after the races and he does say things he doesn't really mean. The blood pressure's high. I respect him very much, but it would make life a lot easier for me if I didn't have to answer back about how the team are looking after both drivers equally. Of course they are. If they weren't, they'd have asked him to let me through so I could have got some good laps in, you know what I mean?

When we're all calm, we work together really well. He helps me, I help him, we look at each other's set-up, we pass on every single piece of information. At this point in the season, it's imperative we do that because the Red Bulls are quick and they're chasing us down.

After not winning my own home grand prix, I can't help but be pleased that Vettel didn't win his at the Nürburgring either!

*'It just goes to show how daft the current scoring is in F1 that Webber even has a sniff having won 1 race to Button's 6.'* Comment posted by Richard S on Times F1 Blog

## GERMAN GRAND PRIX FINAL POSITIONS

| Pos | Driver | Team | Laps | Time |
|-----|--------|------|------|------|
| 1 | Mark Webber | RBR-Renault | 60 | 1:36:43.310 |
| 2 | Sebastian Vettel | RBR-Renault | 60 | +9.2 secs |
| 3 | Felipe Massa | Ferrari | 60 | +15.9 secs |
| 4 | Nico Rosberg | Williams-Toyota | 60 | +21.0 secs |
| 5 | Jenson Button | Brawn-Mercedes | 60 | +23.6 secs |
| 6 | Rubens Barrichello | Brawn-Mercedes | 60 | +24.4 secs |
| 7 | Fernando Alonso | Renault | 60 | +24.8 secs |
| 8 | Heikki Kovalainen | McLaren-Mercedes | 60 | +58.6 secs |
| 9 | Timo Glock | Toyota | 60 | +61.4 secs |
| 10 | Nick Heidfeld | BMW Sauber | 60 | +61.9 secs |
| 11 | Giancarlo Fisichella | Force India-Mercedes | 60 | +62.3 secs |
| 12 | Kazuki Nakajima | Williams-Toyota | 60 | +62.8 secs |
| 13 | Nelsinho Piquet | Renault | 60 | +68.3 secs |
| 14 | Robert Kubica | BMW Sauber | 60 | +69.5 secs |
| 15 | Adrian Sutil | Force India-Mercedes | 60 | +71.9 secs |
| 16 | Sebastien Buemi | STR-Ferrari | 60 | +90.2 secs |
| 17 | Jarno Trulli | Toyota | 60 | +90.9 secs |
| 18 | Lewis Hamilton | McLaren-Mercedes | 59 | +1 Lap |
| Ret | Kimi Räikkönen | Ferrari | 34 | Radiator damage |
| Ret | Sebastien Bourdais | STR-Ferrari | 18 | Hydraulics |

All points are valuable, but my race started badly and didn't get much better today. I had a poor start to drop back to fifth after the first turn and was able to get ahead of Massa at the start of the second lap but just couldn't get past Kovalainen. His pace was way off what we could have achieved at that point of the race but there was just no way through. We struggled with graining and tyre degradation throughout with both tyres not working well for us. The problem with the fuel rig at Rubens's second stop also affected my race as we were so close on the track and he was struggling with the Prime tyre. So overall it has been a tough and disappointing day for the team.

Congratulations to Mark on his first win and I'm really pleased for him because I know how good that feels. I just can't wait to get to Hungary in two weeks where we will have new parts and hopefully warmer weather to take the fight to the Red Bulls.

### OVERALL POINTS

| | |
|---|---|
| Jenson Button | 68 |
| Sebastian Vettel | 47 |
| Mark Webber | 45.5 |
| Rubens Barrichello | 44 |
| Felipe Massa | 22 |
| Jarno Trulli | 21.5 |
| Nico Rosberg | 20.5 |
| Timo Glock | 13 |
| Fernando Alonso | 13 |
| Kimi Räikkönen | 10 |
| Lewis Hamilton | 9 |
| Nick Heidfeld | 6 |
| Heikki Kovalainen | 5 |
| Sebastien Buemi | 3 |
| Robert Kubica | 2 |
| Sebastien Bourdais | 2 |

*'Well done on a great drive in difficult circumstances. I think you drove twice the distance of everyone else because you had to weave to keep tyre temp!'* Sam, sister

*'Well done fella. Drove the hell out of it once again. Bring on Hungary!'* James Williamson

'Should Jenson be worried? Not overly just yet. He has a significant lead and lots of drivers to take points away from Vettel and Webber, not least of all each other. Brawn however should be very worried. I can see Jenson taking the driver's championship still, but the constructor's? I suspect Red Bull, if they keep their heads, know that that is the real prize they're chasing.' Comment posted by Martin P

# Hungarian Grand Prix
## Hungaroring, Budapest
### Friday 24 July – Sunday 26 July

**Number of laps:** 70

**Circuit length:** 4.381 km

**Race distance:** 306.630 km

**Lap record:** 1:19.071
(Michael Schumacher, 2004)

### MY HISTORY AT THE HUNGARORING

**2008 (Honda)**
Grid 12; finished 12

**2007 (Honda)**
Grid 17; retired (throttle)

**2006 (Honda)**
Grid 14; finished 1

**2005 (BAR-Honda)**
Grid 8; finished 5

**2004 (BAR-Honda)**
Grid 4; finished 5

**2003 (BAR-Honda)**
Grid 14; finished 10

**2002 (Renault)**
Grid 9; retired (throttle)

**2001 (Benetton-Renault)**
Grid 17; spun off

**2000 (Williams-BMW)**
Grid 8; finished 9

Hungary is always one of my favourite races. In 2006 I had my first Formula One win here – a thrilling maiden victory in the wet – so the Hungaroring holds special memories. Winning in Hungary again would be an amazing feeling, probably more so than any other race because winning twice at the same track would be spectacular. It's the first time that I've been back with a car that has a chance to win.

With its twisty layout of interlinked corners, it's a low-speed and high-downforce circuit, one of the toughest on the calendar in terms of technical and physical demands. There's no real respite round the lap, but it is a lot of fun to drive. The lap has a good rhythm and mix of low- and high-speed turns. The circuit generates an incredible amount of grip as the weekend gets underway, which can provide a real challenge in finding the right set-up. It will be especially tough with the way that the cars are this year, as they seem to be very twitchy compared with previous years. Overtaking is very difficult. It's always hot for the race here, which is good news for us. Mind you, the year I won it rained!

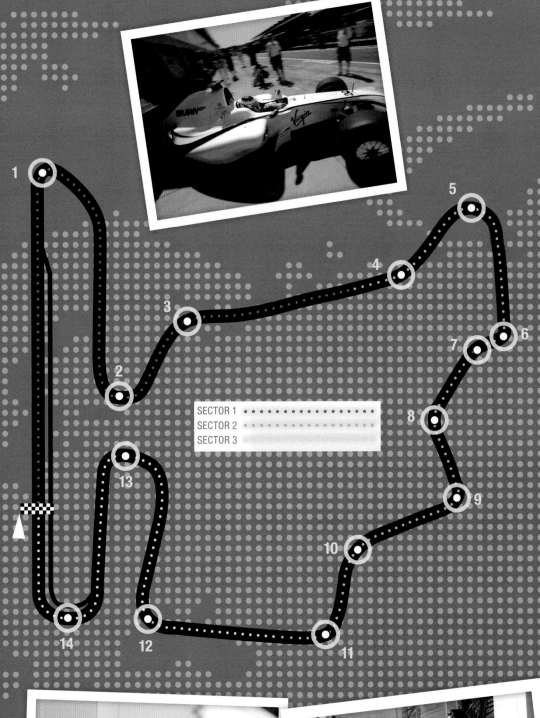

1
5
4
3
6
7
2
8
13
9
10
14 12 11

SECTOR 1
SECTOR 2
SECTOR 3

# Hungary:
## Preparation, practice and qualifying

After the frustrations of the last two races we are looking forward to some true summer temperatures and achieving the full potential of our car. We're pretty confident that the inherent performance of the BGP 001 has not disappeared, and the problems we experienced with the tyres were unique to the cool temperatures in Silverstone and at the Nürburgring. I've been at home in Monaco for the past week concentrating on my training, but I know that the guys in the factory and at Mercedes-Benz have been working incredibly hard on our latest upgrade package. I just can't wait to get back in the car.

I stayed in Le Meridien Hotel in the centre of Budapest. It's a driveable distance to Budapest and I would take my motorhome, but I love the city so much I enjoy staying in town. Of all the host cities on the Formula One calendar, there are a few I've made a mental note to visit again when I'm not racing, and Budapest is top of that list. The buildings are beautiful, the restaurants good and the river traffic adds to the bustle. The whole city looks amazing when illuminated at night. The hotel is on a square, by the river, and in the evening it buzzes with youngsters hanging out and playing guitars. It's very difficult for drivers to walk around the city. Fans seem to know exactly where we all stay. They're friendly, but they do mob you. I settled in at the hotel, and then all the Button gang – with Jessica, too – went out to an Argentinian steakhouse and had a relaxing evening.

### FRIDAY
A hot and sunny day! And it's been a much better Friday for us than at the last couple of races. With the track temperature rising to 47°C, the heat is working in our favour, so it's back to business as usual. Our pace has been very strong on both the harder and softer tyres. Our consistency has been good and Bridgestone tell us we are the only team who haven't damaged our rear tyres. This circuit is notoriously tough on tyres – you normally get graining and oversteer, which makes the car undriveable.

However, we had a productive day completing our test programme. Rubens and I are both feeding back positive reactions to the new aerodynamic updates. We've achieved a lot of important work today

evaluating the tyres and whilst we still have some way to go to get them working at their optimum, we're confident we're looking good and we'll be back to winning ways.

As usual, Friday is a long working day spent setting ourselves up for the weekend. Late afternoon and evening engineering debriefs tend to go on so long that they always culminate in us eating dinner with the team at the circuit in the Brawn motorhome.

### SATURDAY
*Qualifying was overshadowed today by an accident suffered by Ferrari's Felipe Massa towards the end of Q2. Rubens had a problem with the rear of his car, and his best time earned him 13th position. Jenson sat out the first half of Q3 as the team changed a component as a precautionary measure and took to the track with just under three and a half minutes remaining and a heavier fuel load than planned. His one run put him in 8th position on the grid.*

I woke up on a beautiful sunny day excited about the prospect of qualifying. The hotel staff are amazingly attentive. At breakfast, my coffee is ready before I ask for it and the waitress remembers Jessica drinks Darjeeling tea. She also makes a big thing of bringing me 'special' orange juice, which is basically a mixture of orange and grapefruit.

It's a bit of a drive to the circuit, 19km or so, and it's traditional for the drivers to indulge in a spot of crazy racing. Last year, Lewis and I pulled up alongside each other at lights en route to the Hungaroring and then raced each other there (all within the speed limit, of course). He was faster in a Mercedes than I was behind the wheel of a Honda, but there's a slip road off the motorway called Bernie Avenue – built because Bernie Ecclestone was not happy with the original circuit entry road – where you can cunningly drop a wheel off into gravel, kick up some dust, and gain an advantage. Last year when I did that, the little stones flicked up and one cracked Lewis's windscreen.

This year an excitable group of 40 or 50 Hungarian fans escorted me through the last part of the journey from Budapest to the circuit, which also gets

the adrenalin going. There's always such a great atmosphere here. It wasn't until I stepped out of the car that I realised how cold it was. There was a real, and unexpected, chill in the air. I walked into the paddock assuming it would warm up later. Surely we weren't going to have another weekend struggling to get temperature into the tyres?

As it sadly turned out, concern for Felipe Massa dominated the qualifying session. Qualifying is the most stressful hour of a race weekend, but when a driver suffers a bad accident, it's pretty horrible. The car felt reasonably good through the first two sessions, although none of my laps were perfect due to traffic and yellow flags. Even though the Red Bulls were surprisingly good on the tight layout, and Alonso and Hamilton looked strong, I still thought we would be competitive in Q3. However, it was a spring from the rear suspension of Rubens's car that had come off and unfortunately hit Felipe, so the team decided to make a precautionary change to the damper unit on my identical car. The process was pretty time-consuming and meant I sat out a good chunk of Q3.

I saw Felipe's accident because I was on the circuit when it happened. I saw his Ferrari had gone straight on into the tyres, and guessed he'd suffered a brake failure or his throttle had stuck because it was a high-speed corner and a strange place to go off like that. I came back into the garage and saw the footage on the little television screen that gets put on my car so I can see the timing screens and so on. We couldn't see the spring, but the team told me something had hit his helmet and he'd gone on straight into the tyres like that because he was unconscious. As the team worked on my car, the incident kept being replayed on TV. It was horrible to watch under any circumstances, but to see another incident where an object that has fallen off a car becomes a projectile flying into the path of a driver was particularly chilling after the death the week before at Brands Hatch of young Henry Surtees, who was killed outright by a bouncing tyre.

It's not unusual for debris to come off cars, but you rarely get flying or bouncing objects. When I saw the moment of impact on TV, it made me shudder. How unlucky can you be? The spring, which weighs 800g, bounced down the circuit and hit Felipe smack at eye level with twice the force that a bullet-proof vest can take. The incident would probably have been fatal if it had occurred before 2004 when the FIA introduced more stringent helmet safety standards. The helmets are now predominantly carbon-fibre, which allows an impact to be distributed rather than absorbed completely at the point of contact. Felipe's survival shows the strength of our helmets.

It was a rush to get me back out at all for Q3. I was only able to get one run and that was on a heavy fuel load – with four more laps of fuel than we had planned. We were on the edge of the working range for the tyres with the cooler temperatures, so the car wasn't handling as well as in practice. The timing screen system went down so at the end of qualifying, none of us knew our position. We all knew our individual lap time, because that comes up on a screen inside the cockpit, but we had no idea how it compared and where that left us on the grid, so we were all wandering around like boys in a playground swapping times to work out where we had qualified. I knew my one flying lap wasn't quick, but I was really surprised when Fernando Alonso reeled off his time and it was a whole second quicker than mine. Not realising the television cameras and microphones were on us, my reaction went out live to global audiences. Martin Brundle had to explain to BBC viewers that I would have been unaware I was being filmed. I can't tell you how many people posted comments on my Twitter page thinking it very funny!

Starting from 8th on the grid isn't ideal when Webber is on the front row next to Alonso with Vettel in third. And I'm on the dirty side of the track... But we're remaining positive. We have a good strategy and we'll take advantage of any opportunities that arise to score as many points as possible.

We are thinking of Felipe and hopefully we will hear that he is okay. He is a great friend of many in the Brawn team. As a fellow Brazilian, Rubens is very close to him and their families are close too. He's devastated – worried about Felipe and conscious it was a part from his car that did the damage. Ross, too, of course worked with him at Ferrari so the atmosphere in the team is subdued. I don't know him as well. He comes across as quite a funny little chap. In the drivers' briefings he can be quite outspoken and, unintentionally, very funny. I respect him as a fierce competitor and skilled driver.

'Good luck little bruv for tomorrow, team Jones and Marlow are watching the race together on Sunday. big kiss. xxx' Tanya, sister

## BRAWN TECHNICAL UPDATES

Having struggled for pace at the last few races, we brought forward our Valencia upgrade package to make the Budapest Grand Prix. Most of the changes were around the floor and diffuser area, although we did have a new specification of front wing designed to suit the high-downforce requirements of this circuit. The straights are very short and a lot of the corners flow into one another so a good balance is vital to setting a fast lap-time.

On Friday we had track temperatures in excess of 40°C and the car had been working well in those conditions, particularly on a long run. Over Saturday and Sunday it cooled considerably and we struggled to generate grip and had very bad graining during the race. This was our least competitive race of the season so far and 7th place was a reasonable reflection of our pace. It is clear that we have to make progress towards understanding the tyres very quickly.

# Hungary:
## The race

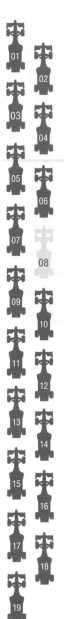

1. **Fernando Alonso**
2. **Sebastian Vettel**
3. **Mark Webber**
4. **Lewis Hamilton**
5. **Nico Rosberg**
6. **Heikki Kovalainen**
7. **Kimi Räikkönen**
8. **Jenson Button**
9. **Kazuki Nakajima**
10. **Sebastien Buemi**
11. **Jarno Trulli**
12. **Rubens Barrichello**
13. **Timo Glock**
14. **Nelsinho Piquet**
15. **Nick Heidfeld**
16. **Giancarlo Fisichella**
17. **Adrian Sutil**
18. **Robert Kubica**
19. **Jaime Alguersuari**

## STRATEGY

The tyres were the same as at Monaco, with Bridgestone bringing the softest compounds (Soft and Super Soft). These tyres aren't the normal two steps apart, and are both low-temperature compounds.

Friday was very warm, and I was back on form with the car in the conditions, running a solid race program on Friday. The tyre comparisons showed that the Super Soft tyre worked very well, even with high fuel, and, with Budapest normally progressing towards the softest tyre over a race weekend, the Super Soft was our primary race tyre.

Unfortunately during qualifying, following Rubens' issues, the team decided to hold me in the pits whilst the mechanics ensured my car was safe. This meant I was only able to complete one of the two planned runs, resulting in a heavier than desirable fuel load for Sunday, combined with a poor position (P8).

The simulations showed a two-stop strategy was best, but with a heavier fuel load than normal due to KERS cars having very good start performance.

*Brawn GP's Jenson Button finished in seventh position at the Hungarian Grand Prix today with team-mate Rubens Barrichello bringing his Brawn-Mercedes car home just outside the points in 10th place.*

We'd heard Felipe was in a stable condition overnight. Once reassured on that, we had to try and put it out of our minds to go racing. It's a strange situation but, concentrating on the day's work ahead, I felt positive that we could get a good result and collect some very valuable points. I was heavily fuelled after qualifying and our plan was to get a good start, stay with the cars in front and then I was going longer at the first stop so I could reel out some superfast laps and jump up the order.

I lost a position to Kazuki Nakajima at the start, but passed him going into Turn 1 on the second lap. I regained 8th position behind Heikki Kovalainen. Our strategy dictated that I'd have a long first stint on the Super Softs, so I thought I'd sit behind the McLaren and take it easy until Heikki peeled off for his first stop and I could put in a few flying laps. But – argh! – my rear tyres grained massively in the first few laps and I was sliding around with no grip. I had no chance of keeping pace with the front-runners. Instead of fighting Kovalainen, I was trying to keep Nakajima at bay. What was going on? It was so

The team put me on the Super Soft tyres for the first stint, the same as most of the other drivers, but we started to get graining very early on. This was the first time over the weekend we had seen this issue, and I was unable to chase the leaders ahead as a result. On the second stint of the race the car was refitted with the Option tyre, with the expectation that with track improvement, they would now be in their working window. Again unfortunately there was a lack of car performance, with the leaders ahead able to pull a gap on me and Trulli. The team called me in a few laps later than Piquet, and gained a place, and earlier than both Nakajima and Trulli. With the fresher Soft tyres, and reasonably low fuel load, I was able to build a gap to all three cars, fending them off for P7.

exasperating, exactly the opposite of Friday when we were the only team not to suffer graining.

From then on, my race turned into damage limitation for our championship challenge. The Toyotas of Jarno Trulli and Timo Glock had the perfect strategy to leapfrog themselves up the order, so, after my first stop, I was stuck behind Trulli. I thought he and Nakajima were stopping three laps ahead of me at the second stops, but it was getting close to my pit-stop and no one pitted! In the end I had two laps to really push. I hammered in two laps and came out ahead of Trulli and Nakajima. That achievement felt like winning the race. The car was just not working. Out of pure frustration I went on the radio to the team and let off steam: 'How, how can this car be so bad?' They said nothing in response. I guess no one knew the answer.

It was disappointing to finish seventh as we had high hopes for this race, but we were fortunate to come away with two points. It was tough accepting the lack of performance, but I knew that I had got the

**How, how can this car be so bad?**

best out of the car. We didn't know what the problem was immediately, but it had to be temperature-related again. Our pace on the Option tyre on Friday was pretty good and we were able to manage the rear end much better than some of the others. By Sunday the car just didn't feel like it did a few weeks ago. Nothing changed between Friday and Sunday except the temperature. We'll have to work hard to identify the problems before Valencia. This was a circuit where, on paper, we were supposed to dominate the Red Bulls but they were fighting for podium positions and we finished 7th and 10th. I started to worry that the performance wouldn't come back and that the Red Bulls were going to overtake us. But, despite their dominance at Silverstone, the Nürburgring and in qualifying, they put in a surprisingly uncompetitive race performance here. Webber's third-place finish, down to consistency more than pace, means he replaces Vettel in second place in the drivers' points table. Sebastian had a poor start from second and retired on lap 27 with a front suspension failure. My championship lead is reduced but I still have a healthy lead of 18.5 points.

McLaren have transformed their car. We knew it would be a good circuit for them. Like us, their car suits low- and mid-speed corners, and they have the advantage of the KERS boost button, but I can't believe I finished 55 seconds behind Lewis's winning McLaren. Lewis is an ally in that he can take points from the Red Bulls, but it's not that simple. With his KERS advantage, he can also take points from us.

We have four weeks now until Valencia. There is a two-week compulsory factory shutdown – part of the new cost-cutting measures – but two weeks where our engineers will be trying to identify the causes of our recent performance issues. I'm sure they'll be queuing to get back into the factory after a fortnight of dwelling on the potential answers in their minds. There is no FIA ban on thinking!

In terms of anxiety, though, there couldn't have been a worse time for Formula One to come to a standstill for four weeks. Having a disappointing race is a bit like falling off your bike. Your instinct is to get straight back into the cockpit and put things right again. I knew I'd dwell on our uncompetitiveness every day unless I spent time with the right friends and with Jessica. I had the London Triathlon to keep my mind focused in the first week, then a period when I was intent on fitness and relaxation.

Holiday fun started with the craziest journey back from the circuit to the hotel with the maddest police escort guy. He loved his job, blowing his whistle, beeping his horn, practically pushing cars and trucks out of the way and slaloming ahead to clear the road for us. At one stage, he led us onto the wrong side of the road and through a red light, beeping manically all the way. The Hungarians are flamboyant about treating F1 personnel as VIPs. One year the police gave us a blue light, attached by magnet, to put on the top of the car so we could just cut a swathe through the traffic ourselves. And you always get a police escort out to the airport. Incredible!

*'Well Done Jenson for getting points yesterday with a difficult car!! STILL the World Championship Leader!!! Lots of Love.'* Mum

*'Good job buddy in Buda. Keep it up for the points!! Have some good rest on holiday break.'* Jean-Michel Tibi (works In F1)

*'Shame about the race weekend mate but your still leading the world champs and I'm sure Ross will sort the car out before the next race!'* Jules

## HUNGARIAN GRAND PRIX FINAL POSITIONS

| Pos | Driver | Team | Laps | Time |
|-----|--------|------|------|------|
| 1 | Lewis Hamilton | McLaren-Mercedes | 70 | 1:38:23.876 |
| 2 | Kimi Räikkönen | Ferrari | 70 | +11.5 secs |
| 3 | Mark Webber | RBR-Renault | 70 | +16.8 secs |
| 4 | Nico Rosberg | Williams-Toyota | 70 | +26.9 secs |
| 5 | Heikki Kovalainen | McLaren-Mercedes | 70 | +34.3 secs |
| 6 | Timo Glock | Toyota | 70 | +35.2 secs |
| 7 | Jenson Button | Brawn-Mercedes | 70 | +55.0 secs |
| 8 | Jarno Trulli | Toyota | 70 | +68.1 secs |
| 9 | Kazuki Nakajima | Williams-Toyota | 70 | +68.7 secs |
| 10 | Rubens Barrichello | Brawn-Mercedes | 70 | +69.2 secs |
| 11 | Nick Heidfeld | BMW Sauber | 70 | +70.6 secs |
| 12 | Nelsinho Piquet | Renault | 70 | +71.5 secs |
| 13 | Robert Kubica | BMW Sauber | 70 | +74.0 secs |
| 14 | Giancarlo Fisichella | Force India-Mercedes | 69 | +1 Lap |
| 15 | Jaime Alguersuari | STR-Ferrari | 69 | +1 Lap |
| 16 | Sebastien Buemi | STR-Ferrari | 69 | +1 Lap |
| Ret | Sebastian Vettel | RBR-Renault | 29 | Suspension |
| Ret | Fernando Alonso | Renault | 15 | Fuel pump |
| Ret | Adrian Sutil | Force India-Mercedes | 1 | Engine |

'The weekend's events must have affected Ross Brawn very deeply. Sure, the cars had a bad race, and the tyres hadn't got up to temperature again, despite the track being hotter. And OK, Mark Webber had taken four points out of Jenson Button's championship lead. But all that paled into insignificance compared to the part Brawn's car had played in the injury to Felipe Massa, a friend and a driver he had nurtured in 2006, Brawn's last year at Ferrari.' Ted Kravitz, BBC blog

### OVERALL POINTS

| | |
|---|---|
| Jenson Button | 70 |
| Mark Webber | 51.5 |
| Sebastian Vettel | 47 |
| Rubens Barrichello | 44 |
| Nico Rosberg | 25.5 |
| Jarno Trulli | 22.5 |
| Felipe Massa | 22 |
| Lewis Hamilton | 19 |
| Kimi Räikkönen | 18 |
| Timo Glock | 16 |
| Fernando Alonso | 13 |
| Heikki Kovalainen | 9 |
| Nick Heidfeld | 6 |
| Sebastien Buemi | 3 |
| Robert Kubica | 2 |
| Sebastien Bourdais | 2 |

# European Grand Prix
## Street Circuit, Valencia
## Friday 21 August – Sunday 23 August

**Number of laps:** 57

**Circuit length:** 5.419 km

**Race distance:** 308.883 km

**Lap record:** 1:38.683
(Timo Glock, 2009)

### MY HISTORY AT VALENCIA

**2008 (Honda)**
Grid 16; finished 13

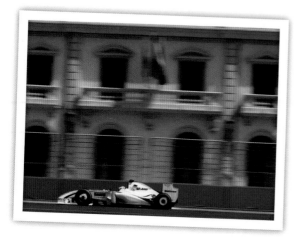

Valencia has a feel of Monaco with its harbour and tight barriers, although the run-off means that it's a lot safer than a normal street track in places. The circuit uses the permanent roads surrounding the Juan Carlos I Marina, which was the base for the America's Cup in 2007. The track closely follows the water's edge for the majority of the lap and uses a specially constructed swing bridge to cross between the north and south sides of the marina. Last year was the first time we went there and I enjoyed it hugely. It's a great setting and a fun track to drive, even though there wasn't a massive amount of overtaking.

It's a very busy circuit for a driver. The lap has a challenging and innovative layout with 25 turns, giving it more corners than any other track on the calendar. Surrounded by high concrete walls and with average speeds of 200kph, and top speeds reaching in excess of 300kph, it is very different from Monaco. There are a few straights where you can relax a bit, but most of the corners are blind. They've put a few extra kerbs in on the corner exits, but it's still a track where you can get caught out.

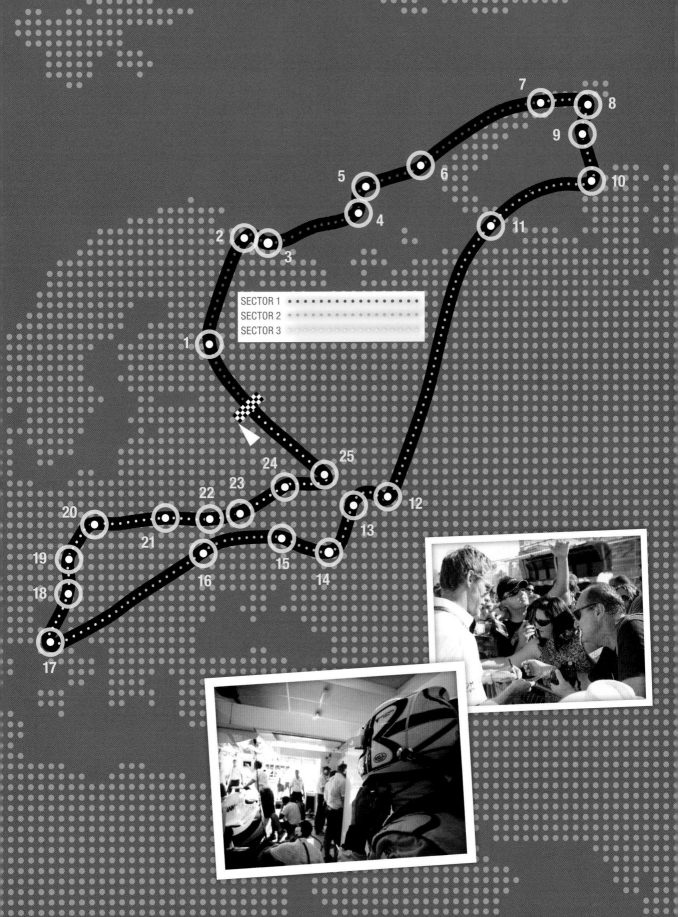

SECTOR 1
SECTOR 2
SECTOR 3

# Europe:
## Preparation, practice and qualifying

I arrived in Valencia refreshed after the summer break. Four weeks is a long time to brood when your previous three races haven't gone to plan, but I was confident that, after the two-week compulsory factory shutdown, the engineers would be desperate to get back to their work stations inside the factory at Brackley to work out just why our car has not been performing as expected. My job was to keep myself busy, fit and relaxed!

That process started the weekend after Hungary when I competed in the London Triathlon in the Docklands for my chosen charity, Make A Wish Foundation, along with my engineers Shov and Bono. I'd entered them in the sprint race on the Saturday – a 750m swim, 20km bike and 5km run – and they both did very well. Bono finished 75th and Shov 102nd, with only a minute between them. I was so pleased for the guys – especially Shov, who had done loads of training. It was so good to get them involved in another competition with me away from Formula One.

The following day it was my go, with a 7.30am start which meant I had to set my alarm for 4.30am. I was a little bit nervous. There were 430 people entered in my 25 to 29 age category – and 430 people treading water together at the start in a dark, cold Dock is an interesting experience... It was freezing, which was probably a good incentive to move fast, and I came out of the swim section in fourth position. I managed to get through transition and onto my bike to be first on the road for the cycle. Wow! That felt good. One guy got past me and I finished the race overall in second place with a time of 2 hours, 7 minutes and 2 seconds, which was a personal best. I was really surprised. I wasn't racing at elite level or against pros,

but it was a great day and satisfying to push yourself to the limit in a different sphere.

The following week I went to the South of France and had a relaxing holiday, truly away from it all, with a gang of friends and Jessica. No one mentioned racing. We were all just in 'off work' mode. I trained, lay in the sun, ate good food and got involved in the cooking too, which was fun. My repertoire now includes some great pasta dishes – freshly made, not with jars of sauce – and the ultimate English breakfast. My missus did lots of Japanese dishes, which were great too.

It was lovely but four weeks off, mid-season, feels like an eternity and I couldn't wait to get back into the car again. Valencia is like a large Monaco, with more boats in the harbour. It doesn't have the glamour of the Principality but there's an excitement arriving in such a huge, buzzy venue. It's also a modern, working harbour and the city itself is beautiful. We were staying in Las Arenas hotel on the beach, with a super-sized pool I found useful for training. It was beautiful staying on the coast, eating lots of paella, the local dish.

I can't believe people find Valencia a dull venue for a race. Put a Formula One car on any road and drive it at speed and, for me, that's pure excitement. True, it's not a fast and flowing track, but it's fun when it goes round the edge of the marina and over the bridge. It's quite challenging for the drivers with so many turns, and the added factor of being surrounded by barriers means you have to maintain watertight concentration. This is only our second year racing here, so it's still a new challenge. I'd enjoy it anyway – and I'm especially keen to get back in the car and get our championship campaign back on track.

## FRIDAY

A lot of work has been going on back at the factory in Brackley following the sport's summer shutdown. The car feels good. We are experiencing very good grip after the set-up changes. It is such a nice feeling – relief, reassurance, excitement – having a driveable car back beneath me again.

In debrief, we concluded we'd had a reasonably good first day of practice. It was encouraging to see the car seems to be on the pace again. The focus of our programme was on set-up checks and back-to-back evaluations to confirm that the work done back at the factory after our shutdown was in the right direction. There is still some work needed on the set-up before qualifying as I'm not completely happy with the balance, but, all in all, the pace of the car seems reasonably good.

Prior to Valencia, I'd viewed the Red Bull drivers as my main championship rivals. Sebastian Vettel and Mark Webber are both very competitive and were busy taking points off each other, which was great for me. Mark is the more aggressive, a bit crazy in exploring the limits as we saw in the way he blocked Rubens at the Nürburgring. Sebastian is a little more circumspect. I'm used to seeing him a little bit worried approaching the start of a race. At the beginning of the season, I rated Sebastian a lot stronger than Mark over one lap (perhaps because Mark hadn't been able to train or test as much as normal after breaking his leg in a cycling accident in the winter). After the first four or five races, though, Mark's consistency was earning him better results and he outraced his team-mate. Now they seem to be taking turns at having productive weekends, alternating good results.

Track temperatures are very high here – reaching 50°C this afternoon – so we've been able to manage our tyre temperatures well and not encounter the issues which have hampered our pace at the past few races. In fact it's extremely hot in the car – good for the tyres but not for the driver! Heat exhaustion is a risk here. It's one of the toughest races physically.

*Good qualifying fella the cars looking better, Remember points win prizes and keep it off the walls!!'*
**Chrissy**

*Go get them little bruv! Xx'*
**Tanya**

## SATURDAY

*Brawn GP's Rubens Barrichello put his Brawn-Mercedes car on the second row today with a strong qualifying effort securing him third place on the grid. Jenson Button completed the team's strong showing with his fifth place.*

It was a pretty good qualifying session for the team today and the car felt strong throughout. In Q1 I posted the fastest time. Q2 was fine, leaving me sixth and through to the pole position shoot-out. In Q3, I made an unfortunate mistake at Turn 4 on my quick lap. I had only the one flying lap in this session, so it all had to come together. However, on Turn 5, where you jump off the kerb on exit, I shifted from 2nd to 3rd but my hand didn't quite come off the lever and it went up accidentally into 4th and I couldn't then get enough acceleration. It was a small mistake, but I was left watching time slip away. I saw two or three tenths of a second disappear... It was agony, and then, however much you try and make up for your error by finding the time on the rest of the lap, you can't because you're already on the limit.

So it was P5 for me, instead of P3, which compromised my position. It's a shame as the potential was there for more, but 5th on the grid is not bad at all. The good news is I start well ahead of Mark Webber's Red Bull and just one place behind Sebastian Vettel. The car is feeling pretty good with fuel so we will see what the race will bring tomorrow. It's not a great circuit for overtaking, but I'll be giving it everything for a good result.

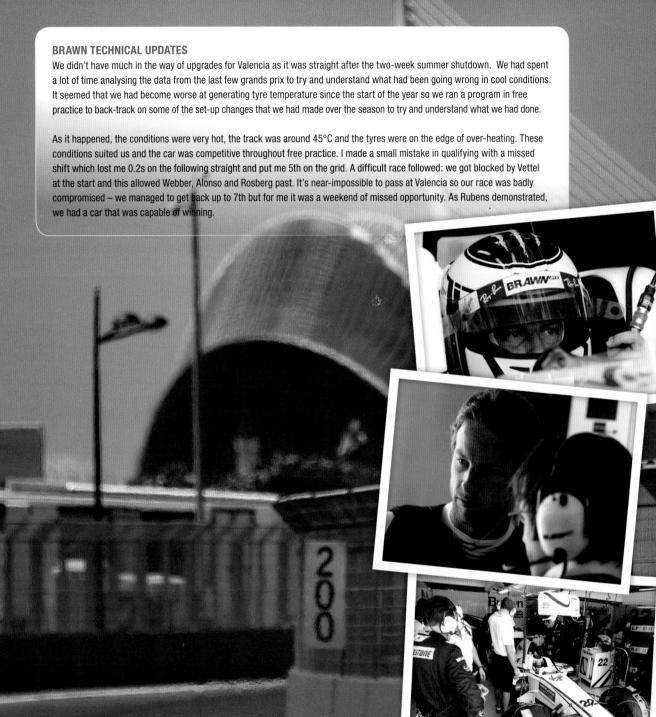

## BRAWN TECHNICAL UPDATES

We didn't have much in the way of upgrades for Valencia as it was straight after the two-week summer shutdown. We had spent a lot of time analysing the data from the last few grands prix to try and understand what had been going wrong in cool conditions. It seemed that we had become worse at generating tyre temperature since the start of the year so we ran a program in free practice to back-track on some of the set-up changes that we had made over the season to try and understand what we had done.

As it happened, the conditions were very hot, the track was around 45°C and the tyres were on the edge of over-heating. These conditions suited us and the car was competitive throughout free practice. I made a small mistake in qualifying with a missed shift which lost me 0.2s on the following straight and put me 5th on the grid. A difficult race followed: we got blocked by Vettel at the start and this allowed Webber, Alonso and Rosberg past. It's near-impossible to pass at Valencia so our race was badly compromised – we managed to get back up to 7th but for me it was a weekend of missed opportunity. As Rubens demonstrated, we had a car that was capable of winning.

# Europe:
## The race

1. Lewis Hamilton
2. Heikki Kovalainen
3. Rubens Barrichello
4. Sebastian Vettel
5. **Jenson Button**
6. Kimi Räikkönen
7. Nico Rosberg
8. Fernando Alonso
9. Mark Webber
10. Robert Kubica
11. Nick Heidfeld
12. Adrian Sutil
13. Timo Glock
14. Romain Grosjean
15. Sebastien Buemi
16. Giancarlo Fisichella
17. Kazuki Nakajima
18. Jarno Trulli
19. Jaime Alguersuari
20. Luca Badoer

*Brawn GP's Rubens Barrichello won the European Grand Prix at the Valencia Street Circuit today – his 10th in Formula One and the 100th GP victory for a Brazilian driver. Team-mate Jenson Button came home in seventh place adding a valuable two points to his lead in the drivers' championship.*

Rubens did a great job this weekend and he deserves the victory, which he has dedicated to Felipe Massa's ongoing recovery. It's been a long time since Rubens has been on the top step, so I'm happy for him – although of course I would rather be receiving the winner's trophy on the podium myself.

I was incredibly excited about racing with a good car again. I got away from the line well, but Vettel, on the dirty side, headed across towards me and 'squeezed' me towards the wall. His aggression surprised me as he's usually more careful at the start. We later learnt that they suspected the engine might not last the race and, in my opinion, that's why he could afford to be aggressive off the start and take a risk. I had to back out of it or risk a ruined front wing and three people flew past me. It annoys me when you hear people say, 'Jenson needs to be more aggressive'. No, I don't, because it would have been a crash and a DNF with no potential to pick up points.

So I was back in 9th. I got past Webber down the inside, but Alonso locked and I had to lift and at that point Webber went up the inside. At Turn 4 we both braked very late. He braked so late I couldn't get around the corner and had to cross the chicane, which meant I came back on track ahead of him. It was more Red Bull aggression. Webber knew what he was doing. Shov came on the radio and said I had to let him back past because I'd officially overtaken him crossing the chicane which is illegal.

That was frustrating on two counts. It's agony giving up a place in the

## STRATEGY

The tyres were once again the same as in Monaco and Budapest (Soft and Super Soft). Valencia is classified as a street circuit, although the track isn't open to traffic during the entire race event, as traditional street tracks are normally.

Friday was warm, with track temperatures in excess of 40°C, and the forecast was for similar weather on Saturday and Sunday. I did a very complete program on Friday, evaluating the tyre compounds and various set-up options in order to understand the tyre temperature issues that have hindered Brawn GP over the last few events. The Super Soft compound showed signs of graining with a number of competitors, whilst the Soft tyre performed well, especially on a longer run, and was therefore to be the default race tyre. The strategy results showed a clear two-stop, with a medium first stint length.

Unfortunately, during qualifying, I pulled for an up-shift twice into T5, losing a few tenths, and dropped to P5 as a result. The start was okay, however Vettel cut across me during the first few corners, resulting in me having to lift off the throttle and straight-line the chicane, losing time and dropping to P8. It was deemed that I had also gained an advantage missing the chicane, so had to give the place to Webber behind, dropping me to P9. I drove a good race with fuel on board from there, jumping Webber again on the last stop of the race to take P7 and two valuable points.

heat of a race, but it also meant that was my race done. To be stuck behind Webber, who was so far off the pace, was extremely annoying. And then Shov was on again saying, 'Go to Mix 2, richer fuel mix, Attack!' I had a go at passing him on Turn 17, but didn't manage it. As anyone who watched the race would observe, it's difficult to overtake here. I thought I'd back off a bit, save some fuel to go a lap longer and then pick up some more places in the pit-stops. My race ended up being a long race to get past Webber, which I did on the second and final pit-stop. I crossed the line in 7th to collect two more useful points.

That messy first lap ruined my race. While I finished seventh, Rubens had won, gaining eight points on me in the championship and leap-frogging Webber into second place in the title race. I now have an eighteen-point lead from my team-mate. Webber lies third, with Vettel in fourth. I'm happy for Rubens, and there are lots of positives to take away from the weekend. The most important being the fact that my championship lead was reduced by only half a point – which is amazing.

Reassuringly, the car's performance was stronger than in the last three races. The engineers had analysed what happened from Silverstone through to Hungary and found the reason we suffered the downturn in performance. Working that out and fixing the problem to immediate effect has really lifted the team. We all knew the issue was to do with tyre temperature. With each new upgrade package, we had been running more downforce and also running certain set-ups with the suspension to help improve the ride quality. Both of these measures have a by-product of looking after the tyres, but the problem was that we then didn't get enough heat into the tyres. We ran back-to-back comparisons here in Valencia and ran with less downforce than the simulator suggested as optimum for this track and found out the best solution. That kind of team effort is so satisfying, the fuel of a great team spirit. I love

> 'Hey, Wishing you all the best for the race today. Hope it's a brilliant one for you. Will be cheering for you in Brackley town' Jules

the way Brawn, our new team, is proving best at pit-stops and at pulling together when things go wrong. It's a fantastic atmosphere.

Who would have predicted the Red Bulls to have such a no-show race? Webber finished 9th, out of the points, and Vettel, as predicted, earned a Did Not Finish classification courtesy of his engine expiring. They must be pretty fed up with the way their championship challenge has hit a brick wall. As championship leader, did a fourth consecutive disappointing race start to affect me? Of course it did! But not in the way some commentators suggested. I haven't lost my nerve or my appetite. How ridiculous to even consider that. There were good reasons why I've not been on the podium for four races – the BGP 001 performance issue, the Massa incident preventing a full qualifying session in Hungary, Vettel's aggression at the start here – and the cumulative effect meant I was starting to think: 'How many points have I got? How many have I lost, and to whom? How many can I afford to lose?' Leading a world championship, and suffering a mysterious downturn in car performance, is not a situation I've ever been in before. I found myself worried about accidents, asking myself 'what if' questions. The bottom line was I had forgotten how to enjoy myself racing, but I recognised that, and was ready to put it right in Spa.

## EUROPEAN GRAND PRIX FINAL POSITIONS

| Pos | Driver | Team | Laps | Time |
|-----|--------|------|------|------|
| 1 | Rubens Barrichello | Brawn-Mercedes | 57 | 1:35:51.289 |
| 2 | Lewis Hamilton | McLaren-Mercedes | 57 | +2.3 secs |
| 3 | Kimi Räikkönen | Ferrari | 57 | +15.9 secs |
| 4 | Heikki Kovalainen | McLaren-Mercedes | 57 | +20.0 secs |
| 5 | Nico Rosberg | Williams-Toyota | 57 | +20.8 secs |
| 6 | Fernando Alonso | Renault | 57 | +27.7 secs |
| 7 | Jenson Button | Brawn-Mercedes | 57 | +34.9 secs |
| 8 | Robert Kubica | BMW Sauber | 57 | +36.6 secs |
| 9 | Mark Webber | RBR-Renault | 57 | +44.9 secs |
| 10 | Adrian Sutil | Force India-Mercedes | 57 | +47.9 secs |
| 11 | Nick Heidfeld | BMW Sauber | 57 | +48.8 secs |
| 12 | Giancarlo Fisichella | Force India-Mercedes | 57 | +63.6 secs |
| 13 | Jarno Trulli | Toyota | 57 | +64.5 secs |
| 14 | Timo Glock | Toyota | 57 | +86.5 secs |
| 15 | Romain Grosjean | Renault | 57 | +91.7 secs |
| 16 | Jaime Alguersuari | STR-Ferrari | 56 | +1 Lap |
| Ret | Luca Badoer | Ferrari | 56 | +1 Lap |
| Ret | Kazuki Nakajima | Williams-Toyota | 53 | Retired |
| Ret | Sebastien Buemi | STR-Ferrari | 41 | Brakes |
| ret | Sebastian Vettel | RBR-Renault | 23 | Engine |

'The deficit between the Red Bulls to Jenson has grown, and his closest challenger is now his team-mate again. Button has two non-finishes in hand before he's overtaken by an 'outsider', and he'll feel a lot more comfortable knowing it's Rubens in second place and not a Red Bull driver.'

David Coulthard, Autosport

The small mistake in qualifying and a difficult start caught behind Sebastian Vettel really cost me today as I got caught in traffic and it's really tough to overtake around this circuit. Still, we did what we came for this weekend and beat the Red Bulls, our main title rivals, so I'm not too disappointed with 7th position. We'll go to the next race in Spa positive and ready to have a good race.

*'Well done Jens, still leading the World champs!! Webber was straight on the radio saying you must let him past after you went off, the commentators didn't think you needed 2. Lots of love, Mum xx'*

*'Mate I was amazed that Vettel's move at the start was legal, it looked very dangerous! At least you got Webber, shame he moaned like a girl about you cutting the chicane! Anyway onward and upward, still a great lead! X'*
Richard

### OVERALL POINTS

| | |
|---|---|
| Jenson Button | 72 |
| Rubens Barrichello | 54 |
| Mark Webber | 51.5 |
| Sebastian Vettel | 47 |
| Nico Rosberg | 29.5 |
| Lewis Hamilton | 27 |
| Kimi Räikkönen | 24 |
| Jarno Trulli | 22.5 |
| Felipe Massa | 22 |
| Timo Glock | 16 |
| Fernando Alonso | 16 |
| Heikki Kovalainen | 14 |
| Nick Heidfeld | 6 |
| Sebastien Buemi | 3 |
| Robert Kubica | 3 |
| Sebastien Bourdais | 2 |

'My money is still on Jenson but Rubens could yet trounce him and, right now, I see the Brazilian as his biggest threat. He showed that, with a slightly different set-up, the Brawn BGP 001 can still do it and he drove a pretty impressive race. In Spa he will want to do it again.'
Edward Gorman, The Times F1 blog

# Belgian Grand Prix
## Circuit de Spa-Francorchamps
## Friday 21 August – Sunday 23 August

**Number of laps:** 44

**Circuit length:** 7.004 km

**Race distance:** 308.052 km

**Lap record:** 1:45.108
(Kimi Räikkönen, 2004)

### MY HISTORY AT SPA

**2008 (Honda)**
Grid 17; finished 15

**2007 (Honda)**
Grid 12; retired (hydraulics)

**2005 (BAR-Honda)**
Grid 8; finished 3

**2004 (BAR-Honda)**
Grid 12; retired (accident)

**2002 (Renault)**
Grid 10; retired (engine)

**2001 (Benetton-Renault)**
Grid 15; spun off

**2000 (Williams-BMW)**
Grid 3; finished 5

Spa is a classic drivers' circuit, and the Belgian Grand Prix is always a race that we look forward to. It's one of my absolute favourite circuits and has a layout which gives everything you could want as a driver. It's one of the fastest and most challenging laps in the world with hills, fast corners and long straights which combine to give you a real buzz to drive, similar to Suzuka and Silverstone. It's also very beautiful with its forest setting in the Ardennes mountains, although that means the weather can be unpredictable. You have to be ready to react, but that unpredictability is part of the thrill of racing at Spa.

Eau Rouge is still a legendary corner. It – and Blanchimont – aren't as crazy-scary as they were a few years ago as they are now an easy flat for us in the dry, but the feeling when you hit the bottom of the hill, touch the ground and shoot straight back up again is amazing. It's a long circuit so there are a lot of corners, some very tricky, and that gives you so many chances to make that tiny mistake that ruins the lap. It's a challenging circuit and normally produces really good racing – the only worry for us is that the cars with KERS are going to have a huge advantage up through Eau Rouge and down the Kemmel Straight.

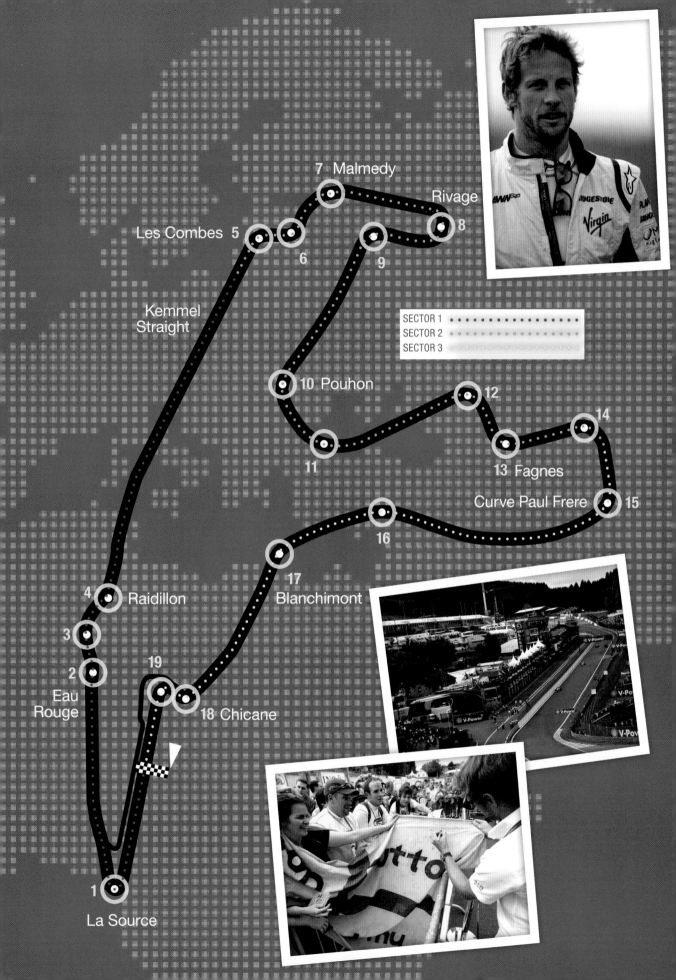

7 Malmedy

Rivage

Les Combes 5

6

9

8

Kemmel
Straight

SECTOR 1
SECTOR 2
SECTOR 3

10 Pouhon

12

14

11

13 Fagnes

Curve Paul Frere 15

16

4 Raidillon

17 Blanchimont

3

2

19

Eau
Rouge

18 Chicane

1

La Source

# Belgium:
## Preparation, practice and qualifying

I was in England visiting the factory on Tuesday and the next day I drove over to Belgium with Chrissy, his brother Al and Richie. We're all racing drivers, so you'd think we'd all be fighting for the steering wheel, but they know I struggle being a passenger so they let me do all the driving. It was great fun, like being on a teenage road trip, but in a slightly smarter car.

We rocked up in the beautiful Ardennes in the evening, dropped my stuff in the motorhome, had a shower and went out to dinner with Shov, Bono, Ron Meadows our team manager and the Mercedes engineers in their lovely, quaint hotel. We had a good evening discussing plans for the weekend over a delicious set menu put together by an amazing chef. Then it was back to the motorhome which, in Spa, is parked in a sorbet and ice-cream factory – not the most picturesque spot, but safe, away from traffic and fans. When I first had my motorhome, there would be a good half-dozen drivers parked together in a designated area close to the circuit. This season it's just been Rubens and me, parked alongside each other, and the weird thing is we never see each other. He's probably inside playing poker!

### THURSDAY
Arriving a day earlier than usual meant I had a lovely, relaxed start. Spa is a seven-kilometre circuit and we were going to walk it as a team group – Ross the Big Bear, Shov, Bono, Ron, James Vowles our strategist, Chrissy, Richie, Al and me. We were all in trainers except Ross who was in travel shoes, which he must have regretted by the end. It's an amazing experience walking this track. Everyone was surprised by how steep the gradient of Eau Rouge is – especially Ross. We set off at 11.30am and got back to the paddock by 1pm for lunch. Other drivers passed us on scooters, but you see so much more on foot.

We had engineering meetings and press obligations in the afternoon, then it was back to the motorhome where we cooked pasta for supper. Boys' pasta, that is – a little less refined than what we'd made on holiday. We open up a tin of pasta sauce, add a few bits and we're well impressed with our cooking. Carbs in!

> 'Keep the faith son! Have a good one, I will be watching dude.'
> Phil Young, former physio

### FRIDAY
It is a real treat to race around Spa in a Formula One car. It's always an unforgettable moment when you hit Eau Rouge on your first lap out, and you do *hit* Eau Rouge. It's rare for the team to get the ride height right first time out. Bam! It unsettles the car... and the adrenalin is running.

The first practice session was interrupted by rain, which gradually intensified. The afternoon session was fine and dry. The combination meant we had perfect practice conditions to prepare ourselves for all eventualities that could be caused by the infamously capricious Spa weather.

The morning was a slightly frustrating session as the rain shower arrived scarcely 30 minutes into practice. It was heavy so we weren't able to get much done apart from some wet running towards the end. However that quick change of set-up experience is valuable here as it is bound to rain during qualifying or during the race itself. The second session this afternoon was much more useful. We worked through a few aero and downforce comparisons as well as looking at the tyres. We collected a lot of information. Finishing the day P17 and P18 shows we're nowhere near as quick as we would like to be, but we know what needs to be done tomorrow to improve on the balance. The potential is there to do that ahead of qualifying. All in all, a good day, with long runs, and we're not experiencing any issues with tyre temperatures so far, which is positive.

### SATURDAY
*Brawn GP's Rubens Barrichello will start the Belgian Grand Prix from the second row of the grid tomorrow having qualified his Brawn-Mercedes car in fourth position at the end of a thrilling qualifying hour in Spa. Team-mate Jenson Button had a more challenging session and will start the race from 14th position.*

Argh, the worst qualifying of the season. I didn't expect to qualify in 14th position today but we really struggled with grip levels, particularly on the softer tyre. We tried different downforce levels,

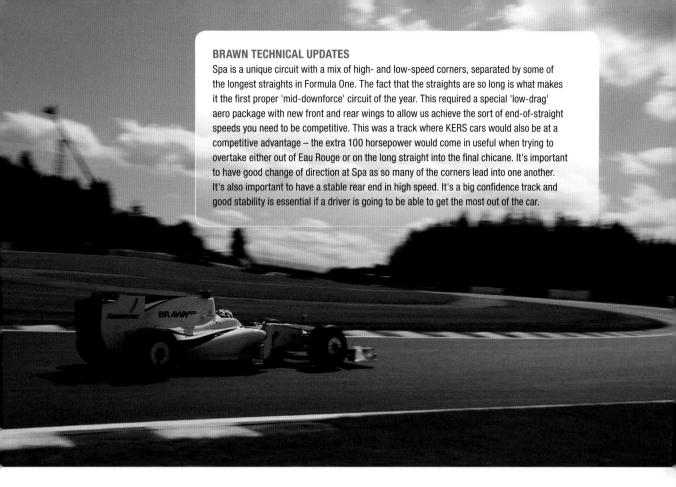

but whatever we did it didn't feel right. With the temperature down, I couldn't find a good balance that worked for 100 per cent of a lap. I particularly didn't like the balance on low fuel so I had a lot of fuel on board which was probably a bit of a mistake. I finished Q1 with a time that left me 15th. In Q2 I was happy with the lap until Turn 9, a little left-hander before Pouhon, where I ran a bit wide onto the Astroturf and lost two tenths.

For some reason the engine on my car was not as powerful. I was losing a tenth of a second on each straight to Rubens – and I didn't make it through to Q3. Rubens was still on low fuel, for the very quick first stint we had both originally planned to do, so his P4 made my performance look worse than it was.

*'Have a good one fella! Missed you this weekend, see you in a bit. X' Richie*

The car hadn't felt right all weekend and I wasn't able to get any more out of it. Rubens and I are usually very closely matched, but he was quick on the Option, and I wasn't, so a priority was to look into the reasons for the disparity that night. I just couldn't find any grip on the softer rubber, which left the rear end unstable and I had no confidence under braking, particularly in the middle sector. It was strange as our set-ups are different but not by much. I'm braced for a very tough race from 14th, but at least we have more time to choose our strategy. We need to get it right and ensure we can score some points tomorrow.

It is the weirdest grid: Fisichella on pole in a Force India, Trulli second in a Toyota, Nick Heidfeld third in a BMW – and Lewis, Fernando and myself all out of the shoot-out. The danger for my championship challenge is the Red Bulls. Vettel and Webber have only qualified in 8th and 9th respectively, but they and Rubens are all ahead of me on the grid.

This evening I am so frustrated. I ate at the circuit with Richie, the old man, my manager Richard Goddard, Shov and Ross. When we got back to the motorhome, the staff from the ice-cream factory had brought over an amazing slab of ice cream with a Brawn car sat on top, made from marzipan with amazingly accurate livery. They'd done a great job, and it was a touching present. It prompted a laugh as Richard ducked down and bit the helmet off the driver.

# Belguim:
## The race

1. Giancarlo Fisichella
2. Jarno Trulli
3. Nick Heidfeld
4. Rubens Barrichello
5. Robert Kubica
6. Kimi Räikkönen
7. Timo Glock
8. Sebastian Vettel
9. Mark Webber
10. Nico Rosberg
11. Adrian Sutil
12. Lewis Hamilton
13. Fernando Alonso
14. **Jenson Button**
15. Heikki Kovalainen
16. Sebastien Buemi
17. Jaime Alguersuari
18. Kazuki Nakajima
19. Romain Grosjean
20. Luca Badoer

### STRATEGY

The tyres for the event were only one step apart (Medium and Soft). Spa is a unique circuit, with Sector 2 alone being the same length as other tracks!

The Friday work was split between tyre evaluations and set-up work, with a few options to work on the tyre-temperature issue we had struggled with in the past. The two tyre options were very similar over a long run, with the Prime being a slightly better tyre.

We were planning to go with an aggressive strategy in qualifying with both cars, but unfortunately I wasn't able to get the lap time out of the Option tyre in Q2, putting myself P14 on the grid for the race. I had a good start, and was up alongside Kovalainen fighting for P11, into T5 on the first lap when Grosjean hit me on the entry to T5 and I had to retire.

*An eventful Belgian Grand Prix for Brawn GP saw Rubens Barrichello finish in seventh position at the end of the 44-lap race to score two points for the team's championship challenge, with team-mate Jenson Button retiring from the race on the first lap after being struck from behind by Romain Grosjean.*

I went to bed brooding on qualifying and woke up wondering if 14th on the grid was just a bad dream. I soon realised it was real enough. When I'm in that mood, nothing anyone says can ever help. I find it best to call Shov and deal with the practicalities of the situation, and we discussed in tactical terms how it was going to be very different starting a race from 14th with KERS cars all around me.

Inside-team rivalry was becoming more noticeable with Rubens in the best form of his life. Each side of the Brawn garage wants to beat the other side. Both sets of mechanics are desperate to win the constructors' championship – their competitiveness is legendary – and that's healthy. It is the turn of Rubens's side to crow a bit, because they had to put up with a lot at the start of the season when I won six out of seven races.

The Sunday morning build-up always leaves me expecting a fun race. I was starting in 14th, but I was thinking of the fun of competing, the potential, the fact that anything could happen at the first corner to ruin the race for the front of the grid! Back in the middle of the starting grid, I realised how very close I was to the Red Bulls, which was odd, because we had expected them to annihilate us. That was a last-minute boost of confidence. I felt sure that I could make my way up to a useful points-scoring position.

My start was great. I had made up a few places in the first few corners to be ahead of Lewis and Rubens. Lewis had problems with the clutch in his McLaren, and I got round him easily. Rubens also had problems when his car went into anti-stall at the start, which left him stranded. It was a great feeling to soar past him. As usual the first lap through Eau Rouge was all pretty crazy, with no one's tyre temperatures up to optimum, everyone a bit nervous and fighting for position. I had a good run going down the straight to Turn 5 just after Eau Rouge. I had exited behind

Kovalainen and stayed in his tow. I had Romain Grosjean in my slipstream. I saw lots of smoke and dust and backed off a little turning in for the corner, but Grosjean just barrel-rolled up and hit my rear wheel. He had outbraked himself, hit my back wheel and spun me around. It's never a nice feeling when you're facing the wrong way on a race track with cars piling into you. Lewis and Jaime Alguersuari, the Torro Rosso new boy, also became tangled up in the incident – and that was that. Race over.

We all got out of our cars and stood waiting for scooters to arrive to take us back to the paddock. Grosjean came up to me and said: 'Did you not see me?!' It was infuriating. Lewis and I both agreed it was a wasted opportunity, a racing incident and no less frustrating for that. I jumped on the scooter and got back to the pits. I said 'sorry' to the guys on the pit-lane wall and they just shrugged. It hadn't happened all season, and as it turned out, it was a

'Good morning Jenson, Today is a different day from yesterday, I know it's gonna be a difficult one for you but remember you are the world championship leader and you will still be after this race.. XxX' Jessica

good race to suffer an unlucky DNF classification. I watched the race from the pit-lane wall. It was the first time this year I'd watched any of the racing live.

The amazing thing was that none of my title rivals had a good day either, and I left Spa with my points lead whittled down by only two points – courtesy of Rubens finishing seventh. The Red Bulls had a disappointing time. At one stage Webber was charging and I thought, 'Here we go', but just as I said it, Webber swerved out after his pit-stop and impeded Nick Heidfeld in the pit lane. I was shouting 'penalty' at the TV screen. It was obvious he would be punished with a drive-through penalty. He was, and it ruined his race. Vettel came through to finish third, which meant he leap-frogged back over his team-mate to lie third in the world championship behind Rubens. I still had a 16-point lead. It wasn't at all as disastrous as it had seemed when I was climbing out of my cockpit at Turn 5 on lap one.

After this race I did not read the papers, but the questions I was being asked – after five disappointing races in a row – suggested the prevailing opinion was that I was finding it difficult to handle the pressure. That wasn't the case at all. What had happened was that the string of bad luck meant I had stopped enjoying myself on the race track and that's never a productive state of mind. I need to relax to drive my best. From that point, I resolved to look at the rest of the season as a mini championship of five races in which I had a fantastic sixteen-point head start. Ross Brawn is quite open about how he had to put an arm around Michael Schumacher and encourage him through the difficult periods in his record number of title campaigns. Even in a successful season, all drivers are going to have their ups and downs. It's the law of averages. Ross knew I wasn't down in terms of confidence; we all knew the reasons for our poor string of performances, but we had a good little sit-down chat after each race when I visited the factory.

I'm told Martin Brundle said on television that sometimes a driver enduring a poor run of luck needs an accident that's not his fault to find the momentum to turn around his fortune. A third-party incident sort of clears the slate. I'd never thought of that before, but maybe it's true. I left Spa with no points, but not because I'd made a mistake... and now I was truly determined to have a great race and revisit the podium in Monza.

We had a decent day on Friday. The lack of testing meant that we had to work through an aero program to assess the various rear-wing options that were available to us. Our long-run pace was not exceptional but we looked like we were a top-three team and given the cool conditions we were reasonably happy. We just had to work on the middle sector to find some time. Saturday was colder again and our issues with tyre warm-up were starting to show. I struggled with the balance through qualifying and, for the first time this year, failed to make the final ten. Rubens was coping better but even so, we were some way off our normal pace. It seemed that we weren't the only team who were struggling. The McLarens of Hamilton and Kovalainen were having similar difficulties.

My race was short and marked my first DNF of the year. We had a good start and I was up to 12th place when Grosjean drove into the back of me at Turn 5. This was disappointing as I was one of the heaviest cars on the grid and should easily have picked up a few valuable points on a difficult weekend.

## BELGIAN GRAND PRIX FINAL POSITIONS

| Pos | Driver | Team | Laps | Time |
| --- | --- | --- | --- | --- |
| 1 | Kimi Räikkönen | Ferrari | 44 | 01:23:50.995 |
| 2 | Giancarlo Fisichella | Force India-Mercedes | 44 | +0.9 secs |
| 3 | Sebastian Vettel | RBR-Renault | 44 | +3.8 secs |
| 4 | Robert Kubica | BMW Sauber | 44 | +9.9 secs |
| 5 | Nick Heidfeld | BMW Sauber | 44 | +11.2 secs |
| 6 | Heikki Kovalainen | McLaren-Mercedes | 44 | +32.7 secs |
| 7 | Rubens Barrichello | Brawn-Mercedes | 44 | +35.4 secs |
| 8 | Nico Rosberg | Williams-Toyota | 44 | +36.2 secs |
| 9 | Mark Webber | RBR-Renault | 44 | +36.9 secs |
| 10 | Timo Glock | Toyota | 44 | +41.4 secs |
| 11 | Adrian Sutil | Force India-Mercedes | 44 | +42.6 secs |
| 12 | Sebastien Buemi | STR-Ferrari | 44 | +46.1 secs |
| 13 | Kazuki Nakajima | Williams-Toyota | 44 | +54.2 secs |
| 14 | Luca Badoer | Ferrari | 44 | +102.1 secs |
| Ret | Fernando Alonso | Renault | 26 | Retired |
| Ret | Jarno Trulli | Toyota | 21 | Brakes |
| Ret | Jenson Button | Brawn-Mercedes | 0 | Accident |
| Ret | Romain Grosjean | Renault | 0 | Accident |
| Ret | Lewis Hamilton | McLaren-Mercedes | 0 | Accident |
| Ret | Jaime Alguersuari | STR-Ferrari | 0 | Accident |

Quite simply, Grosjean outbraked himself and hit my back wheel. That was it for my race today. It's frustrating as I was in a reasonable position having made up some places and with a lot of fuel on board, but it's better to have my first retirement here where I haven't been so competitive than when I'm running at the front. We're determined to get back on the track at the next race and be more competitive there at a track which should be quite good for our car.

**OVERALL POINTS**

| | |
|---|---|
| Jenson Button | 72 |
| Rubens Barrichello | 56 |
| Sebastian Vettel | 53 |
| Mark Webber | 51.5 |
| Kimi Räikkönen | 34 |
| Nico Rosberg | 30.5 |
| Lewis Hamilton | 27 |
| Jarno Trulli | 22.5 |
| Felipe Massa | 22 |
| Heikki Kovalainen | 17 |
| Timo Glock | 16 |
| Fernando Alonso | 16 |
| Nick Heidfeld | 10 |
| Giancarlo Fisichella | 8 |
| Robert Kubica | 8 |
| Sebastien Buemi | 3 |
| Sebastien Bourdais | 2 |

'The most extraordinary statistic now is that Button still heads the table by the same margin he had in his pocket after six races. Despite a lean period collecting 11 points, compared to the 61 he had amassed after Turkey, Button can hardly believe his luck as rivals take turns to stumble in the rush to kick the Brawn driver when he is down.' Maurice Hamilton, Guardian

'Sorry about the weekend, very unlucky but I guess damage limitations. Hopefully Monza will be successful' Spud

# Italian Grand Prix
## Autodromo Nazionale Monza
### Friday 11 September – Sunday 13 September

**Number of laps:** 53

**Circuit length:** 5.793 km

**Race distance:** 306.720 km

**Lap record:** 1:21.046
(Rubens Barrichello, 2004)

## MY HISTORY AT MONZA

**2008 (Honda)**
Grid 19; finished 15

**2007 (Honda)**
Grid 10; finished 18

**2006 (Honda)**
Grid 5; finished 5

**2005 (BAR-Honda)**
Grid 3; finished 8

**2004 (BAR-Honda)**
Grid 6; finished 3

**2003 (BAR-Honda)**
Grid 7; retired (gearbox)

**2002 (Renault)**
Grid 17; finished 5

**2001 (Benetton-Renault)**
Grid 11; retired (engine)

**2000 (Williams-BMW))**
Grid 12; spun off

Monza is a fantastic track situated in the royal park at the heart of the town of Monza, just outside Milan. It is the fastest circuit of the year with four long straights enabling the cars to reach top speeds of 340kph and average lap speeds of 250kph. The emphasis is on engine power and aerodynamic efficiency, which require the cars to be set up with a special low-downforce aero package to minimise drag.

Ascari is probably my favourite part of the track, but also Parabolica, where the challenge is to brake as late as possible, particularly in qualifying when you're on a quick lap. Our car is good under braking and on traction, and we have the power of our Mercedes-Benz engine to maximise speed on the long straights, so it's a circuit that should be reasonably good for us.

I love the electric passion that the fans bring to the race weekend. The atmosphere is supercharged at Monza, with a lot of very emotional Italian fans. The tifosi are big Ferrari fans, of course, and they'll be especially vocal now they have an Italian in the car in Giancarlo Fisichella, fresh from his incredible pole and second-place finish in Spa. Historically, the passion from the fans is also for Formula One as a show so all the drivers get a lift from having packed grandstands cheering us on.

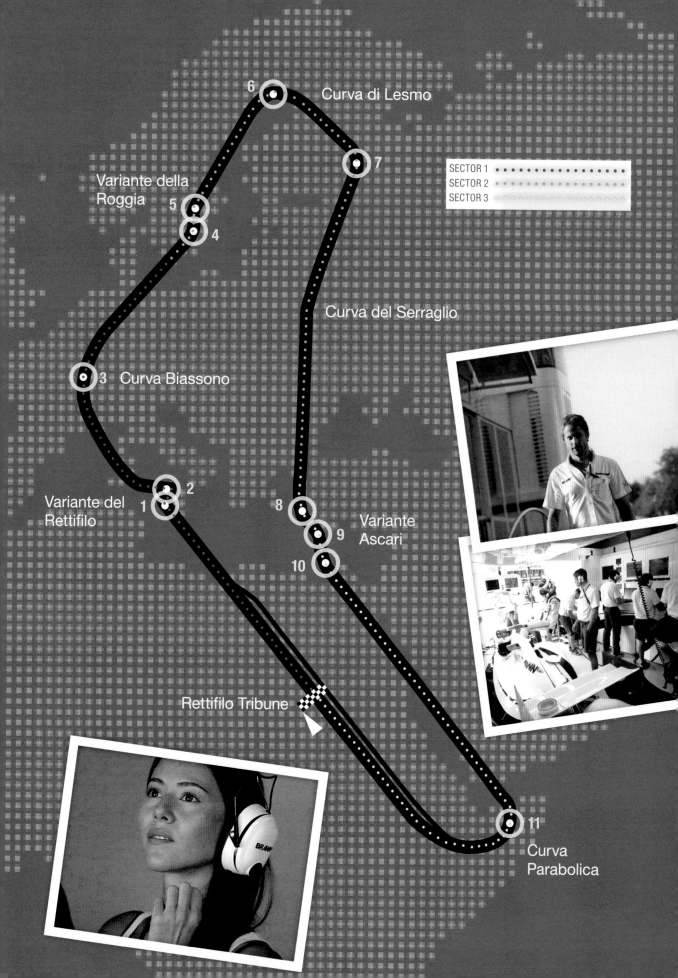

6 Curva di Lesmo

7

SECTOR 1
SECTOR 2
SECTOR 3

Variante della
Roggia

5

4

Curva del Serraglio

3 Curva Biassono

Variante del
Rettifilo

1

2

8

Variante
Ascari

9

10

Rettifilo Tribune

11

Curva
Parabolica

# Monza:
## Preparation, practice and qualifying

The build-up to the Italian Grand Prix was not about the fight for the 2009 world championship at all. Yet again, an off-track story – 'Renault-gate' – dominated the headlines and occupied all media outlets. When the story emerged on the evening after the race at Spa, I was as shocked as anyone. The idea that a team would instruct one of its drivers to fake an accident and crash in a specific place, on a specific lap, in order to bring out a safety car that would benefit his team-mate's race strategy was unthinkable. Reckless of life and limb in the extreme, it would also be the worst form of cheating known in a sport that pushes boundaries all the time. Yet, that is what Nelson Piquet Jr, having been sacked by Renault, alleges happened in Singapore last year – where he did crash and his team-mate Fernando Alonso, on a bizarre strategy, did go on to win the race. And that story is one that the paddock, and the world at large, was soon to learn Renault would not contest. Incredible.

I spent two years at Renault, and the less I say about my experience there the better really. I arrived in only my second year in Formula One and struggled with a difficult car. By the second year I was performing better than my team-mate Jarno Trulli, whose career was managed by Flavio Briatore. However, it was Trulli who Briatore decided to keep in the team at my expense, even though I had finished in front of him and scored more points than him. He brought in Alonso (whom he also managed) instead. The decision shocked me at the time, but I'd been considering other options anyway because there were certain people in the team I didn't get along with that well.

I left Renault at the end of 2002. Seven seasons on, I'm leading the world championship… and I need a strong race here in Monza before we set off for the last four fly-away races. I haven't been on the podium for five races and, come late Sunday afternoon, I fully intend to be looking down on a cheering gaggle of Brawn mechanics to the sound of the British national anthem.

Racing here is going to be tough for everyone this year because, until the ban on in-season testing, we would normally have had a test beforehand. It'll be interesting to see how the teams cope with the limited running because Monza is very different to most of the circuits that we race on. The car will be set up with the lowest levels of drag and downforce possible to take advantage of the long straights. It changes the feel of the car quite a bit and that always takes a few laps to get used to, so the practice sessions will be very important.

I'm feeling very gee-ed up, looking at the remainder of the season as a five-race championship in which I start with a sixteen-point cushion.

I'm in the motorhome this weekend, which is parked next to another factory in one of the many sprawling, light industrial acres of Monza. Again, it's not picturesque, but it has electric gates and security which is the main issue. And I have my favourite pizza and pasta restaurant to visit close by.

### FRIDAY

The woods of the royal park are alive with the buzz of passionate fans. All the way into the circuit car park you pass windows draped with Ferrari flags and messages to Kimi and Fisi, stalls selling Prancing Horse-logo merchandise and campers who have turned their pitches into temples to Ferrari. The atmosphere never fails to excite.

It's a head-down day for us all at Brawn. Thanks to the ongoing Renault-gate story, we drivers and engineers were left alone to concentrate on our work. What with Monza being such a unique low-downforce circuit and the fact that we haven't had the opportunity to test here this year, we were all aware that the day's sessions were crucial towards getting the best set-up on the car.

I completed 53 laps in total with the car in the low-downforce configuration. The main focus has been on race preparation to ensure we understand how the car feels with this set-up. Unfortunately we had a couple of issues, which meant that I couldn't do the long runs that we had planned, so that was a bit frustrating. Everything was sorted out by the end of the day, which is good, but we have a lot of work ahead of us. It feels very different running with such low downforce, but the car has been performing reasonably well. We need to work on the fine-tuning of the set-up overnight to ensure that I'm completely happy with the balance before qualifying.

## BRAWN TECHNICAL UPDATES

Monza is the fastest circuit in Formula One. The average speed for the lap is in excess of 150mph and peak speeds before braking are over 200mph. You run the lowest downforce of the year at Monza. This makes the car difficult to handle, particularly on the brakes for the first and second chicanes. The FIA had made the kerbs at the chicanes much higher (we didn't find this out until after we had done all our simulation work), so ride control was a big factor in setting a good time in the first sector. The rest of the circuit is fast. Lesmos, Ascari and Parabolica are all about balance – if the driver has the right balance then he has the confidence to carry speed through the corner. Parabolica is particularly important as it leads onto the long start–finish straight.

We realised we had a good car on the first run. Considering it is such an unusual track, it was probably the one where we made the least number of set-up changes during Friday. We'd decided to run high fuel to prepare for a one-stop race. This meant that we finished the day in 16th and 19th position but by our calculations, we were as fast as anyone and just had to make minor tweaks overnight to give us better rear stability on a very long stint.

## SATURDAY

*Brawn GP's Rubens Barrichello and Jenson Button qualified their Brawn-Mercedes cars on the third row of the grid for Sunday's Italian Prix at the Autodromo Nazionale di Monza with fifth and sixth positions respectively in today's qualifying session.*

Rubens and I both ran at the front of the field throughout the hour with our cars performing well on both the Prime and the Option tyres. I finished Q1 in P3, progressing easily through to Q2, where I topped the timesheets with a time of 1:22.955. I favoured the harder Prime tyre for the final session.

The car felt great and I completed just one run in Q3 with three flying laps to set my quickest time. Strategy dictated a heavy fuel load and I felt I got the best out of the car to claim sixth position, just fifteen hundredths of a second behind Rubens in fifth.

The great thing to know going into the race tomorrow is that we had the ability to be on pole today, but, strategically, we had to consider the pace of the KERS cars off the line and so we put a lot of fuel on board and focused on what was right for our race: a one-stop strategy. I'm really happy with sixth position today. Rubens and I have been so close on lap times all weekend and he's ended up just fifteen hundredths ahead of me, which is the difference between getting your head down on the straights. I obviously didn't do it enough! It's been a positive day and I'm extremely confident that we can have a good race.

1. **Lewis Hamilton**
2. **Adrian Sutil**
3. **Kimi Räikkönen**
4. **Heikki Kovalainen**
5. **Rubens Barrichello**
6. **Jenson Button**
7. **Vitantonio Liuzzi**
8. **Fernando Alonso**
9. **Sebastian Vettel**
10. **Mark Webber**
11. **Jarno Trulli**
12. **Romain Grosjean**
13. **Robert Kubica**
14. **Giancarlo Fisichella**
15. **Nick Heidfeld**
16. **Timo Glock**
17. **Kazuki Nakajima**
18. **Nico Rosberg**
19. **Sebastien Buemi**
20. **Jaime Alguersuari**

## STRATEGY

The tyres were the same as Spa, with both compounds next to each other on stiffness (Medium and Soft). There are few corners for the relatively long lap distance at Monza and normally you don't experience any significant tyre issues or high degradation.

Friday was warm again, with track temperatures just under 40°C, and the forecast was for similar weather on Saturday and Sunday. I completed a tyre comparison, the results of which showed both compounds to be very similar to one another, with very low degradation of either compound. The tyre results, combined with evidence of KERS cars having the highest performance advantage of the season to date (both in qualifying and during the start) meant a one-stop was the best strategy for our team. However, it was going to be a close race with the one-stoppers ahead.

I started just behind Rubens, on the same one-stop fuel load. Only Kovalainen ahead was also on a one-stop fuel, with the top three on two-stop fuel.

I had a positive start to the race, along with Rubens: both of us got past Kovalainen on lap one, with only Hamilton, Räikkönen and Sutil ahead – all on two-stop fuel. The team managed the pace and gap to Hamilton, beating him by the last stop of the race, to take P1 and P2.

*Brawn GP's Rubens Barrichello won the Italian Grand Prix in Monza this afternoon to score his second victory of the season and his eleventh Formula One win. Team-mate Jenson Button came home in second place in his Brawn-Mercedes car to complete a fantastic weekend which sees the team's eighth victory and fourth one–two finish of the 2009 season.*

A fantastic day for Brawn GP, our fourth one–two finish. After Red Bull's haul of a solitary championship point thanks to Vettel's eighth place, Brawn, mathematically, are close to sewing up the constructors' championship – possibly at the next race in Singapore. That would be a fairy-tale scenario for a team that began the season not knowing if it was ever going to be a competitor on the Formula One stage.

Starting on the third row, behind Lewis Hamilton on pole, Adrian Sutil's revitalised Force India, Kimi Raikkonen's Ferrari, Heikki Kovalainen's McLaren and Rubens, I knew I had to get past Kovalainen, who was also fuelled heavy for a one-stop. The brilliant aspect of qualifying sixth was that the KERS cars – apart from Alonso – were all ahead. So as the lights went out, it was Kovalainen and Rubens I was chasing. It was a messy first lap. Kovalainen made it very tough. Alonso didn't get the jump with his KERS, which was good. I sat behind Kovalainen through the second chicane, then managed to put the nose up the inside in Lesmo One and got through in Lesmo Two. That was a much-needed move. Without that I might have only been third. When you succeed in your aim so early it really sets you up well for the rest of the race. So that little first-lap manoeuvre was very, very important.

In that same lap, Mark Webber, who had only qualified in tenth, went off at Della Roggia after an incident with Robert Kubica. Another nil-point finish from a Red Bull driver was another encouraging marker. I was left to race at a pace that would make the strategy work. That meant pounding out aggressive lap times to maintain the gap to the front-runners prior to the pit-stops. I was due in for refuelling and fresh tyres on lap 28 (Rubens had the more advantageous lap 29 call because he had qualified higher up the grid) and the

'*Monza was a breakthrough race for Button – he must fancy his chances of being able to defend a 14-point lead over a man in the same car over the next four grands prix.*' Andrew Benson, BBC online blog

plan worked out beautifully, with us both jumping the three two-stopping cars at their seconds stops.

In the last stages, I had Lewis chasing me. I was confident I had him covered because it's difficult to overtake here, which might sound silly as this is a circuit with a lot of straights and McLaren has KERS, but you drive accordingly. I had Shov on the radio going crazy, 'We've got to switch to Mix 2. We need all the power we can get to stay in front of Lewis and keep this far from Rubens...'

I was like: 'Shov, just chill out. I'm driving here and I know what I'm doing!'

I felt pretty confident – even with Shov in my ears quite a lot – and duly crossed the line 2.8 seconds behind Rubens. My driving style may not always betray it, but

I was pushing hard. I think Lewis – who, in pursuit of me, lost it and crashed out with only one and a half laps to go – would vouch for that. Monza is a tough circuit to push 100 per cent all the way because of the big danger of locking up the rears under braking with such low downforce. There are two chicanes at this circuit, so you have that issue twice a lap, but both Rubens and I showed a winning consistency.

It was an amazing feeling to be back up on the podium and have a great celebration with the guys in the team afterwards. I earned another eight points today, which, after accruing only 11 points in the previous five races, makes me feel we're back in business. I go to Singapore looking for a victory for sure. There are so many positives for me. I have a fourteen-point lead with 40 more points up for grabs. My closest competitor is my team-mate and we have identical cars. In theory, I can finish behind Rubens for the rest of the season and still win the title. Rubens still has a worry over his gear box (his engineer told the BBC's Ted Kravitz at Monza that he was praying for 52 laps that Rubens's gear box would hold out). Ross Brawn has made it clear that we are allowed to fight for the world championship, but that there are to be no secrets or withholding of engineering information within Brawn GP. It's going to be an exciting battle down to the wire, and I'm relishing the prospect. There are also six or so other drivers capable of winning races, so it's become a game of points accumulation.

## ITALIAN GRAND PRIX FINAL POSITIONS

| Pos | Driver | Team | Laps | Time |
| --- | --- | --- | --- | --- |
| 1 | Rubens Barrichello | Brawn-Mercedes | 53 | 01:16:21.706 |
| 2 | Jenson Button | Brawn-Mercedes | 53 | +2.8 secs |
| 3 | Kimi Räikkönen | Ferrari | 53 | +30.6 secs |
| 4 | Adrian Sutil | Force India-Mercedes | 53 | +31.1 secs |
| 5 | Fernando Alonso | Renault | 53 | +59.1 secs |
| 6 | Heikki Kovalainen | McLaren-Mercedes | 53 | +60.6 secs |
| 7 | Nick Heidfeld | BMW Sauber | 53 | +82.4 secs |
| 8 | Sebastian Vettel | RBR-Renault | 53 | +85.4 secs |
| 9 | Giancarlo Fisichella | Ferrari | 53 | +86.8 secs |
| 10 | Kazuki Nakajima | Williams-Toyota | 53 | +162.163 secs |
| 11 | Timo Glock | Toyota | 53 | +163.925 secs |
| 12 | Lewis Hamilton | McLaren-Mercedes | 52 | Accident |
| 13 | Sebastien Buemi | STR-Ferrari | 52 | DNF |
| 14 | Jarno Trulli | Toyota | 52 | +1 Lap |
| 15 | Romain Grosjean | Renault | 52 | +1 Lap |
| 16 | Nico Rosberg | Williams-Toyota | 51 | +2 Laps |
| Ret | Vitantonio Liuzzi | Force India-Mercedes | 22 | Transmission |
| Ret | Jaime Alguersuari | STR-Ferrari | 19 | Gearbox |
| Ret | Robert Kubica | BMW Sauber | 15 | Engine |
| Ret | Mark Webber | RBR-Renault | 0 | Accident |

'I feel Jenson deserves to be champion. Dare I say he would make the better ambassador for the sport? Jenson is in the middle of his career rather than at the end of it; he is photogenic; less highly strung and emotional than the Brazilian; he carries himself brilliantly and speaks intelligently (no Kimi Räikkönen-esque monosyllabic responses from Jenson); he is also a pretty chilled-out customer. After the race in Monza I was struck by the fact that he had to tell his race engineer to stop getting so worked up by the fast-closing Lewis Hamilton during the closing laps. How cool is that?' David Coulthard, Daily Telegraph

It's nice to be back up here on the podium. I'd like to be where Rubens is sat but he did a better job today. I've lost two points to Rubens but gained seven on Vettel. I still have a fourteen-point lead. I'd much rather win of course, but after the previous five races, we're back at the front. Rubens pipped me by 2.8 seconds over the weekend. He's a tough team-mate, very competitive, and it's going to be tough for the rest of the year, I know that, but I'm up for the challenge and very excited about it. We're going to take it I'm sure right down to the wire... For me it was a great result.

Rubens and I have a great relationship and we've been team-mates for years. We'll work together; we've had to pull our car back to the front and we'll see how it goes from here.

| OVERALL POINTS | |
| --- | --- |
| Jenson Button | 80 |
| Rubens Barrichello | 66 |
| Sebastian Vettel | 54 |
| Mark Webber | 51.5 |
| Kimi Räikkönen | 40 |
| Nico Rosberg | 30.5 |
| Lewis Hamilton | 27 |
| Jarno Trulli | 22.5 |
| Felipe Massa | 22 |
| Heikki Kovalainen | 20 |
| Fernando Alonso | 20 |
| Timo Glock | 16 |
| Nick Heidfeld | 12 |
| Giancarlo Fisichella | 8 |
| Robert Kubica | 8 |
| Adrian Sutil | 5 |
| Sebastien Buemi | 3 |
| Sebastien Bourdais | 2 |

'Something clicked at Monza. He was on the pace throughout the weekend, more comfortable in the car than he had been for some time, and he looked a potential winner for the first time since Turkey in June. In the end, that win didn't happen but the two Brawn drivers were neck-and-neck throughout the grand prix and the result, with a bit of luck, could easily have gone either way.'
Andrew Benson, BBC online blog

'Following Rubens Barrichello and Jenson Button's one–two in Monza, it was significant that team boss Ross Brawn wanted to stress how his drivers are sharing information on their car's set-up. His words sounded like he had recently had to bash the drivers' heads together: "I demand they do it fairly and openly... Everything has to be on the table... They have to work together properly," Brawn told us after the race.'
Ted Kravitz, BBC online blog

'And then there were two. Two drivers, both in the white overalls of Brawn, locked in what has surely now become a private duel for the Formula One World Drivers' Championship. After Sunday's Italian Grand Prix, at which the Red Bulls effectively fell out of contention, the scrap is between Jenson Button, of Frome, Somerset, and Rubens Barrichello, of Sao Paulo, Brazil'
Jonathan McEvoy, Daily Mail

# Singapore Grand Prix
# Marina Bay Street Circuit
## Friday 25 September – Sunday 27 September

**Number of laps:** 61

**Circuit length:** 5.073 km

**Race distance:** 308.950 km

**Lap record:** 1:45.599
(Kimi Räikkönen, 2008)

### MY HISTORY AT MARINA BAY

**2008 (Honda)**
Grid 12; finished 9

Last year's Singapore Grand Prix was the first Formula One night race and an amazing experience – truly one of the highlights of the year. It was great fun to drive at night, with most of the circuit pretty easy in terms of visibility, although there were two or three corners that weren't quite as well lit as the rest. That made it difficult to pick the braking distances when you arrived at the corner.

The Marina Bay Street Circuit is pretty challenging. Made up entirely of public roads with an anti-clockwise layout and lots of first- and second-gear bends in its 23 corners, it is a stop-start layout with an average speed of just 175kph and a track which demands cars run with maximum levels of downforce. A stop-start track isn't usually my favourite type of circuit, but I still enjoyed it.

With the city skyline and more than 1,500 light projectors illuminating the circuit, it's a spectacular event. I remember coming around to the start on the installation lap last year and seeing all the camera flashes as we lined up on the grid – it was a very special moment.

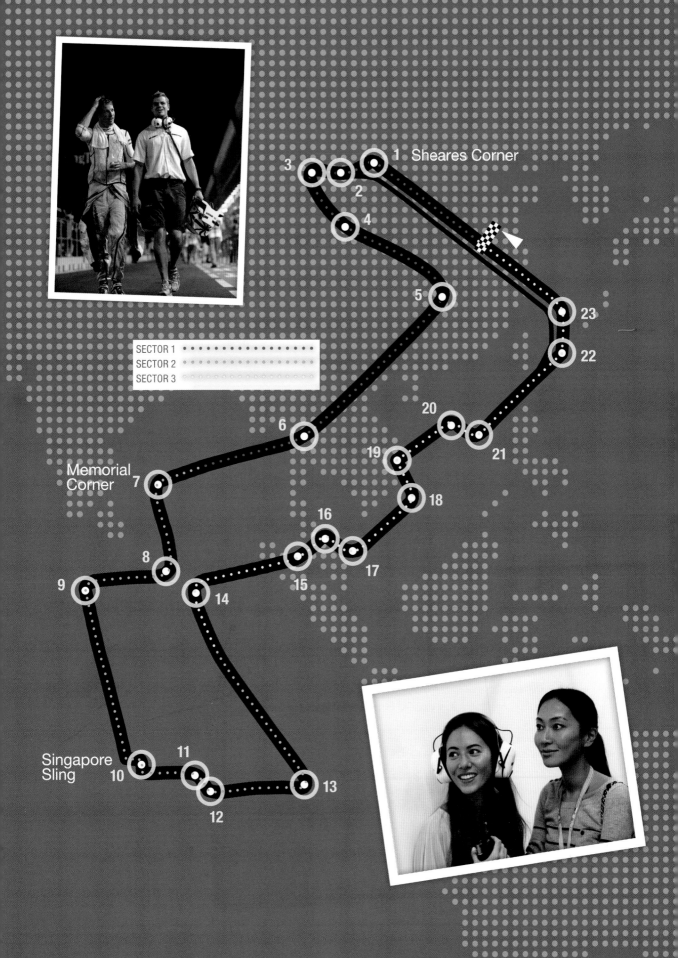

1 Sheares Corner

3

2

4

5

23

22

SECTOR 1
SECTOR 2
SECTOR 3

6

20

19

21

Memorial
Corner

7

18

8

16

9

17

14

15

Singapore
Sling

10

11

13

12

# Singapore:
## Preparation, practice and qualifying

After the jubilation of Monza I flew to Japan for a week's break. Jessica and I are renting an apartment in Midtown, Tokyo – a stylish new urban complex set in green space – for the couple of weeks that cover the two Asian races in Singapore and Japan. For me, it's the best place to relax. I love the city, the people and the food, which is very healthy.

We went for a couple of days to Hakone, a hot spring resort south-west of Tokyo. Our trip coincided with Silver Week, which is a string of five consecutive holidays in the autumn (as opposed to Golden Week which is a similar holiday period in the spring) and a popular time for travel, so it was pretty busy. It was a great place. We had our own little hot spring area attached to our room so we could enjoy it privately. And we had amazing, wholesome food, so it was the perfect relaxed build-up to the next race. People assume Japanese food is all raw fish and sushi, but there's lots of noodles and rice too. I make a point of trying most things. At lunchtime I really got into Soba noodles – a pile of grey/brown noodles we ate cold with a soya-based dipping sauce and chopped spring onions and fresh wasabi. In the evening, I could never resist the beef tepanyaki – beef is delicious here – and I also tried blowfish, which is meant to be deadly poisonous, but I'm still okay!

### THURSDAY
As last year, the race start time in Singapore is 8pm local time, so we will stay on European timing for the race weekend. This means staying awake throughout the night and sleeping most of the day to ensure that we are alert and the body is ready to react in the right way for the evening timetable. It was potentially hard – not least because I was coming from Japan, not Europe – but I had practically been running on European time in Japan, eating late and going to bed at 3am – tough on Jessica, who was working, and had to be up at 7 or 8am. Once in Singapore, though, it was easy. The gang and I were staying in the Swissotel, where they looked after us beautifully. Thick, heavy curtains blocked out the daylight so our sleep plan worked. We ate dinner at 2 or 3am, went to bed at 4am, woke up at midday and breakfasted at lunchtime. It was quite hard to find breakfast at that time, but we pounced on the idea of pancakes and fruit each day. I did change my watch to Singapore local time otherwise I'd never attend meetings at the right time!

I spent a day at the factory in Brackley before flying to Japan, driving the circuit on our simulator, which helps prompt the memory in terms of the track layout, gears and downforce levels, so I feel well prepared and looking forward to getting the weekend underway. That started when, instead of my usual circuit walk, I went out on a scooter with two helmets – one with a light smoke visor, another with a clear visor. Neither was perfect over the course of a lap, but I decided to start off with the tinted one in practice to protect against the glare on the brighter corners.

Excitement in the team is building up because this is the race where, mathematically, Brawn GP has the chance to seal the constructors' championship. To do that here, or in Japan next week, would be incredible considering our team wasn't even an official team just eight months ago. The situation brings its own stresses and I can also detect a natural bit of nervousness within the team. We do expect to be quick. We have brought a new update kit which should gain us four tenths.

### FRIDAY
It's great to be back working in Singapore and everyone is enjoying the challenge of adjusting to our different working hours. A night race is unique and the city looks beautiful as you drive around at high speed. We had a pretty full-on evening with a busy programme of set-up evaluations and tyre testing. This venue is a tough one, physically and mentally, with heat and humidity to contend with as well as the dazzling floodlights. The circuit is enclosed so tightly by barriers that total concentration is required.

The humidity is a real discomfort. The temperature is about 30°C during the day and 28°C at night, but with extremely high humidity. You get very, very sweaty and the air feels so hot and thick you feel you can't breathe enough of it in. I had to have all the air vents of my helmet closed off during practice because I've had issues in the past with carbon flakes lodging in my eye. I thought my helmet was as good

as hermetically sealed, but, even so, I got carbon in my eye yet again and had to go to the hospital at the end of the sessions. It hadn't lodged deep, but it's still alarming when the doctor whips out a needle to prise it out of your eyeball. The medical staff were brilliant, and gave me antibiotic drops and medicine to ensure it doesn't become infected.

The organisers have done a reasonable job with the circuit layout. The key is achieving consistently quick laps and that's what we worked on today. That's hard, though, when the surface is very, very bumpy and the car tends to bounce all over the place. It's an intensely physical experience for a driver trying to control the car from corner to corner over the bumps. It would be too easy to end up in the barriers. The bumps also make it difficult to set up a car. Any change you make is compromised by the bumps. Still, the car feels reasonable and with some more work later tonight, we should be ready for a good weekend. We have shown great pace throughout, topping the time sheets in first practice.

## SATURDAY

*A tough evening for Brawn GP at the Marina Bay Street Circuit saw Rubens Barrichello qualify in fifth position for tomorrow's Singapore Grand Prix with team-mate Jenson Button qualifying in twelfth position. Rubens will start in tenth position on the grid due to a five-place gearbox change penalty.*

I was anticipating a strong showing in qualifying, but today was disastrous. I was all set up to continue from where we left off yesterday. The only change I made was in reverting to a clear visor, because the tinted one was just too dark in three or four corners. Clear wasn't perfect either. The way the light refracts through the layers of tear-offs left a luminous, bright patch at the top of the visor – but that was a minor inconvenience easily forgotten in the excitement of qualifying.

The car felt pretty good in Q1 and I set the second quickest time after Lewis Hamilton, which was a positive start. No alarm bells. We had a bit of understeer, so we made some changes for Q2, but unfortunately it made the car very difficult under braking and I locked the front left tyre up into Turn 7, which lost me a lot of time. With a flat-spotted front tyre, it's impossible to make the time up around here. So that was that. Eliminated in Q2. My qualifying was over.

It was all a bit of a surprise, to put it mildly. We thought it was going to be a walk in the park and suddenly we were in the mix, and then I failed to get out of Q2. It was more than a bit frustrating because in hindsight, as a team, we were a bit complacent. We have four sets of Option tyres and four sets of Prime tyres for qualifying and the race. In Q1, we ran a new Prime tyre and a new Option tyre and we were second quickest. In Q2, we ran an old Option tyre on the initial run and then changed to a new Option. Realistically, if we were uncompetitive, we would have run two new Option tyres, but I was left with only one run with the new tyre to put in a quick lap. We'd lowered the tyre pressure a bit to give more grip, but that meant the car was lower and because of that I hit the bump on Turn 7 when I got on the brakes and both fronts locked solid. It was unbearably frustrating. I went on the radio and said, 'Guys, this is the way to lose the world championship...' I meant me, not them, but as a team – and I mean myself, my engineers and Ross – we should not have been taking big risks in Q2. Our aim should be to ensure we get safely to Q3.

We'll make the best of it tomorrow, of course, but starting from twelfth on the grid is going to make it a tough race. The team had a bad day overall, with Rubens making a mistake by pushing too hard on his second run in Q3 and putting his car in the wall at Turn 5. It is such a strange result for us because we have had very good pace all weekend on a circuit where we thought we would be very quick. The situation is softened slightly for me in that Rubens took a five-place penalty because his car needed a gearbox change. All this on a weekend we'd had such high hopes for. This season really is proving to have peaks of highs and lows.

I wasn't in a great mood on Saturday night. Jessica was fantastic. Generally, I hate talking about major frustrations because my family and friends naturally try and comfort me by saying 'it's not that bad'. And I'm aware that they're hiding their own feelings of disappointment, because of course they're going through exactly the same pain as me. But it really was that bad – I was starting 12th when I'm trying to win a world championship. The Red Bulls are at the front – Vettel on the front row just behind Hamilton on pole, and Webber in fourth – and obviously they still have a chance to challenge us in the championship, so we have made it difficult for ourselves. I went back to the hotel and wished everyone goodnight. I was facing a sleepless night but Jessica told me to lie down and said she was going to give me a foot massage. I have to say she is extremely good at it, and as she rubbed my feet, she said, 'So Jenson, tell me about today and how you're going to make it right tomorrow...' and I found myself opening up, quite therapeutically, and starting to look at my situation from a more positive perspective.

## BRAWN TECHNICAL UPDATES

Singapore is a circuit very much like Monaco. Short straights and lots of first- and second-gear corners require a maximum downforce set-up to give good braking stability and traction. It is by some margin the hardest circuit for the brakes as there are so many braking zones and so few straights to cool them down again. This causes the brake temperatures to rise and that in turn causes high wear. Singapore is also one of the bumpiest tracks; this makes it easy to lock wheels on braking and hard to get on the throttle for corner exits. The race is unique in that it is hosted at night – although the artificial lighting system is very impressive and from the driver's point of view, it is much the same as driving in daylight. This also means that you don't get sunshine warming the tarmac, so, although the air temperature is very high, the track temperature rarely exceeds low 30s and warm-up can be a problem.

We had a good day on Friday. It was difficult to manage the Super Soft tyre as it tended to grain due to the aggressive nature of the circuit, although we were in a better position than most teams and our long runs were competitive. However, we were struggling on single-lap pace with the Super Soft tyre. This was evident on Saturday when I got bumped out in Q2.

In the race, the car was working well. We'd focused on long-run performance and once I was in free air we were able to make good progress for a fifth-place finish, a reasonable result considering our poor performance the day before. On the other hand, we could have achieved much more if we had qualified better. We had our own brake issues during the race, our right front disc had started to get very thin and once you lose material, it heats up quickly and is difficult to keep cool, even when driving slowly. At this stage I was attacking Vettel, but we had to back off and make sure we got to the finish.

# Singapore:
## The race

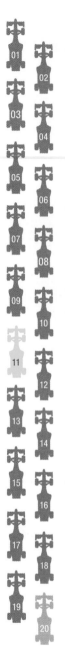

1. Lewis Hamilton
2. Sebastian Vettel
3. Nico Rosberg
4. Mark Webber
5. Fernando Alonso
6. Timo Glock
7. Robert Kubica
8. Heikki Kovalainen
9. Rubens Barrichello (gearbox penalty)
10. Kazuki Nakajima
11. **Jenson Button**
12. Kimi Räikkönen
13. Sebastien Buemi
14. Jarno Trulli
15. Adrian Sutil
16. Jaime Alguersuari
17. Giancarlo Fisichella
18. Romain Grosjean
19. Vitantonio Liuzzi
20. Nick Heidfeld (pit start)

### STRATEGY

The tyres were the same as for Valencia, Monaco and Budapest (Super Soft and Soft), with both compounds having the same low temperature range.

Singapore is unique in that as the sessions progress (P1 and P2 especially) the temperatures actually drop, as the sun goes down and night falls. The track started at 37°C in P1, dropping to 33°C by the end of P2, making a considerable difference to both car and tyre performance. The Friday tyre testing showed the Super Soft tyre to be faster than the Soft for the first three laps, but degrading very quickly, with the Soft tyre being faster during the race as a result. The race tyre plan was therefore two reasonable stints on the Soft tyre, with a shorter stint at the end on the Super Soft. The fuel effect is very high at Singapore, with the cars struggling with the bumpy track with heavy fuel on-board, as well as trouble with brake usage. We opted for a two-stop strategy as a default, based on how competitive we would be.

I qualified P12, behind Nakajima on the grid, with Rubens demoted to P10 following a gearbox penalty. Being outside the top ten, we are able to choose a starting fuel load after qualifying, which represents a reasonable strategic advantage. I was fuelled heavier than all of the cars ahead – since we would be faster running longer than cars stopping earlier and therefore able to make up places in the race.

*Brawn GP extended their lead in the constructors' championship at the Singapore Grand Prix this evening with Jenson Button and Rubens Barrichello bringing their Brawn-Mercedes cars home in fifth and sixth positions respectively.*

I woke up and started to look for positives. As soon as I'm close to the car, I always get a familiar resurgence of optimism for the next session on track, and that was fuelled by the news that Nick Heidfeld's BMW was found to be underweight by the scrutineers after qualifying, and he was penalised fifteen places on the grid. As a result, I moved up one place on the readjusted grid to start from 11th and on the clean side of the track – a welcome little bonus.

The conditions were hot and humid, and the air had that thickness you detect before a thunderstorm breaks. It added to the ominous feeling of having Kimi Räikkönen in his KERS-boosted Ferrari sitting behind me on the grid. KERS, or Kinetic Energy Recovery System, is a boost of power collected from energy built up through braking and supplied at the push of a button. To the cars that are fitted with it, it is worth an extra 80 horsepower, which is more than ten per cent of our engine power. KERS drivers can push the button once per lap, when they're travelling at more than 100km per hour. Our car doesn't have it, but I've spoken to Lewis and he says it makes a significant difference. The classic time to use it is off the start, once the car has reached 100km per hour. If it's a relatively long run down to the first corner, KERS cars can make up at least two grid places.

So it's frustrating if you have a KERS car next to you or just behind you on the grid. Thankfully, at Singapore it's a quite a short run to Turn 1. My priority was to get past Kazuki Nakajima's Williams off the line or as early as possible or my strategy was compromised. I had to keep in touch with Kovalainen, Kubica and Barrichello. It's been a season of important first-lap passes and I enjoyed getting the job done and climbing up a place to run in 10th. That one move made

*'We need to see a champion's drive from Button. Monza was good but he was beaten by his team-mate, but these are impressive laps here from Button. Those few laps [enabling him to jump Rubens at his second stop] could have won him the world championship.'* Martin Brundle, BBC TV

my race. From 10th, I could let our strategy play out, though the first stint was quite frustrating as I could see Rubens getting away from me while I was stuck behind Heikki with a heavier fuel load. I was waiting and waiting behind his McLaren. He made so many mistakes, he was costing me so much time each lap. Heikki was pitting two laps before me and I was so excited about the prospect of putting in a couple of fast laps as soon as he'd disappeared down the pit-lane entrance, but then the safety car came out. Adrian Sutil had had an accident and the timing of the safety car's arrival did not play into our hands. I had to pit on that lap – and wave goodbye to the three places I was due to make up through the first round of stops – and I was still behind Kovalainen. I did jump Webber in the pits so I was up to 8th. The running order was Hamilton, Rosberg, Vettel, Glock, Alonso, Barrichello, Kovalainen, then me. Rubens backed it up a bit and let the front run away, then floored it and Heikki tried to keep up, but he was all over the place. The guy could win a race if he was just consistent.

Rubens pitted, followed by Heikki, and I had four laps before my stop to kick in and pull out some fast laps, which I did. The timing screens went green, green, green – indicating personal best sector times – and I came out in front of Heikki and Rubens, who had pressed the neutral button too late and stalled when he came in for his second stop. Shov was on the radio saying, 'It's going to be very tight. Rubens is going to be on your left when you come out.' And he was, safely behind me. Rosberg, like Vettel, had taken a penalty for exceeding the pit-lane speed limit,

so I was up in fifth and happy with the way the car was working. Vettel was in front of me and I was enjoying putting my foot down and catching him over a second a lap. We didn't have to take any risks, but I kept hustling him in case he faced similar brake issues to Webber, who'd retired with a dramatic explosion of black smoke with a front brake failure. The team came on the radio and told me to slow down, with a warning about our brakes overheating. Then they came on again and told me to back off more, saying the brakes wouldn't last. I complied and slowed two to three seconds per lap, then on the last lap Ross came on the radio and said, 'Jenson, you've got to push, you're racing Rubens. He's right behind you...'

I judged it right and crossed the finish line in 5th, only one place behind Vettel and one ahead of Rubens, collecting four very important points. Considering the awful qualifying session, this was a very satisfying race for me. Somehow, with luck and a shrewd strategy, we saved a potentially damaging situation and I increased my lead even after qualifying in 12th position. The podium finishers – Hamilton, Glock and Alonso – took the most points, but they're not in the title hunt. With Webber's DNF classification, his title hopes are over, and we are back to three title contenders for the remaining three races of the season.

I felt very tired. I had one drink at Amber Lounge and left after ten minutes. The weekend hasn't panned out as we expected at all, but I'll go to Japan tomorrow feeling very positive and looking forward to the next race. I'm fifteen points ahead, three races to go.

## SINGAPORE GRAND PRIX FINAL POSITIONS

| Pos | Driver | Team | Laps | Time |
|-----|--------|------|------|------|
| 1 | Lewis Hamilton | McLaren-Mercedes | 61 | 1:56:06.337 |
| 2 | Timo Glock | Toyota | 61 | +9.6 secs |
| 3 | Fernando Alonso | Renault | 61 | +16.6 secs |
| 4 | Sebastian Vettel | RBR-Renault | 61 | +20.2 secs |
| 5 | Jenson Button | Brawn-Mercedes | 61 | +30.0 secs |
| 6 | Rubens Barrichello | Brawn-Mercedes | 61 | +31.8 secs |
| 7 | Heikki Kovalainen | McLaren-Mercedes | 61 | +36.1 secs |
| 8 | Robert Kubica | BMW Sauber | 61 | +55.0 secs |
| 9 | Kazuki Nakajima | Williams-Toyota | 61 | +56.0 secs |
| 10 | Kimi Räikkönen | Ferrari | 61 | +58.8 secs |
| 11 | Nico Rosberg | Williams-Toyota | 61 | +59.7 secs |
| 12 | Jarno Trulli | Toyota | 61 | +73.0 secs |
| 13 | Giancarlo Fisichella | Ferrari | 61 | +79.8 secs |
| 14 | Vitantonio Liuzzi | Force India-Mercedes | 61 | +93.5 secs |
| Ret | Jaime Alguersuari | STR-Ferrari | 47 | Brakes |
| Ret | Sebastien Buemi | STR-Ferrari | 47 | Gearbox |
| Ret | Mark Webber | RBR-Renault | 45 | Brakes |
| Ret | Adrian Sutil | Force India-Mercedes | 23 | Accident damage |
| Ret | Nick Heidfeld | BMW Sauber | 19 | Accident |
| Ret | Romain Grosjean | Renault | 3 | Brakes |

It was a good race for me and I'm happy with fifth position and four more points today. Getting ahead of Kazuki off the line was key and that really made my race. The first stint was quite frustrating as I could see Rubens getting away from me while I was stuck behind Heikki with a heavier fuel load. The safety car then made it very difficult as I still had fuel for a few more laps and should have been able to make up two places at my first stop. I had to put in some quick laps before my second stop to close up to Rubens and then we were pushing Sebastian before deciding to save the brakes and settle for fifth position. The weekend hasn't been quite what we expected but it's good to come through from 11th on the grid to score points. I'll go to Japan tomorrow feeling very positive.

## OVERALL POINTS

| | |
|---|---|
| Jenson Button | 84 |
| Rubens Barrichello | 69 |
| Sebastian Vettel | 59 |
| Mark Webber | 51.5 |
| Kimi Räikkönen | 40 |
| Lewis Hamilton | 37 |
| Nico Rosberg | 30.5 |
| Fernando Alonso | 26 |
| Timo Glock | 24 |
| Jarno Trulli | 22.5 |
| Felipe Massa | 22 |
| Heikki Kovalainen | 22 |
| Nick Heidfeld | 12 |
| Robert Kubica | 9 |
| Giancarlo Fisichella | 8 |
| Adrian Sutil | 5 |
| Sebastien Buemi | 3 |
| Sebastien Bourdais | 2 |

*'Yo Jens, Brilliant drive mate. You got this!'*
Toby Scheckter

*'Golly gosh nail biting stuff!
Hang in there please Jenson.'*
Jocelyn Broughton

*'That was a work of art bro. I cried when you put in those stunning laps before your pit stop, Congratulations. Hugsx'*
Samantha, sister

*'Oh my god, are you trying to send me to an early grave! Well done for today, big hugs.'*
Natasha, sister

# Japanese Grand Prix
## Suzuka International Racing Course
### Friday 2 October – Sunday 4 October

**Number of laps:** 53

**Circuit length:** 5.807 km

**Race distance:** 307.573 km

**Lap record:** 1:31.540
(Kimi Raikkonen, 2005)

## MY HISTORY AT SUZUKA

**2006 (Honda)**
Grid 7; finished 4

**2005 (BAR-Honda)**
Grid 2; finished 5

**2004 (BAR-Honda)**
Grid 5; finished 3

**2003 (BAR-Honda)**
Grid 9; finished 4

**2002 (Renault)**
Grid 10; finished 6

**2001 (Benetton-Renault)**
Grid 9; finished 7

**2000 (Williams-BMW))**
Grid 5; finished 5

Suzuka is such a fun circuit – I enjoy racing here so much more than Fuji, the other venue for the Japanese Grand Prix. Suzuka's eighteen-turn figure-of-eight layout is unique and I have lots of good memories from competing here over the years. With the famous Spoon Curve and the high-speed 130R corner, it's a real driver's circuit with a thrilling fast-flowing lap, similar to Silverstone and Spa. Everyone has missed having it on the calendar for the last few years.

130R is one of the fastest corners in Formula One and you really have to think about how you approach it. We might not be flat through there this year, but it is still a real buzz to take the corner carrying speeds of 300kph. I've had some moments there in the past! I've always enjoyed great support at Suzuka from the Japanese fans, who are so enthusiastic about the sport. I don't expect the track characteristics to favour our car as much as the Red Bull so it'll be a difficult one, but I can't wait to race here again and put on a great show.

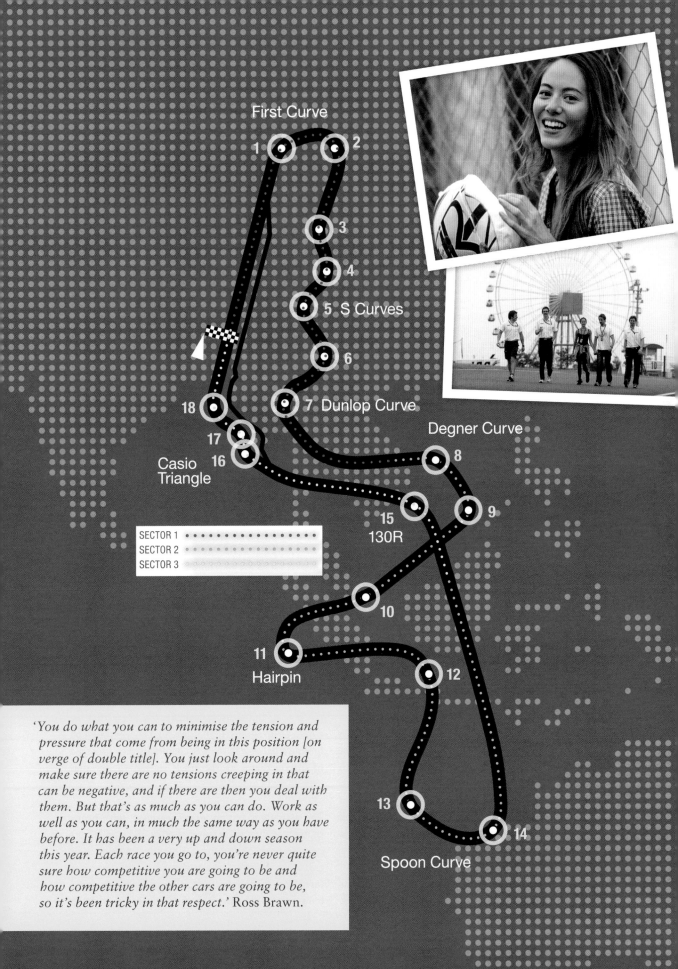

First Curve

1    2

3

4

5   S Curves

6

7   Dunlop Curve

18

17

16

Casio
Triangle

Degner Curve

8

15    9
130R

SECTOR 1
SECTOR 2
SECTOR 3

10

11

Hairpin

12

13        14

Spoon Curve

'You do what you can to minimise the tension and
pressure that come from being in this position [on
verge of double title]. You just look around and
make sure there are no tensions creeping in that
can be negative, and if there are then you deal with
them. But that's as much as you can do. Work as
well as you can, in much the same way as you have
before. It has been a very up and down season
this year. Each race you go to, you're never quite
sure how competitive you are going to be and
how competitive the other cars are going to be,
so it's been tricky in that respect.' Ross Brawn.

# Japan:
## Preparation, practice and qualifying

After Singapore I flew straight to Japan and arrived in Tokyo early on Tuesday morning. I went to the gym to get the flight out of my system and then joined some of the team for a PR event at Bridgestone, which culminated in a trip to an amazing restaurant in Ginza where the speciality is mushrooms and truffles. It's literally a temple to the stuff. The head chef/proprietor is a massive fan of motorsport and helps young drivers find sponsorship through karting, junior formulas and Formula Three. In return they work as waiters in his restaurant. So there were lots of photos taken and exchanges of mini helmets and they showered us with gifts and sweets. We were also given these amazing sushi knives, which are made in the same way as a Japanese samurai sword in a process where the steel is heated, hammered flat, folded, hammered again, and so on, as many as 30 times to add strength to the blade.

Sitting in that kind of supportive atmosphere is galvanising when the world at large is debating the mathematical possibilities both of Brawn taking the constructors' title and me securing the drivers' crown this weekend. I'm aware of the potential scenarios – of course I am! I know I could fulfil my life's dream in Suzuka if 1) I win and Rubens finishes fourth or lower; 2) I'm second and Rubens finishes sixth or lower; 3) I'm third and Rubens finishes eighth or lower; 4) I'm fourth and Rubens does not score. However, I'm not taking all that number-crunching into the race weekend with me. I know this circuit doesn't suit our car and I'm focusing simply on getting the maximum out of it in order to score as many points as possible. Then we'll see how things pan out.

On Thursday morning, Ross, Rubens, his mate, my gang and Nicola Armstrong, who is the Brawn team's media contact, all took the Shinkanshen bullet train from Tokyo to Nagoya, and then another from Nagoya to Suzuka. We arrived at the circuit and began our usual walk around the track at 1pm. Situated on Honshu, the largest of the Japanese islands, the track is owned by our team's former owner, the Honda Motor Company, and was built in 1962 as a test circuit before hosting its first Formula One race in 1987. It's such a beautiful configuration. Whether you've had good, bad or indifferent experiences,

you always remember the thrill of driving here. So there was our little gang – Shov, Bono, Jessica and myself – strolling along and about two-thirds of the way round, I heard the distinctive buzzing noise from the karting circuit where I'd raced in 1996 and 1997. I could see national-standard karters racing around the track, which has similar characteristics to the Formula One track, and all sorts of good memories flooded back.

Suzuka has an incredible history of hosting title deciders. In 1988 Ayrton Senna won his first championship here. The place is entrenched in people's minds as the circuit where Senna and Prost took each other out in consecutive years – notably in 1989 when they were both driving McLaren Hondas – in order to secure the drivers' title. Little did I know when we got to the chicane, the very scene of that incident, that myself and Rubens, one behind the other fighting for title-clinching points, might be in the same sort of situation. A Brazilian and a driver whose style has been compared to Alain's!

### FRIDAY

The weather forecast was poor, with lots of rain predicted, and that's what we woke up to – overcast skies as far as the eye could see. The morning session started on a wet track which began to dry out as it progressed. But even in wet running we could see we were struggling in the first sector with the change of direction at high speed required through the S Curves. The sequence through turns 3 to 6 is like a snake wiggling all the way up the hill and the quick changes of direction cause understeer in our car. If you go down the usual route of dialling out the understeer, the rear of the car gets twitchy. We knew that we would be up against it all weekend. I concentrated on finding a balance in the wet conditions then switched to Intermediates as the track started to dry out, managing 17 laps.

The afternoon session was a washout, with heavy showers leading to a saturated track and small rivers on some parts of the circuit. There was nothing to be gained or learnt by going out again as the weather forecast predicted dry qualifying and race sessions. I hung around, chatted with the engineers to come up

with our run plan, went on Twitter. I felt sorry for the fans, who are so fanatical and have paid to come and watch a washed-out session.

Normally we eat at the track on Friday night, but the washout meant we were ahead of schedule and could pack up earlier. We all went to an amazing restaurant for beef sukiyaki. We are so lucky in this sport in our opportunities to travel. Each host city or circuit always wants to put out their best local facilities, and the restaurants in particular relish looking after Formula One visitors. We all sat around a big table, in the middle of which was a big pan full of boiling stock. You put thin slices of beef, mushrooms, noodles, cabbage and vegetables into it, let it simmer for a bit and then you all eat communally, taking bits out and dipping them in raw egg from individual little bowls in front of you. At the end you're left with a delicious soup. It's so tasty and such a novel way to eat. It was a great 'team' experience.

## SATURDAY

*Brawn GP's Rubens Barrichello and Jenson Button came through a chaotic and delayed qualifying session at the Suzuka circuit today to qualify their Brawn-Mercedes cars in fifth and seventh positions respectively for tomorrow's Japanese Grand Prix. However, both drivers have been penalised with five-place grid penalties for failing to reduce speed under the yellow flag in Q2.*

I arrived at the circuit in crisp sunshine and Ross looked like the happiest man I've ever seen. Rain during qualifying would have really set us back. We knew we were losing five tenths a lap to the Red Bulls, but still we couldn't ignore the thrilling prospect of possibly securing the constructors' title this weekend. We were losing seven-tenths to the quick cars in Sector 1 and, even going well through sectors 2 and 3, we couldn't pull back more than a tenth in each, which left an aggregate loss of five-tenths per lap to the Red Bulls. So that trend, noted early season, about the opposing characteristics of the Brawns and Red Bulls is still there.

When I went out for my run in qualifying, the car came to me and I felt confident of a reasonable result. It was warm and sunny... and then it turned out to be the most stressful qualifying I have ever experienced. That was Rubens's opinion, too. You rarely get three red flags in one qualifying hour, but, with so little practice yesterday, and the fact we hadn't raced here for three years, it was bound to be a bit testing for the new drivers.

Q1 was fine – Rubens and I were second and third fastest. Q2 was heavily disrupted, first with huge crashes by Jaime Alguersuari and then Timo Glock, who had to have a screen put around him whilst being attended to by the medics, but we still finished second or third. I was happy, we put 50-odd kilos of fuel in the car. But Q3 produced another red flag when Heikki Kovalainen put his McLaren in the wall so I had only one flying lap at the end of the session. I was really looking forward to it, but the car felt very, very tricky again in Sector 1. I struggled with rear grip and actually lost three-tenths to Rubens, who was running more downforce. That's where I lost the time, as the car was working well through the rest of the lap.

So I was seventh and, disappointing though it was, I thought I could live with that, get some good points, perhaps even a podium finish. But other drivers, especially Fernando Alonso, had complained that some cars had not slowed down sufficiently under the yellow flags in Q2, so a group of us were brought in before the stewards. The regulations state clearly that you have to reduce speed and I hadn't because, in that split second that you have to react when you see a yellow flag, I could also see the green flag on the other side of where the broken wing mirror was lying on the track and I thought to lift off, on a corner, was more dangerous. But we all got a five-place penalty – Rubens, Adrian Sutil, Alonso (ironically) and myself. Rules are rules and I respect them. Penalties were being doled out by the dozen – Buemi for holding Kubica, Kovalainen for a gearbox change, Glock for not starting. The way the FIA institute the penalties is very specific. They start with the provisional grid, then move back each penalised driver in the chronological order in which each offence was committed. That left a very strange grid and I ended up in tenth, having moved back three positions, while Rubens only moved back one in the re-shuffle – which didn't seem fair. Rubens woke up a happy man on Sunday while I woke up incredibly annoyed.

'Best of luck Button... Give it some now we're at the business end of the season!' Ben Payne

'Keep it going man, you're doing an awesome job, take care, Paul' Paul Ryman

## BRAWN TECHNICAL UPDATES

Suzuka is a very high speed track, the first sector is a sequence of very fast corners and we had struggled to match cars like the Red Bull on this type of circuit. We hadn't expected to be very competitive here so our focus was to make sure we still achieved the best possible result and didn't allow Red Bull to take too much out of our championship lead. It's very easy on the brakes and the smooth surface allows you to run the car low and stiff.

It's one of those circuits where balance is everything – if the car feels good in the high-speed section it is quick. If not, you can be losing nearly a second in the first sector alone. Friday was wet all day, we did some short runs in these conditions but as the remainder of the weekend was forecast to be dry we didn't want to use up engine mileage and stayed in the garage for P2.

Saturday was the first dry day and that meant a busy schedule. We got some balance work done on the Prime tyre. As expected, we were struggling in Sector 1 but had good pace in sectors 2 and 3. Going into qualifying we didn't expect to be on the front row but were hopeful we wouldn't be too far back from it. It was a difficult session due a number of heavy crashes causing a series of red and yellow flags. However, Rubens had managed P5 and I was P7. Unfortunately both of us failed to lift for a yellow flag after Buemi spread debris on the track, and we were penalised meaning we started the race in 6th and 10th places respectively.

# Japan:
## The race

1. Sebastian Vettel
2. Jarno Trulli
3. Lewis Hamilton
4. Nick Heidfeld
5. Kimi Räikkönen
6. Rubens Barrichello (5-place penalty)
7. Nico Rosberg
8. Adrian Sutil (5-place penalty)
9. Robert Kubica
10. **Jenson Button (5-place penalty)**
11. Heikki Kovalainen (gearbox penalty)
12. Jaime Alguersuari
13. Sebastien Buemi (5-place penalty)
14. Giancarlo Fisichella
15. Kazuki Nakajima
16. Fernando Alonso (5-place penalty)
17. Romain Grosjean
18. Vitantonio Liuzzi (gearbox penalty)
19. Mark Webber (pit start)

## STRATEGY

The Suzuka tyre compounds were the Hard and Soft compounds (the same as in Sepang, Barcelona and Silverstone). The track has similar demands on tyres to Silverstone, though it's different in as much as both the left and right tyres are worked hard, thanks to the figure-of-eight layout.

Friday was very wet, with only Wet and Intermediate tyres being used all day. Saturday morning was the first dry running we had, with a small tyre and set-up program being completed. The two compounds looked similar, with the Soft tyre degrading more over a long run, meaning that after just a few laps the Hard compound was faster. We therefore decided that the risk of starting the Soft tyre, even though the track would improve, was too great for the race.

*Brawn GP moved a step closer to securing the 2009 constructors' championship at the Japanese Grand Prix in Suzuka today. Points-scoring finishes for Rubens Barrichello and Jenson Button in seventh and eighth positions see the team requiring half a point from the remaining two races to take the title.*

Starting tenth, with a KERS car behind me and a long drag down to Turn 1, I knew I would have to be aggressive. We'd worked hard to fine-tune the front wing setting – it's difficult to find the optimum working range. I was on a two-stop strategy and I had to make the best job possible of picking up points after our eventful qualifying session.

I had a reasonable start, a bit of wheel spin because we were on the less grippy side of the track, but not too bad, and Heikki Kovalainen in his KERS-boosted McLaren predictably rocketed past me before I took second gear. I was vying with Giancarlo Fisichella's Ferrari into Turn 1 for 12th place, but muscled ahead. Robert Kubica, ahead of me, was stopping longer and I knew I had to get past him early. We were weaving about a bit. On lap three, through 130R and into the last corner, the chicane, I jumped him down the inside – it worked and I was very pleased with myself!

My progress was hindered by the combination of Kovalainen's McLaren and Adrian Sutil's Force India. The pair were all over each other, an accident waiting to happen, and I was suffering from understeer in the choppy air behind them. It wasn't possible to pass them because both cars were fast on the straights, and it was getting frustrating because at the pace they forced I was in danger of being leapfrogged by Kubica and even the Toro Rosso of Jaime Alguersuari at the first round of stops. But their accident finally did happen, at the chicane four laps before my pit stop, and I moved into the points in 8th position. I knew I was stopping earlier so I put my foot down, pulling a second on the cars around me. Shov was filling me in on the gap between myself and Rosberg and Rubens, and I was reeling out qualifying lap after qualifying lap, so I had a good first stint. Shov called me in early for my second stop and I exited and went straight onto another flying lap taking lots of time out of Rosberg and Rubens. Rubens pitted and came out just in

front – and then the safety car intervened, ruining my weekend's work yet again. There's a speed limit we're supposed to stick to and Rosberg obviously didn't – he went round a lot quicker than us, pitted and came out in front of Rubens and Heidfeld. He could not have done that without speeding.

For the rest of the race I pushed hard to get in front of Rubens but I had Kubica behind me. He tried it on me at Spoon and there were a few hair-raising late-braking moves in the hairpin when he nearly went into the back of me, but I held him off and finished in 8th. When you think I finished one place behind Rubens, having started four places behind him, I'd have to say this was a good race. I can't understand why Rosberg was not penalised for speeding under the safety car. It leaves an awkward question for the remaining races this season: What do we do now behind a safety car? Do we stick to the limit, or do we ignore it as Rosberg did and hope we get away with it?

Three points from Rubens's 7th place and my 8th place meant, gallingly, we hadn't secured the constructors' championship for the team. We were just half a point short. We hung around in the evening waiting for the stewards to make a decision on Rosberg, but no action was taken. It was just as well it wasn't won off the track, late in the evening, because all the adrenalin and emotion had drained away. When we do sew up the constructors' title in Brazil, we reasoned, it will be just the biggest, best buzz to cross the line with all the team on the pit-lane wall cheering the Brawn cars as we fly past. I felt sorry for Ross, though. He badly wanted it concluded just to get rid of some of the stress and pressure on the team.

Vettel was imperious, as he should have been in a fast car that was perfectly suited to Suzuka. His victory

emphatically puts him back into the title chase. All the talk has been of Rubens versus me, but I certainly don't underestimate Sebastian. Of course he's a threat. He's a quick driver, he has an awesome car. On a fast circuit he walked it with no team-mate to race against (Webber had started 20th after an accident in qualifying and finished 17th). The reassuring thing for us is that the Red Bulls shouldn't be as dominant in Brazil and Abu Dhabi. The cars will be our equal in Interlagos, but Abu Dhabi should suit us more.

The final stage of the season is going to be exciting. I head into the last two races with a fourteen-point lead over Rubens and sixteen over Sebastian. I've been in the 'chased' position before in Formula Ford in 1998 when I had Dan Wheldon and Derek Hayes hunting me down. Personally, I'd love to win both the drivers' and the constructors' title in Brazil – so I'm praying for dry weather. Our wet pace is not so good.

Over the last four races it's been very close between Rubens and myself. In qualifying he's beaten me, but in races I've had the better pace. A Formula One championship season is a seventeen-race contest. I did all my winning at the start of the year, but to finish on the tail of Vettel's Red Bull in Singapore (when he started from second and I started 11th) was a good example of how I've made the best out of bad situations to keep the championship alive. I'd love to return to going from pole to victory over the course of a weekend, but our car has not been consistently dominant. Apart from a few sessions when I've made a small mistake and suffered, there are rational mechanical reasons, or bad luck, to explain our downturn in performance. To win, you have to get the most out of a great car and you have to extract the best when it's not great – it's all about building up points until you reach an unassailable position.

## JAPANESE GRAND PRIX FINAL POSITIONS

| Pos | Driver | Team | Laps | Time |
|-----|--------|------|------|------|
| 1 | Sebastian Vettel | RBR-Renault | 53 | 1:28:20.443 |
| 2 | Jarno Trulli | Toyota | 53 | +4.8 secs |
| 3 | Lewis Hamilton | McLaren-Mercedes | 53 | +6.4 secs |
| 4 | Kimi Räikkönen | Ferrari | 53 | +7.9 secs |
| 5 | Nico Rosberg | Williams-Toyota | 53 | +8.7 secs |
| 6 | Nick Heidfeld | BMW Sauber | 53 | +9.5 secs |
| 7 | Rubens Barrichello | Brawn-Mercedes | 53 | +10.6 secs |
| 8 | Jenson Button | Brawn-Mercedes | 53 | +11.4 secs |
| 9 | Robert Kubica | BMW Sauber | 53 | +11.7 secs |
| 10 | Fernando Alonso | Renault | 53 | +13.0 secs |
| 11 | Heikki Kovalainen | McLaren-Mercedes | 53 | +13.7 secs |
| 12 | Giancarlo Fisichella | Ferrari | 53 | +14.5 secs |
| 13 | Adrian Sutil | Force India-Mercedes | 53 | +14.9 secs |
| 14 | Vitantonio Liuzzi | Force India-Mercedes | 53 | +15.7 secs |
| 15 | Kazuki Nakajima | Williams-Toyota | 53 | +17.9 secs |
| 16 | Romain Grosjean | Renault | 52 | +1 Lap |
| Ret | Mark Webber | RBR-Renault | 51 | +2 Laps |
| Ret | Jaime Alguersuari | STR-Ferrari | 43 | Accident |
| Ret | Sebastien Buemi | STR-Ferrari | 11 | Clutch |

'You have to assume that Button can take a fifth or two seventh places in Brazil and Abu Dhabi, but he really needs a 'champion's drive' to satisfy the fans and media that he is a worthy title holder. Mind you, David Coulthard and I agree that we would both have loved to "limp home" to become world champion with six victories. Many others have won with more dominant cars and fewer victories.' Martin Brundle, BBC TV

*'Wow Jens! I'm still shaking after that race. Especially after the safety car! Brilliant pass on Kubica and drive to catch Rubens. Love from Mum'*

*'Crazy weekend little bruv, hope next race is more straight forward! PLEASE? Ha ha. Great drive and bring on Brazil. Lots of love xxx'*
Tanya, sister

Starting from 12th place on the grid was always going to make for a tough race but my pace was really good in the race and I was very happy with the performance of the car. I was pulling massive amounts of time out of the guys in front of me but they were on heavier fuel loads which held me up as it's difficult to overtake here. I did the best that I could in the car that we had this weekend and we got the maximum performance out of it with a points-scoring finish. I only lost one point to Rubens which is my main priority. Obviously we lost nine to Sebastian but we were expecting them to be strong here. We go to two circuits now which should suit the characteristics of our car so I'm excited about the end of the season and already looking forward to the next race in Brazil.

## OVERALL POINTS

| | |
|---|---|
| Jenson Button | 85 |
| Rubens Barrichello | 71 |
| Sebastian Vettel | 69 |
| Mark Webber | 51.5 |
| Kimi Räikkönen | 45 |
| Lewis Hamilton | 43 |
| Nico Rosberg | 34.5 |
| Jarno Trulli | 30.5 |
| Fernando Alonso | 26 |
| Timo Glock | 24 |
| Felipe Massa | 22 |
| Heikki Kovalainen | 22 |
| Nick Heidfeld | 15 |
| Robert Kubica | 9 |
| Giancarlo Fisichella | 8 |
| Adrian Sutil | 5 |
| Sebastien Buemi | 3 |
| Sebastien Bourdais | 2 |

# Brazilian Grand Prix
## Interlagos
## Friday 16 October – Sunday 18 October

Interlagos – named after its location between the two man-made lakes that provide water and electricity to Sao Paulo – is a track that has special memories for me as I scored my first world championship points here, for Williams, in 2000. The circuit is the highest of the year at 800 metres above sea level, and it is one of only four anti-clockwise circuits on the calendar.

The track's inner-city location, combined with the electric passion of the Brazilian fans, makes Interlagos one of the most atmospheric venues of the year. The involvement of my team-mate – the local hero, Rubens – in the title fight will only fuel the fever. This year will be the first time for ages that this grand prix hasn't been the final race of the season, but, with the constructors' and drivers' championships still to be decided, it promises to be a fascinating and intense weekend.

**Number of laps:** 71

**Circuit length:** 4.309 km

**Race distance:** 305.909 km

**Lap record:** 1:11.473
(Juan Pablo Montoya, 2004)

### MY HISTORY AT INTERLAGOS

**2008 (Honda)**
Grid 17; finished 13

**2007 (Honda)**
Grid 16; retired (engine)

**2006 (Honda)**
Grid 14; finished 3

**2005 (BAR-Honda)**
Grid 4; finished 7

**2004 (BAR-Honda)**
Grid 5; retired (engine)

**2003 (BAR-Honda)**
Grid 11; retired (accident)

**2002 (Renault)**
Grid 7; finished 4

**2001 (Benetton-Renault)**
Grid 20; finished 10

**2000 (Williams-BMW)**
Grid 9; finished 6

Interlagos provides a great challenge for teams and drivers: the high altitude and the notoriously bumpy surface are two key considerations when setting up the cars. The reduced atmospheric pressure causes a loss in engine power and aerodynamic performance, while the cars have to run with an increased ride height to cope with the bumps, which are particularly noticeable in the braking area for Turn 4.

The lap is characterised by long straights with flowing left-hand corners and a twisty in-field section. The changes in gradient give the circuit an unusual, almost three-dimensional feel, and combined with the anti-clockwise direction and bumpy surface, keep you fully focused. The high-speed left-hand corners add an extra physical challenge. The weather has been known to play its part in races over the years so we will be keeping a close eye on the forecast.

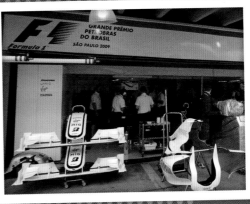

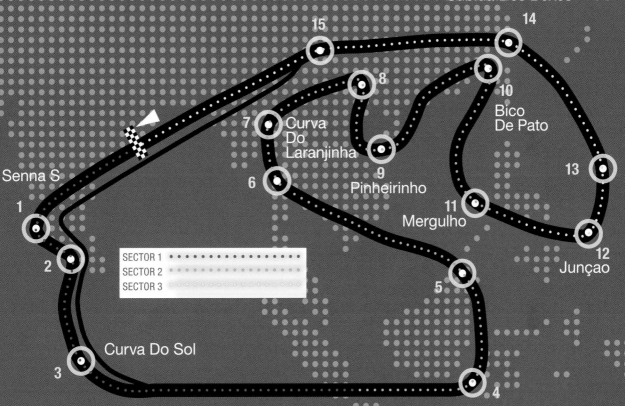

Subida Dos Boxes

14

15

8

10

Curva
Do
Laranjinha

7

Bico
De Pato

Senna S

6

9

Pinheirinho

13

1

12

2

11

Junçao

Mergulho

SECTOR 1
SECTOR 2
SECTOR 3

5

Curva Do Sol

3

4

Reta Oposta

# Brazil:
## Preparation, practice and qualifying

The media build-up to the Brazilian Grand Prix began as soon as the cars were packed up in Suzuka. Sebastian Vettel's victory and Rubens's finish just ahead of me left three of us in contention for the drivers' title with two races to go. A great situation for the fans! There is a lot of speculation about whether Sebastian could bridge a seventeen-point deficit to snatch the title the way Kimi Räikkönen did in 2007, and also about the chances for Rubens, inspired by his home support in Brazil and boosted by an intimate knowledge of Interlagos.

I don't listen to any of that. I know what position I am in. If anyone stops to study the statistics, they will see that none of my rivals has ever got any closer to me than fourteen points. Since the British Grand Prix, Rubens – who is supposed to have had an amazing second half of the season – has only gained nine points on me. When you're in the business of collecting as many points as possible, statistics can be a great comfort. The numbers stack up in my favour; neither Rubens nor the Red Bull drivers have significantly closed the gap on me. My qualifying performances from mid-season onwards may not have done me a great service, but it is from the races that you earn the points. I have gone out for every single point I can get and I have a comfortable fourteen-point lead to show for it. When you consider what Rubens and Sebastian have to do in Brazil and Abu Dhabi, and what I have to fail to do, I feel confident I'll get the job done.

After Suzuka, I spent four days in Tokyo, and then Jessica and I joined two friends in Hawaii for three nights, which was a refreshing change of scene. I did nothing except train, eat good food and chill out before heading to Brazil last Sunday – a journey which took two days. The itinerary involved long flights from Honolulu to LA, LA to Miami, and Miami to Sao Paulo, each with a three-hour stopover. Thankfully I am so used to flying that I knew that I would be able to sleep for a great deal of the journey, and I did. It then took two hours to travel from Sao Paulo airport to the hotel. I woke up on Wednesday feeling awful. I told my physio Mikey that I felt ill and he thought it was probably just the after-effects of the flights. I was worried I was going to be sick over the weekend. Can you imagine? Horrendous! Mikey was right, however, because I bounced back after a good night's sleep.

I needed that mini-holiday leading up to this race because I knew it would be hectic. The Brazilians are extremely patriotic and intensely emotional about sport. Rubens is the focus of their dreams for glory this weekend. It's not a very comfortable situation for me, fighting him for the world championship on his home soil. I love the country, but I don't feel at ease on this visit. I'm probably the most wanted man in Brazil! On advice, we are travelling to and from the circuit in a bullet-proof car. And I didn't want Jessica to come to support me here. I haven't received any threats or anything, but there is an edginess in the air. Whenever I walk into the paddock I get booed, or I get asked for an autograph and then booed to my face. What?! The guys tell me not to rise to it, so I just smile and wave at every opportunity.

I booked myself into a standard room at the Grand Hyatt, where I've stayed for the last couple of years. This time I was not upgraded when I checked in – but I suppose I wouldn't be in Brazil! We spend most of the time away from the circuit in meat restaurants called *fogo de chao*, Brazilian steakhouses where barbecued beef is a speciality. The waiters come around the tables with huge pieces of sizzling meat on skewers and slice bits off onto your plate. It's the first place you go when you arrive in Sao Paulo and the last place you visit before you leave. You eat so much meat it's unbelievable, but I love it. The plan is to go to different restaurants like this three nights on the trot – Tuesday night with the boys, Wednesday with the team and Thursday with the British media.

The Brazilians played a joke on me on Tuesday. At the entrance of the restaurant, they put a ladder up in front of the door because some people are superstitious about walking under ladders. But I don't believe in that sort of bad luck, so that attempt at unsettling me was wasted! The funny thing was that Mikey and I were wearing similar clothes. We got out of the car and the photographers surrounded him, thinking he was me, which was great because I could run around the back and get through the door. Then they tried to push me away, to help the photographers out. That's when Richard, my manager, flexes his muscles as a bouncer. It was fun, even though I couldn't quite work out what they were trying to do.

Despite the tensions, our garage is fun, largely because Rubens, his family and friends fill our team hospitality area here. They are a great bunch of people: very competitive, like Rubens, but very friendly and respectful of the fact that we're both fighting for something so huge. As the local boy at his home grand prix, the cameras are all on him and his side of the garage. Fine by me – I can relax and focus!

## THURSDAY

I left Suzuka praying for dry weather here. When it's dry, you know what you're going to get. If the car's good, it's good. If it's not, it's not. However, when it's wet, you hit one river and you're off the circuit into the wall. In Sao Paulo, it rains properly, none of your English drizzle! Rivers run across the circuit. As soon as you as much as touch it, you slide and you can easily be in the wall before you know it. I woke up on Thursday morning and, guess what? Rain!

I was in to the circuit early for an 11am FIA press conference which featured the three contenders for the drivers' world championship. Rubens and I sat in the front with Sebastian behind us. It was a fun question-and-answer session. Sebastian was saying all the pressure is on me and I was thinking, 'Hmm. I'm leading the championship by fourteen points, how is all the pressure on me? You have to beat me here. The pressure's on you!'

It looked as though the rain would prevent our usual circuit walk, but it stopped and we set off. I was

walking with my engineers and Ross about 200 metres behind Rubens, who was happily entertaining at least fifteen photographers and journalists. The circuit is very short, and it wasn't that hot, but it's so hilly, you're breathing quite heavily when you get to the end of a lap. The surface of the track is better than it used to be, but it's still a bumpy circuit. We were looking at how dirty the track seemed. Normally we'd go out early on the Friday morning practice session, but in Interlagos it's not worth it because the circuit is so dirty we'd get lost with our set-up trials. So there we were, walking on the track on which we could just claim two world championship titles. I said to Ross, 'You seem a little bit stressed, a little bit tense.' He said, 'Do I?' I said, 'Yes, Ross, I could see it at Suzuka and you haven't changed.' He's been carrying such pressure – two potential championship titles and sponsorship interest that needs to be confirmed to steer the future of the team. He said, 'Yes, Jean [his wife] has been keeping her distance from me...!'

## FRIDAY

Today was a businesslike day working as usual on maximising the set-up for the race. The car was working well and I was happy with the balance. We looked very competitive. Morning practice took place with light rain developing into a brief heavier shower half an hour into the session, which kept us in the garage for a short time, but we achieved more running than we initially expected. The afternoon session was largely dry, so we completed most of the day's planned programme. I did 74 laps and ended the day fifth fastest. The car seems to be working well on the Prime tyre, which is encouraging, and the pace was good. I'm struggling a little with the balance on the Option tyre over one timed lap but we hope to resolve that overnight to be ready for qualifying.

## SATURDAY

*Brawn GP's Rubens Barrichello took pole position in the rain-delayed qualifying session at the Interlagos circuit in Sao Paulo today ahead of his home race, the Brazilian Grand Prix, with team-mate Jenson Button qualifying in 14th position on the grid.*

I woke up in a bad mood because I had a dream that I was going to qualify badly, that Rubens was going to be at the front, and that I'd be devastated. I dismissed it as anxiety about the conditions. It was forecast to chuck it down. We hadn't experienced proper rain since Shanghai and we didn't know how it would affect the car. What else can this second half of the season throw at us? Wet conditions are scariest during practice. You know you have to get some laps in, but, if you put it in the wall on Saturday morning, you're not going to be qualifying at all. So it's a tricky one. I went out, gingerly at first, but the pace was good and I was happy with the car. We heard there was a lot of rain in the area and that qualifying was going to be wet, but I was happy about wet conditions now. I'm reassured about the car in these conditions. Rain is fine!

Romain Grosjean had put his Renault in the wall in practice. I'm sure we were all thinking, 'I want to be quick in qualifying but I don't want to make a mistake like that.' There were so many rivers flowing across the tarmac and you have to lift through the rivers or you spin your tyres and head into the wall. As qualifying hour approached, I was assuming the start would be delayed because it was so wet. And then the countdown on the computer screens started and the time started ticking down in green – signalling live track time – and I was thinking, 'You're kidding me, they haven't delayed the start.' Even if nobody posts a businesslike lap time, you've at least got to go out of the pits and come back in to protect your position. If you don't go out, the cars who have gone out will be in front of you on the grid. So we had to go out and put a time in. The times were about 30 seconds slower than a decent time in the dry. In Q1, the car was good and I was sixth quickest. Lewis went off coming out of Turn 5, across the grass, and because of the amount of rain it was like a muddy lake – he ended up losing control and being absolutely caked in mud. So he didn't progress through Q1. That didn't matter to me. The one I was keeping my eye on was Sebastian Vettel – and he didn't get through Q1 either, so that put a big smile on my face.

All the time I was saying to the guys, 'This is too wet, they've got to delay it.' But we started Q2 on time. I was about the eighth car out of the pits and as I finished my out lap Shov came on the radio and said, 'Red flag, red flag, big accident,' so I came straight back in. Then I saw on TV that Liuzzi had lost it on the straight, aquaplaning smack into the pit wall right where Shov was sitting and ripping all four wheels off the car. Shov said it was scary because from the 'prat perch' – as we call the place where the engineers sit – they felt an immense impact through the wall. I said, 'See? see? I told you it was too wet.'

Q2 was interrupted for an hour. It's so frustrating. You can't stay out of the car for long in case they announce a restart. At 4pm local time, it stopped raining – two hours into qualifying – and we went back out for the remainder of Q2. The circuit was wet, but without the rivers we'd encountered in Q1. We'd made a few tyre-pressure adjustments that we thought would help me in the changing conditions. The car was transformed, but not the way we expected. It ended up having so much understeer that I felt like I was driving with no front wing. I had a car in front of me and I thought perhaps that was causing a problem to my downforce. Shov came on radio and said 'Do you think you can go quicker than the time you've just done? Because you need to...' I said, 'Yes, I can, but I need to get this car ahead of me out of the way.'

The car pitted and I went for a quick lap. But the terrible thing was that I didn't actually go any quicker. The front tyres were grained and the rear tyres had started to overheat. I was sliding around and it was too late to come into the pits for new tyres. I had to stay out and try and put a lap in to jump back into the top ten. But I couldn't. The tyres were destroyed. The track was drying out, the standing water had gone, the surface was becoming greasy – perfect conditions for Intermediate tyres. A lot of runners had been called in to put the Inters on, but I didn't get that opportunity. Shov came on the radio. 'P14, I'm afraid, but, to be fair, we should have been on Inters, Jenson.'

Rubens qualified tenth in Q2. It was a tough call for the team. Ross knew that if he put me on Inters at the last minute, he'd have to do the same for Rubens, because if I went quicker, I'd have pushed him out of Q3... It was a difficult situation for them, trying to be fair to both of us. I don't know if that's why they didn't call me in for Inters, but I was out. And absolutely devastated, mainly because Rubens was in the top ten.

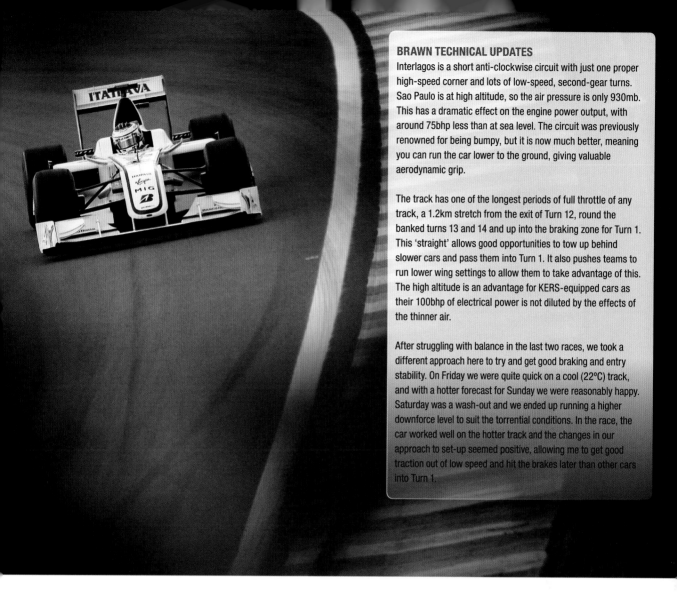

I got out of the car, stalked straight to our hospitality area and sat in my little driver's room watching Q3 on TV. I knew the team were going for an aggressive strategy on fuel because they had wanted to qualify us both on the front of the grid. I saw the circuit had dried further, so everyone went out on Intermediates, and it seemed like our car was transformed compared to others which had worked well on the Wets, like the Williams cars for instance. Rubens was very quick and got pole. That was the worst thing that could have happened, even though I knew he was fuelled short. It was still a humiliating situation for me because I was so far back. I felt sick, physically sick. It was a horrible feeling, knowing that my world championship dream could have slipped away in Brazil because of a bad qualifying session. It's one of the worst situations – when you've done badly in qualifying, and your teammate's done well. I sat down with Mikey and said, 'This is terrible, this is not good.' But after fifteen minutes or so I realised sulking wasn't going to make it better. I had to pick myself up and sort myself out for the race and plot a brilliant strategy to try and win the title tomorrow. I didn't want it hanging over until Abu Dhabi. I spent a lot of time with the engineers, the mechanics, and I was very, very positive, excited about the race. The great thing was, I had started 14th before in Brazil, in 2006, and finished third. I knew it could be done. It is a circuit where I've always enjoyed overtaking.

I went back to the hotel and talked to my mum on the phone. She was very upset, worried for me, so I spent some time reassuring her. 'Don't worry, Mum. I'm going to kick some butt tomorrow.' I then went down to dinner with the gang in the Japanese restaurant in the hotel. I told everyone it was going to have to be one hell of a race to win the championship. I had good meal, a beer to relax me and went to bed early.

# Brazil:
## The race

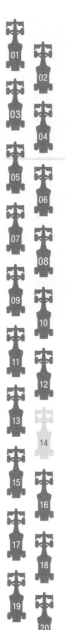

| | |
|---|---|
| 1. | **Rubens Barrichello** |
| 2. | **Mark Webber** |
| 3. | **Adrian Sutil** |
| 4. | **Jarno Trulli** |
| 5. | **Kimi Räikkönen** |
| 6. | **Sebastien Buemi** |
| 7. | **Nico Rosberg** |
| 8. | **Robert Kubica** |
| 9. | **Kazuki Nakajima** |
| 10. | **Fernando Alonso** |
| 11. | **Kamui Kobayashi** |
| 12. | **Jaime Alguersuari** |
| 13. | **Romain Grosjean** |
| 14. | **Jenson Button** |
| 15. | **Sebastian Vettel** |
| 16. | **Heikki Kovalainen** |
| 17. | **Lewis Hamilton** |
| 18. | **Nick Heidfeld** |
| 19. | **Giancarlo Fisichella** |
| 20. | **Vitantonio Liuzzi (gearbox penalty)** |

### STRATEGY

Bridgestone brought the Super Soft and Medium compounds to Brazil. Interlagos has a lot of combined loading (cornering and traction), especially in Sector 2, but it is normally not too hard on tyres. Historically this has been a bumpy circuit, but since 2008 the surface has been significantly improved.

Friday was mostly dry, and the Medium tyre showed low degradation and good warm-up, confirming our suspicion that this would be the primary race tyre. The Super Soft grained, but was controllable. With a very short pit-lane, and an Option tyre that would only be able to run 20–25 laps or so, the race was very much centred on a two-stop strategy.

Qualifying was very wet, with all cars on Wet tyres in Q1. I set the sixth fastest time, with Rubens fifth fastest. The rain then started again, and Q2 was delayed, then red-flagged. It wasn't restarted until 16:10, when all the storms had passed over. The track dried quickly, and some cars switched to Intermediate tyres, with only Rubens, Webber, Sutil, Grosjean, Alguersuari

*Brawn GP secured the 2009 FIA Formula One constructors' championship at the Brazilian Grand Prix in Interlagos today with Jenson Button driving a superb race from 14th position on the grid to a fifth-place finish to wrap up the drivers' championship with one race of the season to go.*

I woke up in a bad mood again. I dreamt I'd won the championship and then realised it was only a dream. The reality was a P14 start. It was a horrible feeling, but I shrugged that off. It didn't make any difference to my normal race-morning routine. I can't say I had any extra adrenalin or determination. I'm always excited about a race and about making the most of a situation. It was business as usual.

Rubens was on pole and his Brazilian fans were rooting for him to dominate the weekend from pole to chequered flag to keep his title hopes alive. The fans were throwing as much flak as they could at me. When I pulled up to my grid slot and got out, thousands of people in the grandstand booed me. I wasn't going to rise to it, so I took my helmet off and waved to the crowd with the biggest smile. They kept booing, but when I walked off, they stopped and didn't do it again. That interaction fired me up. They didn't know that that needle gets me extra-excited, extra-motivated, even though I was lining up on a grid with potential problems all around me. I was surrounded by new boys – Kamui Kobayashi (replacing the injured Timo Glock in the Toyota), Grosjean and Alguersuari. As the engines revved, waiting for the start signal, I knew exactly what I had to do.

I had a good start, passed Grosjean and caught up behind Alguersuari. But then Kobayashi came across and tried to put Alguersuari in the pit wall, and I was stuck behind them with nowhere to go. I didn't gain

and me remaining on Wets. My tyres grained in the drying conditions, leaving me in P14.

Being outside the top ten, we had a free fuel opportunity. Overtaking is very possible in Brazil, especially as we had a 5–10kph advantage over most of the cars ahead. We therefore filled a few laps longer than the top ten, allowing me to fight my way through the field.

any places at turns 1 and 2 because Grosjean was able to get past me again on the outside. Coming out of Turn 5, there was a bit of mayhem up front. That presents a difficult situation because you can see it – cars all over the place, a couple of cars off the circuit – but you don't want to slow down too much because if you lift then cars might hit you from behind, and equally you don't want to lose position, so you have to be controlled. Alguersuari, in front of me, did lift off during the incident and I had nowhere to go, so I had to pass him into the corner where the accident was. You don't want to be side by side with someone going through all the mayhem, but I ended up in front of him, with three cars travelling off circuit. Then, in Turn 8, I got past Kimi, who was limping around with a broken front wing... and suddenly the safety car appeared.

On the opening lap, I'd gone from 14th to 9th, and could only benefit from the field being bunched up by the safety car, because the guys in front who were stopping early (like Rubens) weren't going to be gaining such an advantage. We spent two or three laps behind the safety car and I caught a bit of TV

action on the big screens. I saw Trulli and Sutil have a bit of a finger-wagging scrap after their big smash, which was fun to watch. We need a bit more of that in Formula One!

While the safety car dictated the pace, it was just a question of keeping the tyres warm. Shov came on the radio and said, 'You're behind a few new guys who might not know how much they need to work these tyres to get heat into them.' 'OK Shov, cool.'

I worked harder than ever to warm the tyres and Shov reported back to say the temperatures were good, the tyre pressure was good, and the re-start was imminent. Rubens took us around really slow, trying to get a good jump on the exit onto the straight, which he did. I tried to get on the outside of Grosjean into Turn 1, but that didn't work. Coming out of Turn 3, I had a good run on him, so I towed up behind him. He pulled to the inside for Turn 4, so I went to the outside, I knew he'd brake quite deep into the corner, and I got a good run on the exit out of Turn 4 and got up the inside of him. We went through Turn 5, the full-speed corner, side by side, up the hill to Turns 6 and 7 – a very fast double right-hander – and I thought, 'Right, I've got to get past him here otherwise I might as well call it a day. This is really important to my race.' I was hanging onto him around the outside, the 'wall of death' as Martin Brundle calls it, and held on and clinched the place. So I was very happy. From then on, it was simply a matter of being aggressive, putting laps in, closing people down, pushing them into mistakes (which nobody made) or getting past them.

Six corners later, I was on the tail of Nakajima, so I towed up behind him on the straight and was able to dive down the inside into Turn 1 and get past him. Then I was coming up to Kobayashi, closing in on him corner by corner. I had a go into Turn 1 two laps later. I knew I had to get it done as soon as possible. I got down the inside, sideways, because the guy was moving in the braking zone which you're not supposed to do – it's dangerous at the speeds we race at, when you're all braking so late. If he moves suddenly you're going to launch sky-high – as a couple of other guys later found out when they were trying to overtake him. Kobayashi fought back at Turn 2. It wasn't worth fighting for at that point so I let him go, then had one more go which didn't work and then another go ten laps later when I made it stick.

I gave it the big 'Let's go, let's go' on the radio to Shov. I had to get my head down and push hard for four laps, and I pulled out a big gap on Kobayashi, Vettel and Lewis. All the guys in front had been stopping and they all came out behind me, which was good, except Webber, who emerged from his first stop right in front of me. I had him there for three laps, which made things difficult for me as I couldn't pull away in clean air and create the gap I needed to get some breathing space between myself and Vettel and the other cars behind. I came in for my stop and rejoined in traffic so I knew that after his stop Vettel would probably be in front of me. Next I had to chase down Buemi. The team were shouting, 'Vettel's coming out of the pit lane,' and he dropped in just behind me, which was nice.

I closed in on Buemi, knowing I had to make the move as soon as possible. It was a bit of a do-or-die manoeuvre into Turn 1 from a long way back because he had very good straight-line speed. I made the move and it reminded me of one I executed in 2006 here, passing Kimi Räikkönen for third place – very late on the brakes and diving up the inside. Most of the time the driver doesn't even know you're there, as it's very difficult to see out of these cars until you've got something alongside you, and then it's SHOCK. I was enjoying myself! On the exit I thought, 'I've got to put my foot on it or he'll come back at me.' I did, and got a massive snap of oversteer, lost the car and almost hit him, but he backed out of it and I was on my way, closing in on the cars in front of me.

The next problem was I had Vettel right up behind me. He was definitely quicker than me and I knew he was going to stop later. I was working out the numbers, the cars in front – Webber leading, then Kubica, Rubens in third, myself and Vettel, and Lewis back in seventh or eighth but without another stop to make. The guys came on, 'In this lap, in this lap,' so I stopped in the pits, and had a good out-lap, but again I was caught up, this time with Kovalainen, which ruined my chances of building a gap to maintain my place ahead of Vettel. I was in sixth place, Rubens in third. That's three points difference, not enough for Rubens's title hopes – he needed to get five points on me – so I knew I was in a great position. I had a big smile on my face, but there was still some way to go. Vettel pitted and came out in front of Heikki. I still couldn't get past him, because he's got his KERS boost button. I was on to the engineers, 'When's Heikki stopping?' This was lap 60 or something. They said, 'We don't know if he is stopping again.' I cried, 'What do you mean, you don't know?' 'We don't actually think he is stopping again.' 'You're joking.'

It was getting a bit close with the points and numbers. Then, unbelievably, Heikki turned off into the pits and I almost gave him a thumbs-up as I went past. From then on, it was about being consistent. I was on the Option tyre. I had Kimi behind on the Prime tyre, and he had good pace. It was about matching his lap times so he didn't get closer, but driving within myself, which I achieved. Then I was told Rubens had lost third place to Lewis, so I was in a very strong position. Rubens in fourth, me in sixth. About eight laps to go, Rubens suffered a puncture – the result of a tap from Lewis when he passed him. He had to pit

'Jenson, it's lap 30. Anyone who questions whether you have a world championship drive within you just needs to watch this race back.' David Coulthard

and I saw him in the box as I went down the straight. I took fifth place from him and felt ecstatic. But there were still seven or eight laps to go and anything could happen. It really could. I radioed in to the team. 'Is everything okay with the car? What do I need to do? Do I need to turn the engine down?' They said, 'No, just do what you're doing. It's fine.' Four laps to go, Shov's on the radio saying 'Jenson, you have four laps to go.' 'Thanks, I know that!' Three laps to go, Shov's on again, 'Jenson, you have three laps to go.' 'Shov, I don't need a running commentary...'

Then it was silence, just me and the car. On the last lap I remember thinking, 'Just relax and enjoy this lap.' It felt like the longest lap of Interlagos ever. I came out of the last corner and crossed the line with an enormous smile on my face and looked up at Felipe Massa, chequered flag in his hand, and it was the best feeling in the world. I was crossing the line as world champion.

The great thing about our pit box this year is that it is all the way at the end of the wall so I had time to slow down and register all the mechanics' faces hanging out over the pit wall. In that quick glimpse I registered tears of joy, some very emotional faces, and I thought, 'What can I do to mark the occasion?' I did a couple of burnouts in front of them. I wanted to stop there and get out of the car and give them all a hug and a high five, but that's impossible, and I

> 'There's 6 laps to go still but I just wanted to say congratulations to the new World Champion!!!! I love you, you did an amazing drive, amazing overtaking you so deserve it. Xx' Jessica

came out of Turn 2 and started singing my favourite song, Queen's We are the Champions – which killed my throat! It was a great, great moment. Rubens came alongside me and gave me the thumbs-up, which was a lovely gesture. I know how difficult it must have been for him. And even though, for the whole weekend, the Brazilian fans had been quite tough on me, once I'd actually won, they were cheering for me. That in-lap was my first ever as world champion and I enjoyed it so much. Shov came on the radio and went through the usual formalities, 'Pick up rubber. Mix one. Save fuel.'

'Shov, I am not thinking about any of that right now!'

I pulled up in my spot, got out of the car, and that was the best feeling – being able to jump on the car and know that the reason the cameras were pointing at me was because I AM THE WORLD CHAMPION. The 2009 Formula One world champion. The first person to rush to congratulate me was Rubens, a touching moment. Then no one else had a chance because I was off, like a headless chicken, running around, jumping up and down in front of the photographers. I eventually found my crew, ran over and gave them all a big hug. They picked me up onto their shoulders. There was so much emotion there, such a release of pent-up stress, joy, incredulity that our maiden season as a team had ended like this. You don't expect to see mechanics tearful, but they've worked so hard. If ever a victory felt well-deserved, this was it.

The first person I saw in parc fermé was Mikey Muscles, my physio. He gave me a big hug, picked me up and said, 'You've done it. You are the world champion.' He was the first person to see me after qualifying on Saturday and he knew how down I had been. He had tried so valiantly to be positive when he was hurting too, so it was a great, emotional, turnaround moment. The next minutes passed in a flurry of hugs, handshakes, high fives. I did a few interviews, even though at that point I just wanted to run down the pit lane and jump all over my team-mates who've worked so hard over the last twelve months. Interviews were pretty pointless. My voice had gone. I couldn't talk because I'd been screaming so much. It was like I'd done three days of non-stop karaoke and smoked several big cigars. I ran down to the team, followed by a mass of photographers, high fives all the way down the paddock, and found everyone in the Brawn area already celebrating. Ross was speechless, just as he had been in Australia, and a little bit tearful. I thought words of wisdom were going to come out of his mouth but he just said one word, 'Exceptional,' and broke down in tears. I gave him a hug and a kiss on the cheek, which I don't think he liked but he was going to get it anyway, the

Big Bear! It was mayhem. Everyone enjoying themselves and some of the mechanics screeching, 'Guys, watch out, you're jumping on the gear boxes and the front wings.' It was just going off in there. Crazy. There was not an inch to move in or any air to breathe. I was dehydrated after the race, but Mikey, whose job is to give me a drink, was nowhere to be seen. He was off enjoying himself.

There were so many moments to savour... I had the biggest hug with the old boy. We were locked in a clinch. I didn't let go because I was talking to him, talking about what we've all been through. 'We've done it Dad, what we've all worked for.' He was crying his eyes out and kept me in a hug because he didn't want to have all that emotion pouring out in front of the cameras. Bernie Ecclestone was so funny. He gave me a hug and said: 'You didn't listen. You don't take orders. I wanted it to go to the wire.'

Next up was the press conference featuring the new world champion, but I arrived and there was no one there. I said, 'Where is everyone? I am the world champion! The world champion, baby!' I must have said 'world champion' about twenty times. It sounded good! Bob Constanduros, who mediates the press conferences, said, 'Hello champion.' 'Is that it?' I said. 'Sorry, hello world champion,' he replied, and it became the running gag.

Afterwards I ran back down the paddock again and found the team celebrations were still intense. All the mechanics were grouped outside ready for a picture. They grabbed hold of me, threw me on their shoulders and covered me in Champagne. I really wish I hadn't changed into my normal clothes because I was drenched for the whole journey back to the hotel. It was an unbelievable feeling. We were all fielding so many congratulations. For Ross, it was an exceptional situation. To win the constructors' championship with his name on the car in his first year as team owner. Incredible.

Later that night the team put on a celebration party at 3P4, a Sao Paulo nightclub which a Brawn GP sponsor had booked for a party anyway. I was scheduled to fly back to the UK, but Rubens kindly lent us his private jet so I could continue celebrating with the team. I thought it was just going to be a team party, but it seemed like anyone could get in, so it was hot and hectic. I saw the boys and partied with them for a little while, then left at 1am, heading straight back to the hotel. I know people expected me to stay up all night and go crazy, but I was so tired.

To chill in bed on my own was the best thing. I spoke to Jessica, spoke to some of the family, and I was up until about 4am, lying in bed with a big grin, enjoying the gradual realisation of what I'd achieved. It took a long time to sink in. I needed that bit of 'me time' to savour the fulfilment of a dream that started more than twenty years ago when the old boy gave me my first kart and I discovered the thrill of winning. I am the eighth English world champion in Formula One and it's the greatest feeling.

Tomorrow I fly to Farnborough to appear at a sponsor's function at the Bluewater shopping centre in Kent. The following day I'll travel to the Brawn GP factory in Brackley, where I can't wait to celebrate with everyone who has worked so hard, and through such a difficult winter, to create a fantastic car and brilliant team ethic. What our team has achieved this season after the winter we had is exceptional. I'll also spend time in the simulator, preparing for Abu Dhabi. And that evening I'll be in London to have a few beers with my old mates from Frome. On Friday, I'm so looking forward to meeting up with Jessica in Dubai, where we'll stay for a break and some training before the final grand prix. I can't wait to get back in the car. It's a new circuit, and I love new circuits. The inaugural race at the Yas Marina Circuit looks like being one big celebration for all of us at Brawn GP – and I think we thoroughly deserve it.

## BRAZILIAN GRAND PRIX FINAL POSITIONS

| Pos | Driver | Team | Laps | Time |
|-----|--------|------|------|------|
| 1 | Mark Webber | RBR-Renault | 71 | 1:32:23.081 |
| 2 | Robert Kubica | BMW Sauber | 71 | +7.6 secs |
| 3 | Lewis Hamilton | McLaren-Mercedes | 71 | +18.9 secs |
| 4 | Sebastian Vettel | RBR-Renault | 71 | +19.6 secs |
| 5 | Jenson Button | Brawn-Mercedes | 71 | +29.0 secs |
| 6 | Kimi Räikkönen | Ferrari | 71 | +33.3 secs |
| 7 | Sebastien Buemi | STR-Ferrari | 71 | +35.9 secs |
| 8 | Rubens Barrichello | Brawn-Mercedes | 71 | +45.4 secs |
| 9 | Kamui Kobayashi | Toyota | 71 | +63.3 secs |
| 10 | Giancarlo Fisichella | Ferrari | 71 | +70.6 secs |
| 11 | Vitantonio Liuzzi | Force India-Mercedes | 71 | +71.3 secs |
| 12 | Heikki Kovalainen | McLaren-Mercedes | 71 | +73.4 secs |
| 13 | Romain Grosjean | Renault | 70 | +1 Lap |
| 14 | Jaime Alguersuari | STR-Ferrari | 70 | +1 Lap |
| Ret | Kazuki Nakajima | Williams-Toyota | 30 | Accident |
| Ret | Nico Rosberg | Williams-Toyota | 27 | Gearbox |
| Ret | Nick Heidfeld | BMW Sauber | 21 | Out of fuel |
| Ret | Adrian Sutil | Force India-Mercedes | 0 | Accident |
| Ret | Jarno Trulli | Toyota | 0 | Accident |
| Ret | Fernando Alonso | Renault | 0 | Accident |

Today was the best race that I've driven in my career and I'm really going to enjoy this moment. For the team to win the constructors' and the drivers championships here is just fantastic and they deserve it so very much after all the difficult times that we all went through over the winter. This season has been a rollercoaster ride from the elation of the wins at the start to the hard graft in the second half of the season which has seen us grind out the results needed to take the titles. We have to say a huge thank you to Norbert Haug and Mercedes-Benz High Performance Engines for all of the support that they have given us over the year. Without their commitment and faith in the team, and the fantastic engine that they have provided, we would not have been able to achieve the success that we have today. The list of people that I have to thank personally is too long to mention but they all know who they are and how much their support has meant to me over the years. To everyone back at the factory in Brackley, thank you for all of your hard work and for producing such a fantastic car. It's going to take a while to sink in, but for now I'm just revelling in the achievement of a lifelong dream. It's going to be one hell of a party tonight!

**OVERALL POINTS**

| | |
|---|---|
| Jenson Button | 89 |
| Sebastian Vettel | 74 |
| Rubens Barrichello | 72 |
| Mark Webber | 61.5 |
| Lewis Hamilton | 49 |
| Kimi Räikkönen | 48 |
| Nico Rosberg | 34.5 |
| Jarno Trulli | 30.5 |
| Fernando Alonso | 26 |
| Timo Glock | 24 |
| Felipe Massa | 22 |
| Heikki Kovalainen | 22 |
| Robert Kubica | 17 |
| Nick Heidfeld | 15 |
| Giancarlo Fisichella | 8 |
| Adrian Sutil | 5 |
| Sebastien Buemi | 5 |
| Sebastien Bourdais | 2 |

'What a day! I am so incredibly proud of the team and our drivers and it's so very special to have won the constructors' and the drivers' championships in our first year as Brawn GP. The second half of the year has been tough after such a successful start but getting the results in the difficult times is what counts in a championship season. It's really going to take a while for what we have achieved today to sink in. Jenson is a fantastic racer and he had a great race today, particularly after such a difficult qualifying yesterday. He knew what he had to do and did just that and is a very deserving world champion. Rubens has made a fantastic contribution to this season without which we could not have won the constructors' championship today. The spirit in which our two drivers have fought for the championship makes me very proud. They have been a credit to the team and our sport.' Ross Brawn

'Dear Jenson, finally it is starting to sink in what we have just done. At home with my lovely family and enjoying the fact that we are world champs, the best at what we do on the planet! Keep having to remind myself it is true. My boys are too young to understand it now but I can't wait till they can realise what we have achieved. X' Andrew Shovlin

'Mate, can't tell you how happy I am seeing you as World Champion. You did it, What an awesome job!!' Phil Young

'You are the Champion, you are the champion of the World! God I'm so proud of you, you've done it. Lots of love from me xx' Mum

'Absolute legend, no one deserves it more fella x' Kieran Baker, nephew

'World Champion little bruv, so proud words can't describe what this means, love you so much. Xx' Tanya, sister

'How is the World Champ this morning? How amazing does that sound. I felt like a 4 year old waking up on Xmas morning so can't imagine how it feels for you. Be prepared for the biggest hug when you get back to Europe. x' Sam, sister

'Oh my god, you're the new F1 World Champion, you are amazing. Well done and enjoy celebrating. Sending lots of hugs and kisses from your little sis. xx' Tasha

'World Champion baby – awesome, you're the best!' Fraser

'Son, what can I say. You're a great friend, a superstar and World Champion. I know how much you wanted this and how much you deserve it. This makes all those years chasing your ass on the bike worth it. Love you my boy.xx' Miles, friend

'You the man, big love. X' Brad

'Mate you deserve it, hope you don't think lanzarote training week will be any easier now your Champ of the World. Brilliant mate, you are a real superstar!' John Brame, trainer

BRAWN GP
2009
WORLD
CHAMPIONS
BRAWN GP
JENSON
2009
WORLD
CHAMPION

# Abu Dhabi Grand Prix
## Yas Marina Circuit
### Friday 30 October – Sunday 1 November

I love the fresh set of challenges a new circuit presents. I always seem to do well on them. My preparation is good. I've worked hard to make sure I know Abu Dhabi as well as I can before I get there. I've walked the circuit, but that was after the Bahrain Grand Prix in April, so I've been learning the track characteristics on the simulator at the factory.

The Yas Marina Circuit has been likened to Monaco crossed with Las Vegas, and it is spectacular. The anti-clockwise track, designed by the renowned F1 architect Hermann Tilke, has unique features including a tunnelled pit-lane exit which crosses under the circuit. And turns 18 and 19 take the driver under part of the huge Yas Hotel.

It is low speed, with very few high-speed elements at all. With a tight corner onto the long straight, I'm not sure what it's going to be like for overtaking. They say the temperature may only be mid-20s, but that takes a bit of believing for the United Arab Emirates!

**Number of laps:** 55

**Circuit length:** 5.554 km

**Race distance:** 305.470 km

**Lap record:** 1:40.279
(Sebastian Vettel, 2009)

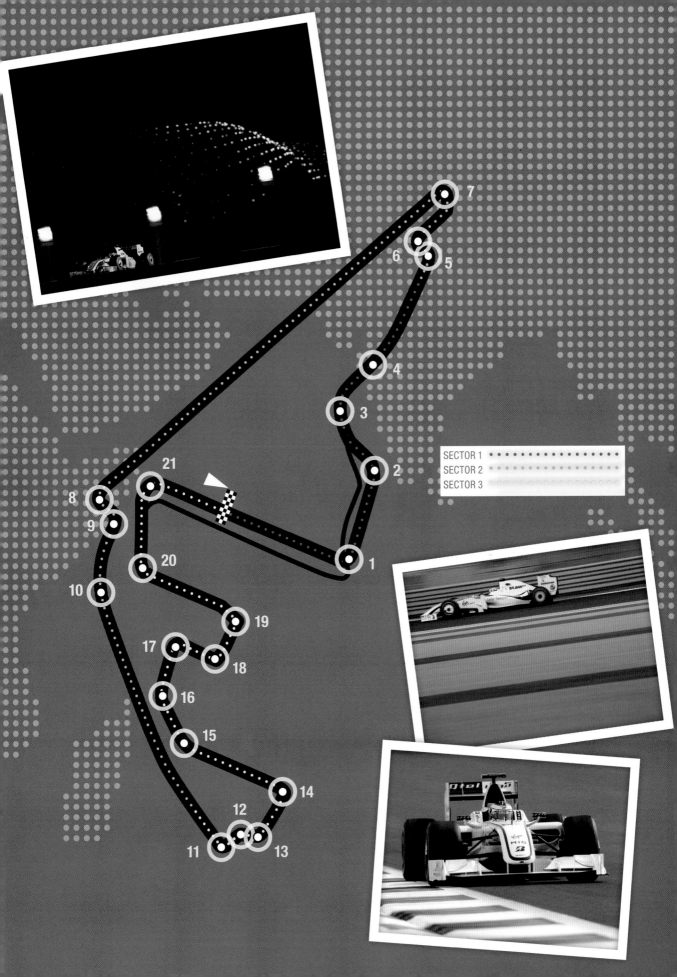

SECTOR 1
SECTOR 2
SECTOR 3

# Abu Dhabi:
## Preparation, practice and qualifying

It's a somewhat surreal but equally incredible feeling to be going into the final race having achieved my ambition of winning the drivers' championship, and with the team having wrapped up the constructors' championship in Brazil. The double whammy! We intend to finish the season in style, but we can be a little more relaxed in our approach to the weekend.

I flew back from the post-race celebrations in Brazil in Rubens' private jet. It was a typically thoughtful gesture from him to lend it to me so I could party properly with the team. I landed back on home soil, as the tenth British world champion, at Farnborough Airport and then went straight to the Bluewater Shopping Centre in Kent. I don't think I ever imagined that my first activity as Formula One world champion would be to visit a shopping mall. Without Jessica, though, I was safe from the shops!

It was a long-scheduled PR day for Virgin. My role was to pose for photographers, give interviews and drive competition-winners around a car park in a four-door, 550hp Mercedes E63AMG. It was good fun, going crazy around a car park flat out, with policemen just staring at me and smiling. I was fulfilling every boy racer's dream in hammering it around a small track. I even made one of my passengers sick! A question-and-answer session with Crofty – BBC Five Live's F1 commentator David Croft – followed. I walked out in front of a sea of Button caps and flags to such a rousing reception. It was a very special moment to acknowledge the claps and cheers and see the words 'World Champion' on Brawn GP and Jenson Button flags.

The following day I travelled to the Brawn factory to learn the Abu Dhabi circuit on our simulator. We use data provided by the FIA to create a circuit map which can be used in our simulator at the factory. We went through this process for the new street circuits in Valencia and Singapore last year and it works well in terms of familiarising yourself with the layout. The idea is that it also allows us to check gear ratios, compare set-up components and understand tyre behaviour, get the balance of the car right and help determine our start set-up for the weekend – but it needs a bit more refining.

After I'd done my 'work', I was led into the auditorium. All the Brawn GP workforce had gathered and we had a mass toasting of our amazing season with Champagne. The scene was set with some footage from the season and we all got quite emotional... until the bit when I started singing 'We are the Champions' after crossing the finish line in Brazil, when everyone just wet themselves laughing! It was an occasion I'll never forget, an incredible contrast to the stresses of where we were ten months ago.

In the evening I drove to London and found I'd been sent hundreds of congratulatory balloons and bottles, including some pink Champagne from Sir Elton John and David Furnish. It was hard to absorb it all – I had messages from David Cameron, Peter Mandelson, Gordon Brown, Lord March, Damon Hill, Nigel Mansell and Sir Jackie Stewart – whose wife told me she'd kissed her television screen when I won! It's so much of a whirlwind that I can only say 'It's strange' when people ask me to describe the sensation of achieving the goal I've worked so hard towards for twenty years. I'm still the same person, doing the same things, but when I go to bed I lie there thinking, 'Yes, all those tough days *were* worth enduring.' I'd experienced a few unhappy times in my karting career, a torrid year at Benetton, frustrating periods at Honda. But however much it hurt at the time, it's all been worth persisting with my ambition. But what do I do now?! The next goal is obviously to win another title, but right now I'm determined to pause and enjoy myself after this incredibly stressful season. The past ten months have been crazy. It's been like my entire Formula One career squeezed into seventeen races – fantastic debut, uneasy mid section, then intense jubilation. I'm so drained.

Later that night I went out to dinner with two of my sisters, my dad, my engineers and their wives and lots of friends – all the gang who have helped carry me through the difficult times. We went dancing and I enjoyed the kind of 'night on the town' I haven't wanted to have during the season. The only negative was that Jessica could not be there. The next morning I flew to Dubai to meet up with her at last, and spend a week on holiday before Abu Dhabi. We had some of the gang there, too, and it was lovely. One day we took a catamaran out. Otherwise we shopped, and lay in the sun. I felt so tired, I had to go to bed early each night. My body needed to lounge around. It was as if the relief of securing the world championship just flooded my system with anaesthetic. I didn't do a lot of training!

One night a good friend, Russell Sheldon, arranged an amazing adventure tour for us into the massive sand dunes of the desert in a 4x4 Jeep. I'm not normally a good passenger, but I was okay. There's not too much danger of hitting anything in the desert! The organisers set up a private camp for ten of us. It was beautifully done with a feast of traditional Arabian food and camel rides laid on. As they say, 'When in Rome...' Getting on a camel must rank as one of the funniest experiences. They lurch forwards and backwards as they get up from their knees and we almost lost Jessica, who was close to being catapulted through the air.

I arrived in Abu Dhabi refreshed to prepare for my first race as world champion – though Bernie says I'm not world champion until he gives me the trophy at the FIA Gala Dinner in Monaco in December. For some reason, it took us two and a half hours to find our hotel, but eventually I went on to join up with the team at the circuit. The facilities at the Yas Marina Circuit are outstanding. There's nothing else like it. It's leagues ahead of any other Formula One venue. The harbour is busy, and feels more like Monaco than Valencia. At night, little lights on the undulating roof over the Yas Hotel that bridges the circuit create a stunning landmark. I could enjoy the sight because, in my budget-cutting year, I certainly couldn't afford to stay under its roof.

The heat was intense – 37°C plus – so our customary track walk became a track scooter ride for Shov and me. We did a couple of laps in daylight. It's difficult to imagine at this stage how a twilight-into-darkness race will feel. Race start time is 5pm on Sunday, just as the sun starts to set.

## FRIDAY

I'm back in the car for the first time since Brazil! On paper, the track layout does not look too exciting, a bit slow perhaps, but when you actually drive it, it's fantastic fun. The track has a bit of everything to keep you on your toes, with high- and low-speed corners, positive and negative camber and walls that are pretty close to you most of the way round. The kerbs are small and low so you can hammer the car over them and drive with aggression. It's quite a technical track, very unforgiving.

The track surface was very dirty at the start of the first practice session, with high track temperatures, but it was a good opportunity for me to familiarise myself with it. It takes two or three laps to get acclimatised to its demands. I had a little spin on Turn 19 – my first spin of the season – and that was great fun because I could carry on with a smile on my face. This is a bonus race for me. The business of winning has been done, and I'm all out to enjoy myself. The simulator is useful for learning the circuit, but it's only when you're actually driving it for real that you work out where your limits are. When you're on a

computer you don't care so much about that kind of precision. Some of the corners have negative camber on entry and exit, so you turn in with oversteer, have understeer at the apex and turn out with oversteer. It must have looked good on television! It's a great idea that works well for this circuit.

The temperatures fell dramatically going into the second session, which is consistent with what we expect to see in qualifying tomorrow and in the race. We worked through our usual Friday programme with the tyres and aerodynamic set-up and collected some good data. All in all, a good first day of practice here, with just a few balance issues to work on overnight. I've been in the top three in every session. The car felt great.

### SATURDAY
*Brawn GP's Rubens Barrichello and Jenson Button qualified in fourth and fifth positions respectively today for the inaugural Abu Dhabi Grand Prix.*

We knew Lewis in his McLaren was the car to beat. In Q1, though, he was four or five tenths quicker than anyone, which was a bigger margin of superiority than we had anticipated. The car has felt good all weekend and the first two sessions went well. Unfortunately, in Q3, when we were running with high fuel and new tyres, I started to get massive vibrations every time I hit the brakes, which made the steering wheel shudder. On such a smooth circuit, any kind of vibration just leads to understeer, which makes the car quite a handful to drive. I ended up P5. I should have been on the front row with Lewis, so I was massively disappointed – though P5 has been my best qualifying performance for ages! I think I showed my frustration, but with a smile.

The funny thing is registering how relaxed my engineers are now we've sewn up the championship. Shov has had a big grin on his face all weekend. Even after qualifying, when we'd hoped for a front-row position, he was saying, 'It's okay, don't worry.' I'm only just realising quite how stressed he was before. He was so uptight about us possibly throwing away our championship lead. I think he's happier that we didn't throw it away than that we actually won it!

I'm looking forward to a good fight tomorrow. I'm enjoying every lap in the car. The fun element disappeared in the intensity of fighting for the championship. Now I'm revelling in it.

## BRAWN TECHNICAL UPDATES

The Abu Dhabi track is new for 2009. It's an anti-clockwise circuit with a lot of slow, second-gear corners and the longest straight in Formula One – the 1.2km run between turns 7 and 8. The only fast corners are turns 2 and 3, which are taken at full throttle, but still exciting as you are at 270kph by the exit. A lot of the corners are off camber on the exits which make it difficult to get on the power without the car going to oversteer. The pit lane is also quite interesting, a tight tunnel that takes you under Turn 1 and rejoins the circuit on the inside of the second corner.

This is a medium-downforce circuit and given the fact that so many of the corners are low speed, the set-up is very similar to what you would run at Interlagos. We didn't have any updates for this event so the car spec was the same as in Brazil. One of the most challenging aspects of this weekend is that the race and qualifying are held at sundown so the track is cooling rapidly. Most of the free practice running is at 35ºC air temperature and 50ºC track temperature (an Abu Dhabi winter!) whereas in the race, the track cools as low as 30ºC. This means the car balance and tyre grip levels are changing throughout the stints so the challenge is to keep correcting wing angles and tyre pressures to keep everything consistent.

# Abu Dhabi:
## The race

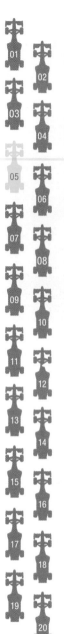

1. **Lewis Hamilton**
2. **Sebastian Vettel**
3. **Mark Webber**
4. **Rubens Barrichello**
5. **Jenson Button**
6. **Jarno Trulli**
7. **Robert Kubica**
8. **Nick Heidfeld**
9. **Nico Rosberg**
10. **Sebastien Buemi**
11. **Kimi Räikkönen**
12. **Kamui Kobayashi**
13. **Kazuki Nakajima**
14. **Jaime Alguersuari**
15. **Fernando Alonso**
16. **Vitantonio Liuzzi**
17. **Adrian Sutil**
18. **Heikki Kovalainen (gearbox penalty)**
19. **Romain Grosjean**
20. **Giancarlo Fisichella**

## STRATEGY

Bridgestone brought the Medium and Soft compounds to Abu Dhabi (the same as Spa and Monza). The interesting factor will be the temperature changes over the sessions; the track dropping 15°C between P1 and P2 and a further 5°C during the race, with the race starting at sunset.

On Friday we focused on running a tyre programme in P2, which starts at the same time as the race. The Medium tyre was a better compound, both for qualifying and the race, but neither tyre was poor; both having very little degradation. With a fairly long pit lane, and a one-stop taking us out of contention in qualifying, we went for a two-stop. The main problem we experienced was tyre warm-up, taking up to five timed laps to get the fastest lap-time out of the tyre, meaning qualifying would be a little different to normal.

The qualifying plan was to go a little longer than in the previous races. Since the tyres hardly dropped performance, we would be a lot faster at the end of a stint than at the start of the next stint, with fresh tyres and heavier fuel. We completed long runs on the Prime tyres in qualifying, a strategy which most competitors adopted by the end of the sessions. Unfortunately I

*Brawn GP's Jenson Button finished his world championship year on a high today with a third-placed podium finish at the Abu Dhabi Grand Prix at the new Yas Marina Circuit. Team-mate Rubens Barrichello came through a first-corner impact to drive a composed race and bring his Brawn-Mercedes car home in fourth position.*

I was determined to enjoy every second of my first race as world champion. With both the drivers' and constructors' championships already decided, there was a very relaxed, end-of-season atmosphere in the paddock, boosted by the spectacular setting. We'd had the comedian James Corden in our garage, filming a hilarious piece for Sport Relief. The guy's a genius! There was a funny moment when Boris Becker was also in our midst, giving an interview. Someone asked him if he thought Sebastian Vettel would win the world championship in 2010, and as Becker said 'yes' – as you'd expect of a supportive countryman – James was in the background pulling funny faces. When he heard the Vettel exchange, he dived in and mock-reprimanded Becker for not talking about Jenson Button, the new 2009 world champion. The look on Becker's face was priceless.

Of course Rubens was still fighting with Sebastian Vettel over second place in the drivers' championship.

had a front wheel weight come off during my last run, which lost a few tenths, dropping me back to P5 from an expected P2.

During the race I made a good start, and I passed Rubens on lap 1 following his contact with Webber. I had slightly less fuel than the cars ahead, but made a good gap to all competitors behind, while saving fuel to get to lap 17, meaning I came out in free air and was able to close the gap down to Webber. We filled for a slightly longer than average middle stint, and were able to close the gap down to just a few seconds to Webber after my last stop, onto Option tyres. The tyre order in the race was Prime, Prime, Option. I was significantly faster on Option tyres (0.5s/lap) than Webber, and was all over him on the last four laps of the race. However, Webber was just able to hold onto his position; I finished P3.

I knew Rubens wasn't going to be with Brawn GP next year, so I went over to him on the grid before the race and wished him luck. We hugged and discussed what we'd been through together as team-mates over the previous four years. We've always been fierce rivals, but we've also worked together well and as friends. It was a touching moment as we wished each other luck for our last race in the same livery.

The first twilight race in Formula One began at 5pm local time in daylight conditions and was scheduled to finish, 55 laps later, in the dark of night under floodlights. It doesn't so much 'grow dark' in this part of the world as 'go dark' almost as if someone has flicked a switch. When the red start lights went out, all of the top five cars had similar starts and we set off in grid formation. Rubens went for a brave move on Mark Webber going into Turn 1 and lost a bit of his front wing. The bit of debris flew back and lodged itself on my car, right next to the cockpit, and I was wondering how on earth I was going to get rid of it. You can't stick your arm out of the cockpit of a Formula One car or it'll get ripped off because of the speed. I was able to get past Rubens in Turn 8 as he struggled for downforce and, as I did, the bit of his

front wing then flew off and almost hit him, so that issue sorted itself out.

I then focused on tracking Mark Webber, but I couldn't get close to the Red Bull. I couldn't get my front tyres working. As the track and ambient temperatures were dropping, I was experiencing our familiar problem of getting heat into the tyres. I was on the Prime tyre for the first two stints and all I could do was push hard and stay as close as possible to Webber, while all the time Rubens was gaining on me.

I knew I'd beaten Rubens at my second stop as I'd built up a five-second lead on him. The guys put on the Soft tyres for our final stint and the car felt transformed. I had bags of front-end grip which meant I could carry more speed into the corners and really attack. I had a bit more oversteer on the exits, but, overall, I could be more aggressive. The last few laps were intensely exciting. I was giving everything to take second place from Mark. The team came on the radio and said: 'Jenson, you have eight laps. Webber is four seconds ahead of you' – and I went for it. I closed on the Red Bull quickly and had a thrilling battle with Mark. On one of the final laps I went into Turn 4 completely sideways. On Turn 8 I tried again but suffered a massive snap of oversteer. Mark is very good at defending and he covered his line defiantly. Over the last five corners we were dicing desperately – him running wide, me almost alongside him, so many times – but I could never gain quite enough ground to make the move stick. It was fun, if frustrating, but great to watch I imagine, with the sparks flying off our wheel-to-wheel manoeuvres into the dark desert air. We were really on the edge. When I saw the television pictures afterwards it reminded me of the late 1980s, when Nigel Mansell and Ayrton Senna delivered those iconic wheel-to-wheel scraps.

I was disappointed not to beat Mark, but it was rewarding to end the season in style, on the podium, and totally enjoy myself spraying the Red Bull guys with the sparkling rose-water we have instead of Champagne in Abu Dhabi. It was a truly special way to end an amazing 2009 season. Rubens missed out on second place to Sebastian, but after seventeen races, Brawn GP end the year as winners of the constructors' championship with 172 points and the history books will show I won my first drivers' title with a clutch of 95 points. Wow.

There was a good end-of-season celebration with the team at the circuit, but it's been a long season, and we were all absolutely drained – particularly the mechanics who work so late into the night when

> 'It isn't just the story of the season, it's the story of motor racing, the story of all sport. The only thing you can say about Brawn is that their world title success was fully deserved and an absolute fairytale. For a new team to come back from the brink of obscurity and ruin to win both the constructors' and drivers' championships is absolutely fantastic.' Eddie Jordan, BBC TV

the race time is offset for an evening start. The team headed immediately back to Dubai, which was a pity, as I'd like to have spent more time sharing the brilliant feeling of achieving so much after the traumatic winter of 2008/09. I went back to the hotel with my gang – Jessica, my manager Richard, my PA Jules, my physio Mikey, Chrissy and Richie. We had fantastic food from the hotel buffet, washed down with the Jeroboam of podium Champagne that had been replaced with sparkling rose-water during the trophy ceremony. I had quite a few other drinks handed to me before we left at 1am, slightly swaying, to party at Amber Lounge.

The next day I was due to fly to Beijing to take part in the Race of Champions in the Birds' Nest Stadium. It's a great concept, matching champions from all branches of motorsport, but it wasn't going to be a 100 per cent serious display of skill from my point of view. I was feeling a bit delicate after the post-

## ABU DHABI GRAND PRIX FINAL POSITIONS

| Pos | Driver | Team | Laps | Time |
|-----|--------|------|------|------|
| 1 | Sebastian Vettel | RBR-Renault | 55 | 1:34:03.414 |
| 2 | Mark Webber | RBR-Renault | 55 | +17.8 secs |
| 3 | Jenson Button | Brawn-Mercedes | 55 | +18.4 secs |
| 4 | Rubens Barrichello | Brawn-Mercedes | 55 | +22.7 secs |
| 5 | Nick Heidfeld | BMW Sauber | 55 | +26.2 secs |
| 6 | Kamui Kobayashi | Toyota | 55 | +28.3 secs |
| 7 | Jarno Trulli | Toyota | 55 | +34.3 secs |
| 8 | Sebastien Buemi | STR-Ferrari | 55 | +41.2 secs |
| 9 | Nico Rosberg | Williams-Toyota | 55 | +45.9 secs |
| 10 | Robert Kubica | BMW Sauber | 55 | +48.1 secs |
| 11 | Heikki Kovalainen | McLaren-Mercedes | 55 | +52.7 secs |
| 12 | Kimi Räikkönen | Ferrari | 55 | +54.3 secs |
| 13 | Kazuki Nakajima | Williams-Toyota | 55 | +59.8 secs |
| 14 | Fernando Alonso | Renault | 55 | +69.6 secs |
| 15 | Vitantonio Liuzzi | Force India-Mercedes | 55 | +94.4 secs |
| 16 | Giancarlo Fisichella | Ferrari | 54 | +1 Lap |
| 17 | Adrian Sutil | Force India-Mercedes | 54 | +1 Lap |
| 18 | Romain Grosjean | Renault | 54 | +1 Lap |
| Ret | Lewis Hamilton | McLaren-Mercedes | 19 | Brakes |
| Ret | Jaime Alguersuari | STR-Ferrari | 17 | Gearbox |

season partying. But it's not every year you win the world championship, is it? After that, my plan is to spend a week in Japan with Jessica to relax and enjoy the feeling that I have fulfilled my lifetime ambition. I am the world champion, and it sounds so, *so* good to say that.

I'm restless by nature. I'm already contemplating my future. I want to be in a winning car next year. This has been an incredible year for Brawn GP. I have been with this team since 2003. It might have changed names, and shrunk in size, but I love the atmosphere, the way we all pull together in difficult times – and we have been through a lot of those. We have been working for a long time on next year's car. That comes with good leadership. You will see the likes of Ferrari, McLaren and Red Bull at the front, but you'll also see Brawn there as well. I want to be a part of that. I want to arrive next season with number one on the car in a Brawn. I hope that's how the contract negotiations will pan out. It's sad, but a driver has to be selfish and my priority is to be with a winning team that can provide the most competitive car.

Our success is sinking in slowly, in waves. It gives me a tingle every time I stop to think that I've achieved the ambition that's fuelled me all my life. That phone call I received from my manager Richard at Gatwick, informing me of Honda's withdrawal from Formula One, seems a lifetime ago. Who could have predicted it would turn into this fairytale ending? Who would have thought that Brawn GP would win both championships with a less-than-fully dominant 001 car and with battling drivers? And what next?

Winning back-to-back titles is the ultimate dream. I know how hard it is to win one, so successfully defending my title will be a hell of a challenge. The experience of this season – from the grey days last winter when I could not see a way forward to the incredible release of emotion in winning in Brazil on 18 October – has made me a stronger person and a more experienced driver. The taste of winning is indescribable. My first victory in a kart at the age of eight started the addiction. Nothing equals the thrill of a victory. My appetite has been sharpened for 2010, big time. So watch out!

'*Button is a worthy world champion and nobody this year deserved the title more than him in my view. There were some truly tremendous drives and, among his six victories in 2009, Monaco and Turkey were exceptional. Some of the drivers are still scratching their heads about how Button managed to beat them in Istanbul by such a huge margin. He also had four pole position laps of excellent quality, but the way he overtook, in an era when overtaking is rare, stood out for me.*' Martin Brundle, BBC TV

It was a fun race today and to be on the podium for the last race of the year is fantastic. I've really enjoyed driving here at the Yas Marina Circuit this weekend and Abu Dhabi has done a fantastic job for its first grand prix. We expected the Prime tyre to be the better tyre in the race but I was struggling for balance, especially as the track temperatures started to fall and it became more difficult to get heat into the front tyres. The car felt great when we switched to the Soft tyre for the final stint. It really felt transformed and suddenly I had a great front end and could carry more speed into the corners. The last few laps were really exciting and I was giving everything to take second place from Mark. I couldn't quite make the moves stick, and he's a very difficult guy to overtake, but it was a good clean fight and we were really on the edge. I'm a little bit disappointed not to get second but it's still great to finish on the podium. I would like to say a huge thank you to everyone in the team at Brackley and at Mercedes-Benz High Performance Engines. It really has been a fantastic year and they should all be very proud of what we have achieved together. It's nice to end the year on a high after what has been a very competitive and challenging season.

## FINAL POINTS

| | |
|---|---|
| Jenson Button | 95 |
| Sebastian Vettel | 84 |
| Rubens Barrichello | 77 |
| Mark Webber | 69.5 |
| Lewis Hamilton | 49 |
| Kimi Räikkönen | 48 |
| Nico Rosberg | 34.5 |
| Jarno Trulli | 32.5 |
| Fernando Alonso | 26 |
| Timo Glock | 24 |
| Felipe Massa | 22 |
| Heikki Kovalainen | 22 |
| Nick Heidfeld | 19 |
| Robert Kubica | 17 |
| Giancarlo Fisichella | 8 |
| Sebastien Buemi | 6 |
| Adrian Sutil | 5 |
| Kamui Kobayashi | 3 |
| Sebastien Bourdais | 2 |
| Kazuki Nakajima | 0 |
| Nelsinho Piquet | 0 |
| Vitantonio Liuzzi | 0 |
| Romain Grosjean | 0 |
| Jaime Alguersuari | 0 |
| Luca Badoer | 0 |

'Who can forget the thousand-yard stare plastered to Jenson Button's face as he careered around the paddock in Brazil, pursued by hordes of snappers, screaming "I am the world champion" over and over? Button had just produced a sensational performance to silence the doubters who said he was a fine driver but an average racer. By his own admission he struggled to cope with the expectation in the second half of the year but his performance drop-off was largely down to Brawn cutting back on development and his own pragmatic approach. Unfailingly polite, refreshingly articulate and humble, Button is a hugely deserving world champion.' Tom Cary, Daily Telegraph

# Acknowledgements

There are so many people I would like to thank, all of whom have played their part in getting me to this point in my life as a person and in my career as a driver, and to all of them I will be eternally grateful. From family to friends, from colleagues to competitors, to my team, team-mates, mentors and more, there are so many people who have been part of this rollercoaster of a journey – a journey which in many respects has only just begun. To thank everyone individually would triple the size of this book, but you all know who you are and so do I and you'll always be a part of this story. For those of you whose cheques have cleared, please find your names below.

My whole family, who I love dearly, and especially Mum, Papa Smurf, Tanya, Samantha and Natasha – no matter what, you've always been there for me. Knowing what to say, when to say it, and always believing. I hope I've made you all very proud; your love and support means more than you'll ever know.

Richard 'The God' Goddard, no matter what challenges I've faced, you've faced them with me, as my manager and also as one of my best friends, and we've always come out on top. Your extortionate fees and your objectionable behaviour are small prices to pay to have, unquestionably, the best manager out there.

Mikey 'Muscles' Collier, a great phsyio and a true friend, always smiling, always laughing, always posing. Whether we're training or racing, you're always there and pushing me to make me better.

Jules 'Me Julie' Kulpinski, everyone should have a 'Jules' but they can't, simply because you're mine! You've gone above and beyond since the very beginning and I'd be lost without you, literally!

James 'Blainey' Williamson, the PR guru. You make my life a whole lot busier but only because you care. Keep eating and one day you'll be full.

Team Ichiban, Chrissy B and Richie Wee. Two of the best friends anyone could have. Whether it's a place to stay or emergency meetings in the office you boys are always there. And to all the boys from home who have always helped me keep it real, big love to you all.

Team Brawn GP – the Big Bear, Shov, Bono and all the boys and girls, whether in the garage or back at the factory, and to everyone, past or present, who helped this team to achieve all it has. We've been through a lot together and as a true team we overcame it all and achieved our lifelong ambitions together. We will always remember the day we became World Champions!

All my fans. You've seen it all and you've always been there through the tough times and the great times. It means, and always will mean, so much to have your support. Thanks to you all.

And last but by no means least, Jessica. The one who is with me when I close my eyes to sleep and when I open my eyes in the morning. You've seen me at my lowest and at my best and no matter what your love has never wavered. You mean the world to me and I love you dearly.

In addition, Sarah Edworthy would like to thank the following people for bringing this book to the starting grid (as in the bookshop shelves): my agent David Luxton for putting the idea on the drawing board; Jules Kulpinski, for her inimitable organisational feats in managing the project; Andrew Shovlin and James Vowles of Brawn GP for technical input and strategy summaries. Thanks also to Kevin Wood, Autosport magazine archivist; Mark Wilkin, executive producer of BBC F1 coverage; Rory Ross, perfectionist in chief; Martin Smith for his constant reminder that it is focused, not focussed; Geertrude and Marja at Le Frelut in the Allier, France, for finding quiet writing locations; Debbie Woska and Michael Dover at Orion for their unflagging enthusiasm.

Weidenfeld and Nicolson would like to thank the following sources for their permission to pubish the photographs in this book.

Front cover: Clive Mason/Getty Images  Back cover: AP Photo/Andre Penner  Inside pages: 1 Mark Thompson/Getty Images; 6 Peter Parks/AFP/Getty Images; 8-9 Jasper Juinen/Getty Images; 12t Andrew Ferraro/LAT Photographic; 12c, b Glenn Dunbar/LAT Photographic; 13, 15 Mark Thompson/Getty Images; 19main Glenn Dunbar/LAT Photographic; 19tr Steven Tee/LAT Photographic; 21main Mark Thompson/Getty Images; 21tr Andrew Ferraro/LAT Photographic; 21tl Drew Gibson/LAT Photographic; 23t Drew Gibson/LAT Photographic; 23c Alastair Staley/LAT Photographic; 23b Steven Tee/LAT Photographic; 26-27 Paul Gilham/Getty Images; 28 Charles Coates/LAT Photographic; 29tl Andrew Ferraro/LAT Photographic; 29cr Mark Thompson/Getty Images; 29br Charles Coates/LAT Photographic; 31main Clive Mason/Getty Images; 31t Charles Coates/LAT Photographic; 32 Charles Coates/LAT Photographic; 33main Clive Mason/Getty Images; 33tr Greg Wood/AFP/Getty Images; 33br Charles Coates/LAT Photographic; 35tl, br Charles Coates/LAT Photographic; 35tr Alastair Staley/LAT Photographic; 35bl Steve Etherington/LAT Photographic; 36 Scott Wensley/LAT Photographic; 37main Alastair Staley/LAT Photographic; 37tl Steven Tee/LAT Photographic; 37bl Mark Thompson/Getty Images; 38 Glenn Dunbar/LAT Photographic; 39-41 Charles Coates/LAT Photographic; 42tl Glenn Dunbar/LAT Photographic; 42tr Charles Coates/LAT Photographic; 43bl Charles Coates/LAT Photographic; 43br Glenn Dunbar/LAT Photographic; 45 Glenn Dunbar/LAT Photographic; 46cr Paul Gilham/Getty Images; 46br Steve Etherington/LAT Photographic; 47main Peter Fox/Getty Images; 47b Clive Mason/Getty Images; 49tl, c Mark Thompson/Getty Images; 49bl, br Steven Tee/LAT Photographic; 51main, t Andrew Ferraro/LAT Photographic; 51tc Steve Etherington/LAT Photographic; 51bc Charles Coates/LAT Photographic; 51b Andrew Ferraro/LAT Photographic; 52tl Charles Coates/LAT Photographic; 52tr Steven Tee/LAT Photographic; 53main Steven Tee/LAT Photographic; 53br Charles Coates/LAT Photographic; 54 Charles Coates/LAT Photographic; 55tl, br Charles Coates/LAT Photographic; 55tr Mark Thompson/Getty Images; 56 Charles Coates/LAT Photographic; 57 Clive Mason/Getty Images; 58 Charles Coates/LAT Photographic; 59tl Diego Azubel/AFP/Getty Images; 59cr, bl Peter Parks/AFP/Getty Images; 59br Glenn Dunbar/LAT Photographic; 60tr Charles Coates/LAT Photographic; 60cr Lorenzo Bellanca/LAT Photographic; 61 Clive Mason/Getty Images; 62-63 Steve Etherington/LAT Photographic; 64tl Charles Coates/LAT Photographic; 64tr Steve Etherington/LAT Photographic; 65bl Charles Coates/LAT Photographic; 65br Andrew Ferraro/LAT Photographic; 66tr Mark Thompson/Getty Images; 66ac Bertrand Guay/AFP/Getty Images; 66bc Charles Coates/LAT Photographic; 66br Clive Mason/Getty Images; 67 Charles Coates/LAT Photographic; 68l Steve Etherington/LAT Photographic; 68r Mark Thompson/Getty Images; 69 Guillaume Baptiste/AFP/Getty Images; 71tr Steven Tee/LAT Photographic; 71cl Andrew Ferraro/LAT Photographic; 71main Steve Etherington/LAT Photographic; 73main, cl, br Charles Coates/LAT Photographic; 73bl Clive Mason/Getty Images; 74 Charles Coates/LAT Photographic; 75main, br Charles Coates/LAT Photographic; 75bl Bertrand Guay/AFP/Getty Images; 76tl, tr Charles Coates/LAT Photographic; 76b Steven Tee/LAT Photographic; 77cr, bl Charles Coates/LAT Photographic; 77br Andrew Ferraro/LAT Photographic; 79 Charles Coates/LAT Photographic; 80 Josep Lago/AFP/Getty Images; 81main Steve Etherington/LAT Photographic; 81t, b Charles Coates/LAT Photographic; 81c Jessica Michibata; 83t Steve Etherington/LAT Photographic; 83c Charles Coates/LAT Photographic; 83b Manu Fernandez/AFP/Getty Images; 84t Fred Dufour/AFP/Getty Images; 84c Clive Mason/Getty Images; 85main Fred Dufour/AFP/Getty Images; 85t Steven Tee/LAT Photographic; 86 Josep Lago/AFP/Getty Images; 87main, tl Steve Etherington/LAT Photographic; 87br Charles Coates/LAT Photographic; 88 Charles Coates/LAT Photographic; 89t Steven Tee/LAT Photographic; 89c, b Steve Etherington/LAT Photographic; 91 Steve Etherington/LAT Photographic; 92 Charles Coates/LAT Photographic; 93 Glenn Dunbar/LAT Photographic; 95tl Steven Tee/LAT Photographic; 95tc Andrew Ferraro/LAT Photographic; 95tr Steve Etherington/LAT Photographic; 97main Paul Gilham/Getty Images; 97t Glenn Dunbar/LAT Photographic; 97ac, bc Steven Tee/LAT Photographic; 97b Andrew Ferraro/LAT Photographic; 98t Andrew Ferraro/LAT Photographic; 98c, bc Charles Coates/LAT Photographic; 98bl Glenn Dunbar/LAT Photographic; 99main Glenn Dunbar/LAT Photographic; 99b Paul Gilham/Getty Images; 100 Steve Etherington/LAT Photographic; 101tl, br Charles Coates/LAT Photographic; 101cl Andrew Ferraro/LAT Photographic; 101bl Glenn Dunbar/LAT Photographic; 102 Charles Coates/LAT Photographic; 103 Bulent Kilic/AFP/Getty Images; 105main Steve Etherington/LAT Photographic; 105tr Charles Coates/LAT Photographic; 105cr Steven Tee/LAT Photographic; 106 Glenn Dunbar/LAT Photographic; 107 Charles Coates/LAT Photographic; 108tl Charles Coates/LAT Photographic; 108tr Steven Tee/LAT Photographic; 109main Charles Coates/LAT Photographic; 109bl Steve Etherington/LAT Photographic; 109br Glenn Dunbar/LAT Photographic; 110 Charles Coates/LAT Photographic; 111bl Andrew Ferraro/LAT Photographic; 111bc Charles Coates/LAT Photographic; 111br Glenn Dunbar/LAT Photographic; 112bl Steve Etherington/LAT Photographic; 112br Charles Coates/LAT Photographic; 113main Guillaume Baptiste/AFP/Getty Images; 113tr Steven Tee/LAT Photographic; 113cr Katrianna Rich; 113br Jules Kulpinski; 114cl Andrew Yates/AFP/Getty Images; 114cr Shaun Curry/AFP/Getty Images; 114bl Mark Thompson/Getty Images; 114br Clive Mason/Getty Images; 115 Mark Thompson/Getty Images; 116 Paul Gilham/Getty Images; 117tl Fred Dufour/AFP/Getty Images; 117main Clive Mason/Getty Images; 118 Jakob Ebrey/LAT Photographic; 119main Jakob Ebrey/LAT Photographic; 119br Charles Coates/LAT Photographic; 120t Steve Etherington/LAT Photographic; 120b Paul Gilham/Getty Images; 121 Jakob Ebrey/LAT Photographic; 122tl Andrew Ferraro/LAT Photographic; 122br Charles Coates/LAT Photographic; 123 Charles Coates/LAT Photographic; 124 Gary Hawkins/LAT Photographic; 125main Steve Etherington/LAT Photographic; 125tl, cl Charles Coates/LAT Photographic; 127main, tl Glenn Dunbar/LAT Photographic; 127cr, br Charles Coates/LAT Photographic; 129main Steve Etherington/LAT Photographic; 129cl Steven Tee/LAT Photographic; 129tr Andrew Ferraro/LAT Photographic; 129br Steve Etherington/LAT Photographic; 130tl Glenn Dunbar/LAT Photographic; 130tr Steven Tee/LAT Photographic; 131 Charles Coates/LAT Photographic; 132tl Andrew Ferraro/LAT Photographic; 132tr Charles Coates/LAT Photographic; 133t Dimitar Dilkoff/AFP/Getty Images; 133bl Steve Etherington/LAT Photographic; 133br Charles Coates/LAT Photographic; 135 Charles Coates/LAT Photographic; 137main Steven Tee/LAT Photographic; 137t Dimitar Dilkoff/AFP/Getty Images; 137c Steve Etherington/LAT Photographic; 137b Attila Kisbenedek/AFP/Getty Images; 139tl Charles Coates/LAT Photographic; 139c Steve Etherington/LAT Photographic; 139cr Steven Tee/LAT Photographic; 141main Fred Dufour/AFP/Getty Images; 141cl, b Dimitar Dilkoff/AFP/Getty Images; 142tl Charles Coates/LAT Photographic; 142tr Steven Tee/LAT Photographic; 142bl Glenn Dunbar/LAT Photographic; 143bl, cr Charles Coates/LAT Photographic; 144 Richard Blake/rb-create/©2009; 145main Charles Coates/LAT Photographic; 145tl Richard Wearne/rb-create/©2009; 145cl, bl Richard Blake/rb-create/©2009; 146 Charles Coates/LAT Photographic; 147main Steve Etherington/LAT Photographic; 147tr, cr, br Charles Coates/LAT Photographic; 149tl Charles Coates/LAT Photographic; 149tr Andrew Ferraro/LAT Photographic; 149c Glenn Dunbar/LAT Photographic; 150tr Steven Tee/LAT Photographic; 150cr Glenn Dunbar/LAT Photographic; 151 Glenn Dunbar/LAT Photographic; 152tl Steve Etherington/LAT Photographic; 152tr Steven Tee/LAT Photographic; 153 Glenn Dunbar/LAT Photographic; 154 Andrew Ferraro/LAT Photographic; 155 Charles Coates/LAT Photographic; 157 Andrew Ferraro/LAT Photographic; 159tl Andrew Ferraro/LAT Photographic; 159c Glenn Dunbar/LAT Photographic; 161 Glenn Dunbar/LAT Photographic; 162tl Charles Coates/LAT Photographic; 162tr Steve Etherington/LAT Photographic; 163 Charles Coates/LAT Photographic; 164 Clive Rose/Getty Images; 165bl Mario Laporta/AFP/Getty Images; 165tr Glenn Dunbar/LAT Photographic; 165br Charles Coates/LAT Photographic; 167t Steve Etherington/LAT Photographic; 167br Charles Coates/LAT Photographic; 169main Steve Etherington/LAT Photographic; 169tl Andrew Ferraro/LAT Photographic; 170 Glenn Dunbar/LAT Photographic; 171-172 Steve Etherington/LAT Photographic; 173 Charles Coates/LAT Photographic; 174tl Steve Etherington/LAT Photographic; 174tr Steven Tee/LAT Photographic; 175 Charles Coates/LAT Photographic; 177t, c Glenn Dunbar/LAT Photographic; 177b Steve Etherington/LAT Photographic; 178br Steve Etherington/LAT Photographic; 179 Steven Tee/LAT Photographic; 181tl Steven Tee/LAT Photographic; 181tr Andrew Ferraro/LAT Photographic; 182 Charles Coates/LAT Photographic; 183 Steve Etherington/LAT Photographic; 184 Charles Coates/LAT Photographic; 185tr Charles Coates/LAT Photographic; 185cr Andrew Ferraro/LAT Photographic; 187main Glenn Dunbar/LAT Photographic; 187tl © Sutton Motorsport Images; 187 tr Charles Coates/LAT Photographic; 189 Charles Coates/LAT Photographic; 191tl Andrew Ferraro/LAT Photographic; 191tr Steven Tee/LAT Photographic; 192 Glenn Dunbar/LAT Photographic; 193 Andrew Ferraro/LAT Photographic; 194-195 Charles Coates/LAT Photographic; 197bl Glenn Dunbar/LAT Photographic; 197br Steve Etherington/LAT Photographic; 199 Steven Tee/LAT Photographic; 201tl Glenn Dunbar/LAT Photographic; 201tr, bl, br Charles Coates/LAT Photographic; 203l Andrew Ferraro/LAT Photographic; 203tc Charles Coates/LAT Photographic; 203bc Steve Etherington/LAT Photographic; 203r Glenn Dunbar/LAT Photographic; 204t Andrew Ferraro/LAT Photographic; 204c Steve Etherington/LAT Photographic; 206 Glenn Dunbar/LAT Photographic; 207 Steve Etherington/LAT Photographic; 209 Charles Coates/LAT Photographic; 210tl Glenn Dunbar/LAT Photographic; 210tr Steven Tee/LAT Photographic; 211tl, br Andrew Ferraro/LAT Photographic; 211cr Glenn Dunbar/LAT Photographic; 213l, tr Charles Coates/LAT Photographic; 213br Steve Etherington/LAT Photographic; 214-215 Steve Etherington/LAT Photographic; 217tl Glenn Dunbar/LAT Photographic; 217tr Steve Etherington/LAT Photographic; 217bl Charles Coates/LAT Photographic; 217br Clive Mason/Getty Images; 219t, b Andrew Ferraro/LAT Photographic; 219c Charles Coates/LAT Photographic; 220 Charles Coates/LAT Photographic; 221 Fred Dufour/AFP/Getty Images

First published in Great Britain in 2009 by Weidenfeld & Nicolson

10 9 8 7 6 5 4 3 2 1

A CIP catalogue record for this book is available from the British Library.

ISBN: 978 0 297 86011 2

Design by Dan Smith (www.bionicgraphics.co.uk)
Edited by Sarah Edworthy and Debbie Woska
Colour reproduction by DL Interactive Ltd
Printed and bound in the UK by Butler, Tanner and Dennis Ltd

Weidenfeld & Nicolson
The Orion Publishing Group Ltd
Orion House
5 Upper St Martin's Lane
London WC2H 9EA

An Hachette UK Company

The Orion Publishing Group's policy is to use papers that are natural, renewable and recyclable products and made from wood grown in sustainable forests. The logging and manufacturing processes are expected to conform to the environmental regulations of the country of origin.